I have been warning of the ...... for some time. I have produ...... .... troubled that parts of the free world want to make government their god. That has tremendous consequences, which Mike LeMay talks about in his book. Glorifying government or making man into a god only leads to disaster. Listen to the warnings!

Jan Markell
Olive Tree Ministries

Mike LeMay writes with the monitory force of a prophet, the accessibility and conviction of an apostle, and the erudition of a biblical scholar. His teaching and writing about scripture are always thought provoking and spirit inspired, and his new work, *The Death of Christian Thought: The Deception of Humanism and How to Protect Yourself*, is an urgent, necessary, and altogether timely analysis of the myriad ways contemporary culture pushes a Marxist/Humanist agenda to undermine rational thinking and subvert biblical truth. Making astute philosophical and theological distinctions among such concepts as deception, opinion, fact, and truth, LeMay challenges Christians to reject the animalistic and irrational trends that underpin progressive ideology and return to correct interpretations of the Word based on godly and soul-affirming thought processes.

Dr. Duke Pesta
Professor of English and Academic Director of Freedom Project

Mike LeMay is a modern man of Issachar – a man who understands the times and knows what America is to do (I Chron. 12:32). In *The Death of Christian Thought*, Mike shows how American Christians have been sold and have bought devastating lies. But Mike isn't just cursing the darkness. In his book, he gives the antidote: godly thinking. Using the Bible as his authority, Mike clearly shows us what the problem is and how to fix it. This is an excellent primer on how to "gird up the loins of your mind" and make a difference now and for all eternity.

Julaine K. Appling
President, Wisconsin Family Action

As biblical ignorance in the professing church continues to grow to unprecedented heights, Mike's book is an urgent wakeup call for Christians to take a stand for the truth of God's Word against secular humanism. Many are unaware that the true gospel has been compromised with humanist teachings, which has produced many false converts in the church. Mike's extensive knowledge and research reveals how and why Christianity is experiencing such a widespread crisis. Most importantly, Mike's book, *The Death of Christian Thought*, gives us excellent biblical council as to how we can protect ourselves from the growing end-times deception. I highly recommend this book for Christians who desire to reflect the light of Christ in an ever darkening world.

Mike Gendron
Founder, Proclaiming The Gospel

America has gone through many changes, some of them ungodly. America's government, liberal media, and progressive liberals are fulfilling what Isaiah 5:20 predicted: *"Woe to those who call evil good, and good evil; Who substitute darkness for light and light for darkness; Who substitute bitter for sweet and sweet for bitter!"* Unfortunately, many Christians are going along blindly with these changes. They are practicing American Christianity instead of Biblical Christianity, allowing the culture to influence the church instead of the other way around.

Mike LeMay addresses these issues beautifully in this book. He identifies the issues that lead many churches to stray. His focus is continually on the gospel and Word of God. Mike has been in tune to the changes America and the church are going through, and has been a faithful Watchman on the Wall, warning the church about the cultural and spiritual changes and attacks. This book is a must read and a helpful guide to the spiritual growth of every believer and a warning of the pitfalls that must be avoided.

Elijah Abraham
Founder, Living Oasis Ministries

Mike LeMay has a burning desire to know and obey God and to love others by passing on what he has learned to everyone he meets. Stand Up for The Truth radio, which he has hosted for years, has provided the conduit for his passion, but from time to time God allows him to share his thoughts via written text. I am confident that *The Death of Christian Thought: The Deception of Humanism and How to Protect Yourself* will stimulate your thoughts, and be the catalyst for discussions and challenge areas of thought that must be challenged.

I encourage you to set aside the time necessary to read, think, discuss and apply the challenges set forth in these pages and firmly believe that your investment will yield great dividends.

Dave Wager
President, Silver Birch Ranch

It is no secret to thoughtful observers that we live in the perilous times the Apostle Paul spoke of in II Thessalonians 2. The atheistic opposition is perhaps now the most brazen the Church has faced since its inception nearly twenty centuries ago and few are up to the task of refuting the outpouring against biblical truth as we race toward the culmination of the Church Age. This is why I thank God for Mike LeMay and his fearless new book *The Death of Christian Thought*. It will not be easy devotional reading, nor will it find acceptance with the feel-good crowd wishing to be told the next pleasantry masquerading as Christianity in our day. However, it will encourage remnant believers to remain resolute in our stand, opposed to the growing darkness, and vigilant in evangelism while we still have opportunity. Bravo Mike!

Eric Barger
Take A Stand! Ministries

THE DEATH OF CHRISTIAN THOUGHT

THE DEATH OF CHRISTIAN THOUGHT

The Deception of Humanism and
How to Protect Yourself

MICHAEL D. LEMAY

ANEKO PRESS

Visit Michael's website: www.michaeldlemay.com
The Death of Christian Thought – Michael D. LeMay
Copyright © 2016
First edition published 2016

All rights reserved. No part of this book may be reproduced, stored in a retrieval system, or transmitted in any form or by any means – electronic, mechanical, photocopying, recording, or otherwise, without written permission from the publisher.

Unless otherwise indicated, all Scripture quotations are from the ESV® Bible (The Holy Bible, English Standard Version®), copyright © 2001 by Crossway, a publishing ministry of Good News Publishers. Used by permission. All rights reserved.

Cover Design: Natalia Hawthorne, BookCoverLabs.com
Cover Photography: Name of Artist/Shutterstock
eBook Icon: Icons Vector/Shutterstock
Editors: Sheila Wilkinson and Michelle Rayburn

Printed in the United States of America
Aneko Press – *Our Readers Matter*™
www.anekopress.com
Aneko Press, Life Sentence Publishing, and our logos are trademarks of
Life Sentence Publishing, Inc.
203 E. Birch Street
P.O. Box 652
Abbotsford, WI 54405

RELIGION / Christian Life / Spiritual Warfare
Paperback ISBN: 978-1-62245-419-8
eBook ISBN: 978-1-62245-420-4

10 9 8 7 6 5 4 3 2 1

Available where books are sold

Share this book on Facebook:

CONTENTS

Introduction IX

Ch. 1: The Enemy Within...1

Ch. 2: Starting Point: The Gospel of Salvation 19

Ch. 3: The Pursuit of Happiness...45

Ch. 4: Our Eternal Road Map to Happiness.......................................57

Ch. 5: Humanism's Corruption of our Thought Process 115

Ch. 6: Improving our Thought Process 143

Ch. 7: Strength in Numbers: Real Christian Fellowship................ 171

Ch. 8: Guarding Our Thought Process.. 193

Ch. 9: Focusing on Eternity 245

Ch. 10: Living as Christians in a Dying World 269

Meet the Author 279

INTRODUCTION

Humanism: hu·man·ism –

"An outlook or system of thought attaching prime importance to human rather than divine or supernatural matters. Humanist beliefs stress the potential value and goodness of human beings, emphasize common human needs, and seek solely rational ways of solving human problems."[1]

America is in a crisis. The greatest nation in the history of the world, founded upon the wisdom of Judeo-Christian principles, is on the verge of total economic and social collapse as our leaders and people have abandoned God and His Word.

America, a unique endeavor of human government that attempted to establish its roots with biblical principles, has decided the religion of Humanism is far more preferable to God and His Word. Over the past one hundred years, an enemy has infiltrated the hearts and minds of American leaders and people, convincing us we know better than God how we should live in and govern our nation.

> *For although they knew God, they did not honor him as God or give thanks to him, but they became futile in their thinking, and their foolish hearts were darkened. Claiming to*

---

[1] http://www.oxforddictionaries.com/us/definition/american_english/humanism.

be wise, they became fools, and exchanged the glory of the immortal God for images resembling mortal man and birds and animals and creeping things.

Therefore God gave them up in the lusts of their hearts to impurity, to the dishonoring of their bodies among themselves, because they exchanged the truth about God for a lie and worshiped and served the creature rather than the Creator, who is blessed forever! Amen.

For this reason God gave them up to dishonorable passions. For their women exchanged natural relations for those that are contrary to nature; and the men likewise gave up natural relations with women and were consumed with passion for one another, men committing shameless acts with men and receiving in themselves the due penalty for their error.

And since they did not see fit to acknowledge God, God gave them up to a debased mind to do what ought not to be done. They were filled with all manner of unrighteousness, evil, covetousness, malice. They are full of envy, murder, strife, deceit, maliciousness. They are gossips, slanderers, haters of God, insolent, haughty, boastful, inventors of evil, disobedient to parents, foolish, faithless, heartless, ruthless. Though they know God's righteous decree that those who practice such things deserve to die, they not only do them but give approval to those who practice them. (Romans 1:21-32)

Welcome to America, 2016! America, "One Nation under God," has sanctioned the murder of 58,000,000 unborn children through abortion, and is now the easiest nation in the world for homosexuals to marry. We are embroiled in a ridiculous debate about people being allowed to use bathrooms and shower facilities that correlate with their "gender identity." On Monday a biological fourteen-year-old male can wake up, decide he feels like a girl, and choose to shower with young girls. If the next day he feels like a boy again, no problem; he just showers with other boys that day.

Truly born-again Christians in America must understand a sad but stark reality: Our nation and its leaders are becoming the enemy of Christianity and will one day soon do all it can to muzzle and even destroy biblical Christianity in our nation. The government already has every tool it needs to begin the elimination of the Christian church in America. Bible-believing Christians are in a shrinking minority in this nation, and a growing percentage of Americans now see the Bible as hostile toward mankind. Public opinion is rapidly turning against us. The government also has the economic leverage to neutralize most churches through the Internal Revenue Code Section 501(c)(3) that many rely upon for economic stability.

But humanists have one more ally to undermine and dismantle the Christian church in America: They have sympathetic collaborators within the church itself, many of whom have risen to positions of power and leadership in the church. So when the government decides the Christian church needs to "get with the humanist program," they will probably find little resistance from a church that has become addicted to "nickels and noses." Biblical truth is being sacrificed for church growth in a growing number of churches who view money and popularity as the standard of success in American Christianity.

Serious Christians must start praying and planning right now for life in post-Christian America. We must prepare committed Christians now for life in a world and nation that hates us and the One we serve, Jesus Christ. I believe the next decade or two will see the emergence of two classes of Christian churches in America: the ones that surrender biblical truth to survive financially, and the ones that are driven underground because they refuse to compromise the truth of God.

We will take a brief historical look at how America has slowly turned from God and embraced humanist thought, but the focus of this book is a wake-up call from the hypnotic trance being perpetrated upon us by the systems of this world: government, public education, and media. In addition to these world systems, many Christian churches have allowed humanist thought to infiltrate the church, leading many naïve, professing Christians into a false sense of eternal security.

Jesus said:

On that day many will say to me, "Lord, Lord, did we not

prophesy in your name, and cast out demons in your name, and do many mighty works in your name?" And then will I declare to them, "I never knew you; depart from me, you workers of lawlessness." (Matthew 7:22-23)

Understand, Jesus is speaking to professing believers in these passages. These people call Him "Lord" and boast of the good deeds they did in His name, yet they will hear the most horrifying words any man will ever hear: *"Depart from me you workers of lawlessness."*

As Hitler rose to power in Nazi Germany, he met with Christian leaders, urging them to support him for the good of Germany and its people. He also let them know that if they did not support him, there would be serious consequences. They capitulated, and within six months every Bible in every church was gone, and only Nazi party officials were allowed to give sermons in churches. We are at the threshold of history repeating itself in America. I believe a large majority of churches and their leaders will capitulate, when enough economic and social pressure is applied, and they will abandon the truth of God's Word for Humanism.

The Christian church in America has become a fractured institution with strangely diverse beliefs, many directly contradicting the clear teachings of the Bible. Homosexual marriage has become acceptable in a growing number of denominations, and the horror of abortion hardly raises a whisper of concern in most churches. The church, which is supposed to stand up against a corrupt, godless culture, now opens its arms and welcomes that culture in to influence its members.

Christians are called to be light and salt to the world – to influence culture, media, education, and government. When those institutions oppose the teachings of God, we are called to hold them accountable to the Christian law and principles on which our nation was established. But the sad truth is that the behaviors of many professing Christians mirror those of godless humanists. Studies show professing Christians divorce as often as unbelievers.[2]

Pornography is now an issue that also deeply affects pastors. Fifty-one

---

[2] http://www.barna.com/research/new-marriage-and-divorce-statistics-released/#.V8GvdXg8Kh8

INTRODUCTION

percent of pastors say pornography is a possible temptation. Of pastors surveyed in one poll, 54% said they had viewed internet pornography within the last year, 30% having done so within the last 30 days.[3]

Many Christian business owners are just as apt to use unethical practices as their pagan counterparts. How are we supposed to call out and fight evil in the secular culture when the church cannot even keep its own members from participating in the same practices? The bottom line is this: the word *Christian* has lost any real meaning. Barack Obama and Hillary Clinton have publicly professed to be Christians, yet they look for every available opening to advance legislation that will kill more unborn children and advance the LGBT cause. And a growing number of ordained pastors see absolutely nothing wrong with these two sins that God calls abominations.

As I complete this book, we are entering another heated presidential election. Donald Trump and Hillary Clinton are the choices we have been given to *save* our nation. Both have claimed their leadership and policies will make America great again. Both also claim to be Christians. But Hillary Clinton has always supported the murder of more innocent children through abortion and has been an ardent supporter for the LGBT movement. Donald Trump has publicly said he has never had a need to confess his sins to God. These are the 2016 choices to *save* America! It is time for a reality check; America is in steep decline, and nothing Donald Trump, Hillary Clinton, or you and I can do will permanently reverse America's march toward ungodliness. America, and every other earthly nation, is on an irreversible road to apostasy, and we will one day oppose God. Through our votes and influence, we may be able to slow down America's fall into apostasy, but the Bible is clear that our nation is headed to a final war against almighty God Himself. With each presidential election cycle, I watch as some conservative Christians again confuse patriotism with citizenship in the kingdom of God.

> *But you are a chosen race, a royal priesthood, a holy nation, a people for his own possession, that you may proclaim the*

---

[3] http://www.expastors.com/how-many-pastors-are-addicted-to-porn-the-stats-are-surprising

excellencies of him who called you out of darkness into his marvelous light. (1 Peter 2:9)

Born-again Christians must understand we are God's people, not Americans. Yes, we love this nation and what it once stood for, and we hope and pray it could someday return to its Christian roots, but we belong to God first and foremost. Our allegiance must be to God, not men. We must accept the truth of the Scriptures: America will one day stand with all humanity, shaking its collective fists in defiance of God. The Christian church must begin to prepare itself for the fact that this nation we love will one day persecute and seek to destroy us, because we pledge allegiance to God, not to America or the world.

We must prepare ourselves as a church for the inevitable: that we are increasingly hated by the world, and we will one day undergo real persecution. The battle Christians fight these days is not for our nation; it is for the eternal souls of men. Jesus warned that the deception in the final days would be so great that many will be deceived. If we are not anchored in the truth of God's Word, we are susceptible to the great falling away Paul warned about. The day is coming when all we will have is God and each other, so we'd better start living now as the Christian church is supposed to live.

Can we depend on the leaders of our churches to prepare us for what lies ahead? Don't count on it, because over the past fifty years, Marxist Humanists have infiltrated our religious seminaries, and that has given us a substantial number of Christian leaders whose beliefs and values align more with humanists than with the Word of God. And by the way, this tactic is a written part of the Communist Manifesto: Infiltrate the seminaries and churches with leaders who can lead people away from God as they depend on human institutions like government instead of our Lord and Creator.

We will start by seeing how it got this bad, and how, through government and public education, people have been trained like Pavlov's dogs to settle for the scraps the government decides we deserve. We will learn how Christian thought has been eroded in our nation and how even the professing church has fallen into the trap of humanist thought.

We will contrast humanist psychology being perpetrated on people with what the Word of God says about improving our thought process, which leads to our beliefs and actions. Psychology is "the scientific study of the human mind and its functions, especially those affecting behavior in a given context."[4] Psychology by itself is not wrong or evil, but humanists have influenced it and turned it into a tool of the enemy to destroy our thought process.

We will discuss the four thought processes revealed in the Bible – evil, fleshly/animal, human, and godly – and how to use a godly thought process to combat the animal and evil thought processes spreading throughout our nation. You will learn how to differentiate between biblical doctrine and flawed, deceptive human doctrine that is taking over many of our churches. You will learn how to use the Word of God to have a godly thought process that will give us excellent marriages, strong biblical churches, and true Christian fellowship – the foundations for true spiritual revival in our nation. This understanding is critical to guarding your heart and mind against the deception permeating our nation and churches, and it will help you stand strong.

We will also discuss how Christians can have meaningful fellowship and discipleship with one another as our nation and the world become more and more hostile toward God and His Word. Serious, Bible-believing Christians are in the minority, and as Humanism continues its march through our nation, we will soon be in the extreme minority. We will need meaningful discipleship and fellowship to strengthen and encourage one another for the days ahead.

But this book will also teach you the most important things of all: how to know for sure you are a born-again believer and not a false convert, and how to share the gospel effectively with family, friends, and strangers to bring them into the eternal family of God.

When all is said and done, these last two things are the only things that matter for eternity. Our nation may or may not be beyond the point of another Christian revival. But the souls of men will live forever, either in heaven with God or in the torment of hell for eternity. That is the only fact that will truly matter for eternity.

Our nation is turning away from God, and the church faces critical

---

[4] http://www.oxforddictionaries.com/us/definition/american_english/psychology.

choices. Will the church capitulate to earthly leaders, as it did under Hitler? Or will it stand firmly on the truth of God and His Word? Will Christian leaders lead us toward or away from God? We must accept the possibility that many of our religious leaders will get in line with the government when their tax-exempt status is threatened, and it affects their finances. But true, born-again believers have received the mind of Christ (1 Corinthians 2:16) and can take our thought process captive to obedience in Christ (2 Corinthians 10:5). We are His chosen instruments to share the gospel and reach the lost.

We can find peace and joy in spite of all that is happening around us, but it will require the will and desire to use a godly thought process by taking our thoughts captive to the obedience of Jesus. Paul taught us we have received the mind of Christ, and we are able by the indwelling of the Holy Spirit to see things as God sees them. The early church met in fellowship and grew in spite of persecution from both Jewish leaders and the Roman government. The believers were committed to the teaching of the apostles and true Christian fellowship. Many were tortured and killed for their beliefs, yet remained faithful to God and His promises.

When America falls under the judgment of God, and economic and social chaos ensue, people around us will be losing their minds and looking for some shred of hope. As the body of Christ, we can point them to the eternal hope of Jesus Christ, but this requires us to be solidly grounded in the Word and promises of God. If we are not, we might be among those who lose their minds when all hell breaks loose in our nation.

We must fight the enemy who seeks to kill and destroy the eternal souls of men. But to fight an enemy, we must first know that enemy and his tactics. Just how did it get this bad in America and the professing church?

Chapter One

THE ENEMY WITHIN

Chapter objective: to understand the enemy's power and position.

What you are about to learn might be a shock to you. As we go through life, we get distracted and don't see the big picture coming together around us. In fact, the enemy that is slowly infiltrating our nation and churches hopes we are so preoccupied with our daily activities that we have not noticed how he is dismantling our nation and the Christian church. Many are being systematically conditioned to reject truth and embrace deception with grave eternal consequences. The eternal fate of millions of Americans, including your family, friends, and neighbors, hangs in the balance. These serious times are calling for a rebirth of Christian thought in our nation.

• By every measurable standard America is in serious decline. Financially, we are stagnant while the government artificially props up the economy with massive spending and borrowing. Morally, we have sanctioned the murder of 58,000,000 children since 1973 through the legalization of abortion. In 2015, the U.S. Supreme Court legalized homosexual marriage. And now the federal government has mandated that students can use whichever bathroom or shower facilities that coincide with their gender identity on any given day. The United States, established on Judeo-Christian principles, has become the easiest nation in the world to murder an unborn child and for homosexuals to marry. And we are drowning in a massive sea of debt. We have rejected the truth and teachings of God in the Bible: the very same God our politicians ask to bless us when they give their carefully scripted speeches asking for our support.

A crisis like this does not happen overnight or by accident. In fact, the conspiracy to undermine our way of life can be traced back to the earliest part of the twentieth century with the establishment of the Federal Reserve and the implementation of the progressive income tax. The early seeds of destruction were being sown, and nobody noticed. We slowly turned to Keynesian economics, which promotes aggressive government intervention into the free enterprise system, the first step toward implementing the socialist economic principles that now dominate our nation. In all probability the candidate who wins the presidential election in progress as I write this will be the candidate who promises the most with the least pain to an electorate addicted to government handouts. In fact, 50 percent of Americans are now dependent on government programs for their economic lifestyle, and their financial future is based on trusting the economic condition of a government that is the largest debtor nation in the history of the world. Our nation is bankrupt, and the American dollar is poised for a fall from grace.

Assuming we are still here, Christians will not be exempt from economic chaos. Each one of us still has time to choose where we want to spend eternity: in the presence of God or separated from Him in hell. We must start to view the future with eternal, spiritual eyes and expose the deception around us to share the eternal hope of Jesus Christ with those we know and love, instead of focusing on our current circumstances.

We start by understanding the depth of the crisis we face and how it came to this point. A quote from Vladimir Lenin says it all:

> "Hundreds of thousands of Rouble notes are being issued daily by our treasury. This is done, not in order to fill the coffers of the State with practically worthless paper, but with the deliberate intention of destroying the value of money as a means of payment... Experience has taught

us that it is impossible to root out the evils of capitalism merely by confiscation and expropriation...The simplest way to exterminate the very spirit of capitalism is, therefore, to flood the country with notes of a high face-value without financial guarantees of any sort....[T]he great illusion of the value and power of money, on which the capitalist state is based will have been definitely destroyed."[5]

This is exactly what is being done through the Federal Reserve over the past several decades. The dollar today has lost 98 percent of its value compared to when the Federal Reserve was established. The "full faith and credit" of the American dollar is a mirage. Christians are warned about the love of money:

No one can serve two masters, for either he will hate the one and love the other, or he will be devoted to the one and despise the other. You cannot serve God and money.
(Matthew 6:24)

But Marxism's influence hardly stops with our faltering economy. Another quote by Lenin has become sadly prophetic in America: "Give me four years to teach the children and the seed I have sown will never be uprooted."

John Dewey, considered to be the Father of Public Education, was an avowed humanist and communist. And his "baby," the National Education Association (NEA), has done him proud. It successfully lobbied to throw God and His teachings out of public education, and to replace them with evolution and humanism. The NEA, the union of public teachers, is one of the most powerful unions in the country and often directs the agenda and platform for the modern Democratic Party: the party of godlessness, socialism, and big government. This party insists on a woman's right to murder her unborn child without restriction. The NEA and government education system will not be satisfied until every student has been completely indoctrinated into godless humanism. While it puts on a public persona of caring for our children, the real agenda is betrayed by two quotes from NEA spokespersons.

---

5   C. W. Kellogg, "Men Who Made the World," Stone & Webster Public Service Journal 24 (May 1919): 360.

NEA General Counsel Bob Chanin said, "It is not because we care about children; and it is not because we have a vision of a great public school for every child. The NEA and its affiliates are effective advocates because we have power" (2009).

Addressing the United Nations in 2011, NEA Spokeswoman Diane Schneider said:

> "How can we teach sex education without including terms such as orgasm, oral sex and masturbation? We are here today because of the chasm that exists when it comes to addressing issues of sexual orientation and gender identity within the educational forum . . . With this in mind, how can we expect to obliterate homophobia in this country? The question comes to mind; how we as educators conserve to eradicate homo- and trans-phobia through education? This is an awesome task.
>
> "The key to the answer lies in the realization that both gender identity expression as well as sexual orientation is a spectrum and not a box that houses our demons. We must teach our children at a very young age that the male, female and intersex come with the presence of genitalia and no further expectation. That one needs to grow up and be their authentic self, free of society's gender expectations. The same could be true of our sexual orientation. Homophobia exists when those stocked in the binary box of strictly hetero, find themselves slipping out of that role that religion and family promote."

Our government education system embraces this agenda to which Christian parents are entrusting the future of their children. In 1963, the Supreme Court effectively banished prayer from public schools. One year later President Johnson gave his "Great Society" speech to eradicate poverty, and the centerpiece was the Elementary and Secondary Education Act that pumped massive government spending into a public education system that had become a front for secular humanism and Marxist ideals. Lenin wanted four years to indoctrinate our children.

We are now reaping the effects of our children undergoing twelve years of humanist and Marxist propaganda. The public education system, with the support of a godless media and government, has systematically destroyed the thought process of an entire generation of Americans. They are systematically being taught to think like animals instead of rational human beings.

- How successful has the NEA and public education been in indoctrinating youth into godless socialism? According to a recent Gallup poll, 53% of Americans under the age of thirty view socialism favorably.[6]

Studies show in 1980:
- 40% of Americans considered themselves conservatives.
- 10% of Americans considered themselves liberals.
- 50% were moderates/undecided.

In 2012:
- 30% of Americans considered themselves conservative.
- 30% of Americans considered themselves liberal.
- 40% considered themselves moderate/undecided.

2028 Projections:
- 10% will be conservative.
- 70% will be liberals.
- 20% will be moderates/undecided.

This is nothing short of a pending death sentence for America and the Christian church in our nation. But there is another culprit that is complicit in the moral and spiritual decay of our nation. This one was entrusted as a guardian to ensure our nation and its people would not neglect the Judeo-Christian principles upon which our nation was established, and on which it would need to rely to remain a moral

---

6   http://www.gallup.com/poll/191354/americans-views-socialism-capitalism-little-changed.aspx

nation. This guardian was strangely silent as prayer was thrown out of our public schools. It was mute as our nation legalized the murder of innocent children. And it is once again largely silent as our nation decides we know better than God how to define marriage. This silent culprit is the Christian church in America. Why has it remained silent? Because fractions of it had been infiltrated by Marxist ideology more than one hundred years ago, which has been subtly undermining the foundations of the Christian church in America ever since. It is feeding the very beast that is out to destroy Christian thought in our nation.

Marxists started infecting the Roman Catholic Church in South America in the nineteenth century and exported their social justice theology to America shortly thereafter. And now they have one of their own as Pope. This man, Pope Francis, is the greatest gift to a godless, one-world government the world has seen since Marx and Lenin. Behind his gentle demeanor is a call to world socialism and a universal religion that worships the god of climate change more than the God of spiritual change. He is working tirelessly to bring unity to the world's religions through his climate change and social justice agenda.

But the Roman Catholic Church, led by a closet Marxist, is hardly the sole culprit. The Evangelical Church in America has slowly been aligning with the social justice movement over the past twenty years; its governing body, the National Association of Evangelicals, is naively playing right into the hands of global Marxists. It also is more interested in climate change than spiritual change.

The Communist Manifesto identifies churches as a primary vehicle to undermine individualism. In the 1940s, socialists starting infiltrating Christian seminaries, and today many of these seminaries dismiss the infallibility of Scripture, teaching a form of humanism that allows for a broad interpretation based on individual morality. The Bible is seen as antiquated and unable to speak to current issues such as abortion and homosexuality. In reality, the Bible speaks clearly on these and every issue man will ever face.

Mr. Manning Johnson, a former official of the Communist Party in America, testified in 1953 to the House Un-American Activities Committee, saying:

"Once the tactic of infiltration of religious organizations was set by the Kremlin . . . the Communists discovered that the destruction of religion could proceed much faster through infiltration of the church by Communists operating within the church itself. The Communist leadership in the United States realized that the infiltration tactic in this country would have to adapt itself to American conditions and religious make-up peculiar to this country. In the earliest stages it was determined that with only small forces available to them, it would be necessary to concentrate Communist agents in the seminaries. The practical conclusion drawn by the Red leaders was that these institutions would make it possible for a small Communist minority to influence the ideology of future clergymen in the paths conducive to Communist purposes."

With the influence of organizations such as the World Council of Churches, the National Council of Churches, and leaders from Evangelical, Catholic, and mainline Protestant Churches, the nature of God and the message of the gospel have been slowly perverted into a movement of Humanism. A false god (a god of love only, but not righteous and just) and a false gospel (social justice instead of individual spiritual transformation) have combined for a false mission (saving the planet instead of saving eternal souls).

Many denominations and churches have opened their doors and given aid and comfort to this enemy, allowing it to infect the thought process of American Christians who were supposed to guard our nation through our Christian morality, influence, social activism, and voting power. Instead, the Christian conscience of our nation is being destroyed, and many churches are guilty co-conspirators in this crime against God, our nation, and its people.

Studies by George Barna Research, a leading Christian research firm, show that the biblical ignorance of professed, born-again Christians has hit heights that were unimaginable just thirty years ago. Barna starts by defining a biblical world view:

"Believing that absolute moral truth exists; the Bible is

totally accurate in all of the principles it teaches; Satan is considered to be a real being or force, not merely symbolic; a person cannot earn their way into Heaven by trying to be good or do good works; Jesus Christ lived a sinless life on earth; and God is the all-knowing, all-powerful creator of the world who still rules the universe today."[7]

These are the basic principles and tenets of the Christian faith – Christianity 101. So let's see what the research discovered about those who call themselves born-again believers:

- Only 19% hold a biblical world view.
- Only 46% believe in absolute moral truth.
- Only 40% believe Satan exists.
- Only 62% believe that Jesus lived a sinless life.
- 53% believe our human works can earn us entry into heaven.

So what is the answer to stop this spiral away from the truth of God to humanism? Is it going to church more often to hear our pastors teach us a watered-down version of the Bible? Well, look at this additional finding from Barna Research: "In a recent survey of Protestant pastors conducted by the Barna Research Group, only half (51%) passed the test on whether they possess a biblical worldview."[8]

The Christian church is supposed to stand up against secular humanism and proclaim the truth of God, teaching His Word to lead people to saving grace and eternal life with God. Instead, the exact opposite is happening: Secular humanism is invading the church and leading millions of professing Christians down the path of eternal damnation. The enemy has succeeded in infiltrating the church with spies and propagandists who are weakening the church when America and its people need it most.

Now the Spirit expressly says that in later times some will

---

[7] https://www.barna.org/barna-update/transformation/252-barna-survey-examines-changes-in-worldview-among-christians-over-the-past-13-years#.V3w5LfkrLIU.

[8] http://www.christianheadlines.com/news/survey-only-half-of-pastors-have-biblical-world-view-1240810.html.

depart from the faith by devoting themselves to deceitful spirits and teachings of demons, through the insincerity of liars whose consciences are seared. (1 Timothy 4:1-2)

True Bible-believing, born-again Christians are fighting a two-front spiritual war these days: First, we must use the truth of God and the power of the Holy Spirit to do all we can to influence America to return to the ways of God, before He completely abandons our nation. Second, and most importantly, we continue to fight the eternal battle for the souls of men that Jesus commissioned us to fight:

And Jesus came and said to them, "All authority in heaven and on earth has been given to me. Go therefore and make disciples of all nations, baptizing them in the name of the Father and of the Son and of the Holy Spirit, teaching them to observe all that I have commanded you. And behold, I am with you always, to the end of the age." (Matthew 28:18-20)

Because Christian thought is being co-opted by Marxist/Humanist thought, many professing Christians continue to vote for candidates who directly oppose God's principles. Many others have become frustrated with the choice of candidates and have decided to sit on the sidelines, wasting the influence of their votes. And now in 2016 we witness the latest group of presidential candidates claiming they are the next savior who can restore this once-great nation. But no matter how good their intentions or ideas, they have no chance of restoring our nation to a righteous standing before God, because we have collectively told God He is no longer welcome in our schools and government. So here is the depth and severity of the crisis we face:

- A government that has abandoned free-market capitalism for massive government spending, leading our nation to the verge of economic bankruptcy.

- A public education system that has trained generations of young people to abandon rational thought in favor of Marxist Humanism.

- A Christian church that has failed to warn our nation

and people, and worse, has invited the enemy into our camp to spiritually neutralize us.

What is the Solution?

- The Bible says that one day every nation will gather in defiance of God. Our nation is no exception to this prophecy. And while true believers look forward to eternity with God, He has given us work to do while we are here on earth: To share the gospel of salvation and obey the Great Commandment Jesus gave us – to love God with all our heart, mind, soul, and strength and to love one another. We are commissioned to be light and salt to the world, influencing secular culture with Christian morals and principles.
- Just because America's biblical fate is to turn in defiance against God, this does not reduce our responsibility to stand up for the biblical principles upon which this nation was founded. I visualize America and this world as the Titanic; it has hit an iceberg and is slowly sinking. But we still have time to get as many people as possible off the sinking ship by sharing the gospel and living the life Jesus calls us to live as His disciples. The sad fact is that many professing Christians do not even understand what being a disciple of Jesus Christ entails. This book will help you understand the privilege and responsibility of being a disciple of Jesus and equip you with understanding and wisdom for how to live a life that shares the hope of Jesus Christ with others.

I understand that the message of America's fate is not an easy one to embrace, but the Bible is clear about the direction our nation will take in the final days. The battle we fight is not to restore this nation to a Christian nation; our battle is for the eternal souls of men, women, and children. But in the interim we must use the Word of God and our Christian influence to slow down the moral decay of our nation, allowing us more time to share the gospel freely. This battle begins in Christian families and churches.

> *The natural person does not accept the things of the Spirit of God, for they are folly to him, and he is not able to understand them because they are spiritually discerned. The spiritual person judges all things, but is himself to be judged*

by no one. "For who has understood the mind of the Lord so as to instruct him?" **But we have the mind of Christ.** (1 Corinthians 2:14-16, emphasis added)

What then shall we say to these things? If God is for us, who can be against us? (Romans 8:31)

True Christians have the mind and authority of Jesus Christ as our weapons against the evil institutions of this world. But as a result of fifty years of godless public education that has destroyed our ability to think and reason, we have been systematically trained to think like Pavlov's dogs. The government, media, and Hollywood ring the bell, telling us what they think we want, and we come running looking for our reward. The government dangles the 501(c)(3) non-profit tax exemption in front of our church leaders, and they do what the government tells them to do. But the reward we are being fed by these earthly masters of our minds is slowly killing us. Unless true Christians, and the clergy that lead us, decide once and for all to stop thinking like animals and start using the mind of Christ within us, many professing Christians will fall for the deceit of a clever enemy who seeks to destroy the souls of men.

- Satan has succeeded in getting us wrapped up in the busyness of life and pursuing things that draw us away from God. We live our lives, full of chaos and confusion, wrapped up excessively in social media, entertainment, and the pursuit of worldly things we think will make us happy. Jesus warned us in the parable of the virgins not to get caught sleeping or with lamps empty of oil. He also warned us that He will come like a thief in the night, when few expect Him. He could call us home at any time, yet many professing Christians have been lulled to sleep by a world that has us chasing our tails with unproductive activities. We are taking our eyes off God and losing our correct focus and emphasis as believers.

- So how do we fight these battles, when we see people being systematically trained to think like animals? We fight it one person and one church at a time, by helping Christians embrace a godly thought process, rejecting the animal and evil thought process the secular culture and its leaders are using to slowly poison us. We take a step back and slow down, returning to the basics of the Christian faith and doctrines taught in the Bible. We step back from the busyness of life that has us chasing what secular humanists tell us will make us happy, and we focus on what God says will make us truly and eternally happy. Once we have returned to these biblical basics, we effectively teach them to our family, friends, and neighbors.

God is a God of order, giving us His Word to help us keep things simple. Life is really not complex at all:

- Every human being ever created by God has two things in common:
  - First, we want to be happy and we choose a thought process we think will make us happy.
  - Second, we all choose one of three journeys in life with eternal destinations:
    - In hell – by pursuing things we think will make us happy but actually make us miserable.
    - In heaven – with little earthly joy or eternal reward.
    - In heaven – with a life of joy and abundant eternal reward in heaven.

Recent statistics show a strong majority of Americans still identify themselves as Christians, believing in an eternal life. Every professing Christian will claim they want destination number three: a life of joy and eternal reward in heaven. But are they living a life consistent with what the Bible teaches about reaching that destination? When we can learn to use a godly thought process to reject the subtle lies of this world, we can learn how to help other professing Christians do the same. We can show them that they alone choose their final eternal destination and the level of happiness they will achieve in this lifetime.

The person who chooses the life of abundant joy and reward, both now and for eternity, is called a disciple of Jesus Christ. He realizes God has given us freedoms and restrictions on those freedoms for our benefit. These biblical conjunctives are where a biblical freedom and a biblical responsibility/restriction overlap to lead us to the narrow path of truth. Those who tout the restrictions without the freedoms are legalists, and those who tout the freedoms without the restrictions are emergents. The truth lies in the overlapping, in the conjunctives, so we must understand the difference between biblical doctrine that leads to true happiness and human doctrine that leads to frustrations.

The Bible refers to four different thought processes every man can choose to act from: evil, fleshly/animal, human, or godly. The thought process you choose to use will determine the earthly path you walk and your final eternal destination. If your thought process is mastered by your flesh, you will end up in hell. If your thought process is mastered by your own human understanding, you might get saved but you will not lead a life of joy and abundant reward and will be unable to help others. But if your thought process is mastered by the Holy Spirit, you will experience a life of happiness, joy, and abundant reward on earth and for eternity in heaven, and you will be able to help others join you on the journey. Jesus said: *"It is the Spirit who gives life; the flesh is no help at all. The words that I have spoken to you are spirit and life"* (John 6:63). Scripture also says:

> *For to set the mind on the flesh is death, but to set the mind on the Spirit is life and peace. For the mind that is set on the flesh is hostile to God, for it does not submit to God's law; indeed, it cannot. Those who are in the flesh cannot please God.* (Romans 8:6-8)

> *For the one who sows to his own flesh will from the flesh reap corruption, but the one who sows to the Spirit will from the Spirit reap eternal life.* (Galatians 6:8)

The thought process we choose every day proves our heart's real intent: to love and serve God or serve our flesh. Satan and his minions corrupt the thought processes of people, convincing them to feed their flesh and ignore using a godly thought process. I will show you that the Word of God can teach you *how* to take your thoughts captive to be truly happy. Most importantly, I'll use God's Word to show you how you can know for sure if you are saved or if you are deceived like many professing Christians. We will discover principles God gave us to be truly happy, both now and for eternity. And we will have the ability to help others get saved and become disciples of Jesus through the Great Commission.

Sadly, much of what passes as Christianity today in America is little more than secular humanism with a little Jesus sprinkled in. But God has given us His Word to discern error from truth. We must understand we are ultimately responsible for our eternal destination, and the choices we make through the thought process we use will determine our eternal fate. In the Sermon on the Mount, Jesus said:

> *Enter by the narrow gate. For the gate is wide and the way is easy that leads to destruction, and those who enter by it are many. For the gate is narrow and the way is hard that leads to life, and those who find it are few. . .Not everyone who says to me, "Lord, Lord," will enter the kingdom of heaven, but the one who does the will of my Father who is in heaven. On that day many will say to me, "Lord, Lord, did we not prophesy in your name, and cast out demons in your name, and do many mighty works in your name?" And then will I declare to them, "I never knew you; depart from me, you workers of lawlessness."* (Matthew 7:13-14, 21-23)

How do you know **for sure** you are on the *narrow path*? Do you know for sure you will not be one of those who hear Jesus say *depart from me, I never knew you*? If you are sure you are on the narrow path, can you state *why* you are certain? And does your "why" line up with the biblical "why"?

How are so many allowing themselves to be deceived? Who is the "father of lies"? Satan: the one who is seducing many into a false sense of security that leads them to eternal doom. His methods have not changed; he is consistent with how he tempted Eve and Adam, which allowed sin and death to enter the world:

- Twisting the Word of God ever so slightly, assigning wrong definitions to the words God spoke.

- Appealing to our pride.

- Assuring us God did not really mean what He said.

While Satan was on his own in Eden, he has now accumulated a mighty army to do his bidding in these finals days: secular humanists, governments, public education systems, entertainment, and media. His minions are being used for one purpose: to convince people to think like animals, to abandon reasoning, understanding, and the truth of God's Word for desires of the flesh.

He has succeeded in getting us to focus on the things of this world that take our focus off God. Just like Peter walking on the water, we take our eyes off Jesus and begin to sink as we focus on our circumstances and the things around us. We are being lulled to sleep in a fantasyland of social media, sports, and entertainment, all with the intent of getting us to stop thinking and blindly follow our flesh.

Satan has elevated false teachers who have reinterpreted God's Word to support their personal desire for earthly wealth and popularity. Some of these teachers do not intentionally deceive us. They only teach what they have been taught by others as right. And because we are too busy to take the time to carefully read and understand the Word of God, we outsource our spiritual growth and development to leaders who are deceived themselves and are leading us to a dangerous place. Jesus said:

> *But woe to you, scribes and Pharisees, hypocrites! For you shut the kingdom of heaven in people's faces. For you neither enter yourselves nor allow those who would enter to go in. Woe to you, scribes and Pharisees, hypocrites! For you travel across sea and land to make a single proselyte, and when he becomes a proselyte, you make him twice as much a child of hell as yourselves.* (Matthew 23:13-15)

But if you stand before God on judgment day and try to blame others for misleading you, your argument will be eternally rebuked by a Holy God. You alone are responsible for the choices you make that lead to either eternal salvation or eternal damnation. I will give you the tools necessary to correctly interpret and live the Word of God and protect your mind and heart against the deception that is rampant these days. And I will help you understand how to use these tools to help others come to saving faith in Jesus Christ. As disciples of Jesus Christ, we are given the command to share the gospel and make more disciples for Him as we await His glorious return.

We face an enemy who is older and more experienced than we are.

He deceived Adam and Eve in the Garden of Eden, and sin and death entered the world. He uses the same tactics over and over because they continue to work! Satan's greatest tool is that he uses deception to corrupt our thought process, and many professing Christians are not heeding the Word of God, which warns us against these deceptions:

> *But I am afraid that as the serpent deceived Eve by his cunning, your thoughts will be led astray from a sincere and pure devotion to Christ.* (2 Corinthians 11:3)

While the visible battle is taking place in government, education, and media, the real battle is in the hearts and minds of professing Christians. We must stop buying what the world and false teachers sell and must use the Word of God as our standard of truth. We can no longer allow humanists to redefine the words God has given us in the Bible. We must become good Bereans, testing everything we are taught against the Bible (Acts 17:11).

We will use the Word of God to help us know for sure we are truly born again, or if we have been lulled into a false sense of security through the teachings of secular humanism masquerading as Christianity. We will share the truth of God in His words, using His definitions.

We will see how the Word of God, correctly interpreted and applied, will guard our mind and heart against deception and help us effectively share the gospel with family, friends, neighbors, and strangers, leading them to salvation and eternal life with God.

We will simplify how we read and understand the Bible. Once we understand its basic storyline and principles, we will find its wisdom and application teaching us to reject sin and walk in increased righteousness, joy, peace, and happiness, confident of our journey and final destination.

We will see how God created our human brain, heart, and conscience to work, and we will learn how to take our thoughts captive before sin disrupts our life and robs us of joy. We will learn the four thought processes discussed in the Bible – evil, fleshly/animal, human, or godly – and how to elevate our thought process and that of people we are in relationship with.

We will discuss issues that often divide Christians and emphasize the importance of true Christian fellowship. When do we break fellowship and when do we accept differences of doctrinal beliefs within fellowship?

Last, we will cover biblical teachings that help develop excellent relationships with our spouses, other Christians, friends, family, and co-workers. We'll learn how to effectively lead people to a saving relationship in Jesus Christ and help other Christians live out their faith boldly and effectively.

We will use the story of a journey to illustrate the principles of this book. Every journey has five major components: a starting point, a road map with directions, a vehicle to get us safely to our destination, a skilled driver of that vehicle, and of course a final destination.

- Our **starting point** is where we are right now in our relationship with God. Once we know for sure we have been reconciled to Him through Jesus Christ, we can prepare for our journey.

- Our **road map** is the Bible. We must study and understand this road map thoroughly, so we will not stray from the most efficient route to our destination.

- Our **vehicle** is our brain, heart, and conscience, which God gave us to process information using understanding and rational Christian thought. If our vehicle is not in proper working condition, we will face serious trouble and delays on our journey.

- Our **driver** is our mind/soul, the part of us that will exist for eternity. The best of automobiles can crash if the driver is not skilled and experienced.

- And our **final destination** is a life of peace and joy and eternity in heaven with abundant reward.

The day is coming when true Christians in America will be mocked and persecuted financially and socially and will even be seen as a threat to American values. While we love this nation and the founding principles, we must understand our nation is abandoning Judeo-Christian values and is embracing humanism. And the time is coming when anyone who tries to oppose humanist values will be seen as a threat. Like the first-century church, we will only have God and each other for strength, friendship, and encouragement.

Satan and the world are out to destroy you. God wants to save you, to help you find peace and joy, and to give you eternal life. He wants you to teach others how to attain the same thing. The thought process you choose to use will ultimately decide your life and eternal future.

If we are going to start our journey to eternal life with God, we must first know who He is. He is *not* the "god" that is being presented by a growing number of Christian churches – one that is all love and allows everyone to go to heaven regardless of their beliefs and behaviors. He is a God who loves us, but He has also given us clear teachings, principles, and rules. He will forgive us of our sins and grant us eternal life, but we must do things His way, not our way.

Chapter Two

STARTING POINT: THE GOSPEL OF SALVATION

Chapter objective: to know if we're saved.

To arrive at our desired destination, we must first know the starting point of our journey. If I blindfolded you, dropped you off in the middle of a desert, and told you to go to Omaha without a road map or instructions, how could you possibly begin your journey? Without a starting point or instructions, you wouldn't know how to get to your destination. This is what has happened to many professing Christians: no initial point of reference, no correct starting point, to begin their journey to eternal life with God.

> *Then Abraham drew near and said, "Will you indeed sweep away the righteous with the wicked? Suppose there are fifty righteous within the city. Will you then sweep away the place and not spare it for the fifty righteous who are in it? Far be it from you to do such a thing, to put the righteous to death with the wicked, so that the righteous fare as the wicked! Far be that from you! Shall not the Judge of all the earth do what is just?" And the Lord said, "If I find at Sodom fifty*

righteous in the city, I will spare the whole place for their sake." (Genesis 18:23-26)

God was willing to spare Sodom, if He could find fifty righteous men, and Abraham negotiated God down to as few as ten righteous men. Yet they could not be found, and God destroyed the wicked city. Sodom's sins pale in comparison to the sins of modern day America! This presents us with a challenge: What exactly is a *righteous* man? The Hebrew word in the passages above for righteous is *sadiyq*: "lawful; just; vindicated by God." The church is God's vessel to spread the gospel by teaching the Word and leading sinners into a righteous standing before God. But the surveys I shared earlier show that the church is failing to carry out this Great Commission.

We cannot share a gospel that we neither know nor have accepted ourselves. The greatest mission field today might be within our own churches. When our nation's leaders decide that biblical Christianity is a danger to its people, we will see persecution come against the true church. And if professing Christians are not truly saved, they will do whatever they deem necessary to survive, including turning their backs on the truth of God in favor of secular humanism. Church leaders, threatened with the removal of their tax exempt status, will be tempted to compromise on the truth of God's Word, so the church can remain open and their income stream will continue. If this sounds harsh, consider this: many are already compromising the truth without persecution, so what makes us think they will stand faithfully when persecution does come?

The seeds of secular humanism have already been planted in many of our churches, and they are beginning to spread like an invasive species of weeds. We must confront lies and deception with the truth, giving every professing Christian the opportunity to choose whom he will serve: God or man. Will he choose the path to eternal damnation or the path to eternal life? Evangelism, inside and outside of the church, must become a priority for every true believer.

Every journey has a starting point, a destination, and a path that connects the two. But sadly, a growing number of professing Christians in America are seeking a destination without knowing where they are right now, so they don't know how to get to their desired destination. Satan has blinded them to the truth of the gospel, and the church is preaching a watered down version of the gospel that cannot remove the blinders.

On a warm, sunny day in Wisconsin, our ministry had a booth at a Christian youth event that attracted people from around the nation. Tens of thousands came, many of them young people who wanted to hear some of the most popular Christian bands perform their latest hits.

For some time we had been meeting as a group of evangelists, discussing the most effective ways to share the gospel with people. We discovered through experience that when we used heavy-handed techniques, preaching fire and brimstone, most people walked away and rejected our message. We learned to ask people questions to gain greater understanding of what the person believed, using their answers as a starting point for more effective dialogue. On this particular day, I opened our discussion with youth who came to our booth with a simple question: "Are you a Christian?"

About 190 youth came to our booth and all answered, "Yes, I'm a Christian." I asked how they knew they were Christians.

All but three said, "Because Jesus died for my sins."

And then the big enchilada: "Why did Jesus have to die a brutal death on the cross for your sins?"

Only one could give the biblical answer: because of the righteous wrath of God against the sinful nature of man. Almost all of the others answered, "I don't know."

Houston, we have a problem! Most professing Christians know *what* Jesus did, but they do not know *why* or *how* Jesus accomplished God's purpose for the salvation of men. They do not understand why God found it necessary for Jesus to die a brutal death on a cross for our sins.

Perhaps you have never pondered this dilemma. Why would God send Jesus to die a cruel death at the hands of evil men? Why didn't God just issue a new command that all men from this point forward are saved? Because the nature of God our Creator would not allow it. Knowing who God is and who we are is the starting point of our journey to eternal life.

Who Is God?

- To understand God's nature we must first <u>understand the difference between who someone is and what they do.</u> Who someone is can be called their nature; what they do is their behavior that stems from that nature (their characteristics). Let's see what the Word of God says about who God is (His nature).

God is always <u>Righteous</u> — HOLY, SET APART

> From the ends of the earth we hear songs of praise, of glory to the Righteous One. (Isaiah 24:16)

> Henceforth there is laid up for me the crown of righteousness, which the Lord, the righteous judge, will award to me on that Day, and not only to me but also to all who have loved his appearing. (2 Timothy 4:8)

> God is a righteous judge, and a God who feels indignation every day.

> If a man does not repent, God will whet his sword; he has bent and readied his bow. (Psalm 7:11-12)

> For the Lord is righteous; he loves righteous deeds; the upright shall behold his face. (Psalm 11:7)

> If you know that he is righteous, you may be sure that everyone who practices righteousness has been born of him. (1 John 2:29)

This is by no means an exhaustive list of the Scriptures that show God's nature is always righteous.

God is <u>Just</u>

The Lord spoke these words to Jeremiah:

- *For I am with you to save you, declares the Lord; I will make a full end of all the nations among whom I scattered you, but of you I will not make a full end. I will discipline you in*

> *just measure, and I will by no means leave you unpunished.*
> *(Jeremiah 30:11)*

The word of the Lord came to Ezekiel:

> *Yet you say, "The way of the Lord is not just." Hear now, O house of Israel: Is my way not just? Is it not your ways that are not just? When a righteous person turns away from his righteousness and does injustice, he shall die for it; for the injustice that he has done he shall die. Again, when a wicked person turns away from the wickedness he has committed and does what is just and right, he shall save his life.*
> *(Ezekiel 18:25-27)*

Jesus said:

> *I can do nothing on my own. As I hear, I judge, and my judgment is just, because I seek not my own will but the will of him who sent me.* (John 5:30)

> *If we confess our sins, he is faithful and just to forgive us our sins and to cleanse us from all unrighteousness.* (1 John 1:9)

> *And they sing the song of Moses, the servant of God, and the song of the Lamb, saying, "Great and amazing are your deeds, O Lord God the Almighty! Just and true are your ways, O King of the nations!"* (Revelation 15:3)

> *And I heard the angel in charge of the waters say, "Just are you, O Holy One, who is and who was, for you brought these judgments. For they have shed the blood of saints and prophets, and you have given them blood to drink. It is what they deserve!"* (Revelation 16:5-6)

> *After this I heard what seemed to be the loud voice of a great multitude in heaven, crying out, "Hallelujah! Salvation and glory and power belong to our God, for his judgments are true and just; for he has judged the great prostitute who corrupted the earth with her immorality, and has avenged on her the blood of his servants."* (Revelation 19:1-2)

- **God's nature (who He is) is always righteous and just, which makes Him holy (set apart; of one substance).** His actions and behaviors are consistent with His nature, and He does not contradict Himself or lie. If God were not always righteous and just, He would not be a perfect God, and man would be left to arbitrary means of judgment, salvation, and righteousness, which is secular humanism. Today, many in progressive Christian circles are preaching this exact doctrine.
- God's personality includes being loving, patient, kind, merciful, and long-suffering. But these personality characteristics (what God *does*) are governed by His right and just nature. We must understand this crucial difference. If we do not, we will be deceived by false doctrines such as universal salvation and Gnostic/Emergent theology, which are leading many astray in these final days. There is a deadly spiritual movement within progressive Christianity, claiming God's nature is always love and He is incapable of not acting out of love. But God in His own Word refutes this false teaching:

    The boastful shall not stand before your eyes; you hate all evildoers. (Psalm 5:5)

    For I the Lord love justice; I hate robbery and wrong; I will faithfully give them their recompense, and I will make an everlasting covenant with them. (Isaiah 61:8)

    The Lord tests the righteous, but his soul hates the wicked and the one who loves violence. (Psalm 11:5)

- *There are six things that the Lord hates, seven that are an abomination to him: haughty eyes, a lying tongue, and hands that shed innocent blood, a heart that devises wicked plans, feet that make haste to run to evil, a false witness who breathes out lies, and one who sows discord among brothers.* (Proverbs 6:16-19)

    Yet this you have: you hate the works of the Nicolaitans, which I also hate. (Revelation 2:6)

The admonishment in this last verse of Revelation 2:6 is important. The Nicolaitans were church leaders who would lord their position over those they led, bringing in human teachings they claimed were from God. Jesus accused the Pharisees of doing this exact thing, and we see it today as secular humanism infects the church. Some pastors position themselves as the CEO of the church, insulated against confrontation when they teach erroneous doctrine. Our growing biblical illiteracy negates even our ability to question doctrinal error, leading many to a false sense of eternal security.

Many times we will hear misled people state this: "A loving God would never send anyone to hell!"

First of all, does God truly "send us to hell"? Or do we choose to go there by rejecting His plan of salvation? Jesus said:

> *For God so loved the world, that he gave his only Son, that whoever believes in him should not perish but have eternal life. For God did not send his Son into the world to condemn the world, but in order that the world might be saved through him. Whoever believes in him is not condemned, but whoever does not believe is condemned already, because he has not believed in the name of the only Son of God. And this is the judgment: the light has come into the world, and people loved the darkness rather than the light because their works were evil. For everyone who does wicked things hates the light and does not come to the light, lest his works should be exposed. But whoever does what is true comes to the light, so that it may be clearly seen that his works have been carried out in God.* (John 3:16-21)

God has provided a means for eternal salvation, but it is up to each of us to accept or reject His plan. We can't save ourselves, but we can reject the saving work of Jesus Christ and choose eternal damnation. When we are given a choice and reject God's plan for salvation, we send *ourselves* to eternal damnation. When people say, "A loving God never sends anyone to hell," they prove they don't know God or the gospel.

The problem comes when Christians cannot correctly reconcile God's love with His just, righteous, and holy nature. God could not love perfectly if he wasn't righteous and just, because His love would then be arbitrary and contradictory. Does God love all men? Yes, He loves His creation. But God's love does not solely decide who is saved or condemned. He loves all men but has a special father-son relationship for His children, who are adopted through the sacrifice of Jesus Christ. Only those who have been justified by grace through complete faith in Jesus Christ are God's sons who will inherit eternal life.

> *But now that faith has come, we are no longer under a guardian, for in Christ Jesus you are all sons of God, through faith. (Galatians 3:25-26)*

> *But when the fullness of time had come, God sent forth his Son, born of woman, born under the law, to redeem those who were under the law, so that we might receive adoption as sons. And because you are sons, God has sent the Spirit of his Son into our hearts, crying, "Abba! Father!" So you are no longer a slave, but a son, and if a son, then an heir through God. (Galatians 4:4-7)*

The key is to understand an important biblical truth: every man is a *creation* of God but God's *sons* are only those adopted by His grace through our faith in Jesus Christ as the only atonement between a righteous, just God and sinful man. When you hear someone say, "Every person is a child of God," they have either been deceived (ignorant) or are intentionally deceiving others (lying).

We sacrifice biblical truth for human understanding when we believe God's dealings are the same for every person He created and that His love alone assures us of salvation and eternal life. The Scriptures clearly refute these false premises. Salvation by God requires that God's just wrath against sin is satisfied by the offending party.

> *So the angel swung his sickle across the earth and gathered the grape harvest of the earth and threw it into the great winepress of the wrath of God. (Revelation 14:19)*

> *The Father loves the Son and has given all things into his hand. Whoever believes in the Son has eternal life; whoever does not obey the Son shall not see life, but the wrath of God remains on him. (John 3:35-36)*

For the wrath of God is revealed from heaven against all ungodliness and unrighteousness of men, who by their unrighteousness suppress the truth. (Romans 1:18)

But because of your hard and impenitent heart you are storing up wrath for yourself on the day of wrath when God's righteous judgment will be revealed. He will render to each one according to his works: to those who by patience in well-doing seek for glory and honor and immortality, he will give eternal life; but for those who are self-seeking and do not obey the truth, but obey unrighteousness, there will be wrath and fury. (Romans 2:5-8)

God's wrath against sin must be satisfied before sinful men can be reconciled to God, and Jesus Christ, God in the flesh, paid the price on the cross, satisfying God's wrath against sin and allowing men to come into a righteous relationship once again with God.

In the Old Testament, a spotless animal was periodically offered as a sacrifice to God for sin. The animal had to be *blameless*. It committed no sin, but God, being holy and perfect, required the sacrifice to be blameless and perfect. This sacrifice was a temporary atonement for the wrath of God against sin. People continued to sin, and the sacrifice of the spotless animal had to continue over and over. This was only a temporary appeasement in the Old Testament sacrifice, for Hebrews 10:1-4 tells us that the sacrifice of animals was only a shadow of things to come, that is, Jesus Christ's death, burial, and resurrection.

The next day he saw Jesus coming toward him, and said, "Behold, the Lamb of God, who takes away the sin of the world!" (John 1:29)

Jesus was God in the flesh. Because He was God, He was spotless and perfect. Because He was human, He was able to absorb the wrath of God against sin: because He was one of us. The only way God could be just was by punishing the guilty party (humanity). And *this* sacrifice could last for eternity because the wrath of God that satisfies His just nature could be poured out on one who was spotless, yet "guilty":

Therefore, if anyone is in Christ, he is a new creation. The old

> has passed away; behold, the new has come. All this is from God, who through Christ reconciled us to himself and gave us the ministry of reconciliation; that is, in Christ God was reconciling the world to himself, not counting their trespasses against them, and entrusting to us the message of reconciliation. Therefore, we are ambassadors for Christ, God making his appeal through us. We implore you on behalf of Christ, be reconciled to God. **For our sake he made him to be sin who knew no sin, so that in him we might become the righteousness of God.** (2 Corinthians 5:17-21, emphasis added)

We must make an important distinction: Jesus did not sin while He was on earth, but the Scriptures say He *became* sin, so God could pour out His just wrath against the guilty party who had actually sinned – humanity. The guiltless sacrifice took our guilt upon Him in our place.

As Christians we must embrace this truth: God's love alone is not enough to save sinful man from eternal damnation. He does not simply love us into heaven. Man has to be seen as righteous in God's eyes, before we can be granted eternal life with Him. The eternally sufficient sacrifice of Jesus Christ on the cross satisfied the wrath of God against sin, which was poured out on Jesus Christ in our stead. He took our sin and gave us His righteousness.

Without a correct understanding of who God is according to His own Word, we can never get an accurate picture of anything else. We cannot understand His ways, *what* He is trying to teach us, *why* He is teaching it to us, and *how* we can live out His teachings. In fact, without understanding who God is, we can know nothing about His most intricate creation: man.

Who is Man Before Salvation?

The Bible says much about the nature and character of sinful man, and it isn't very flattering. Things started out well, as man was to be the crown jewel of God's creation and take over all the earth (stewardship).

> *So God created man in his own image, in the image of God he created him; male and female he created them. And God blessed them. And God said to them, "Be fruitful and*

> *multiply and fill the earth and subdue it, and have dominion over the fish of the sea and over the birds of the heavens and over every living thing that moves on the earth."*
> (Genesis 1:27-28)

God desired that men would love and glorify Him by managing His creation, being fruitful, and multiplying His family. But love must be a choice, not forced upon another. So God gave man a free will to choose to love and obey Him or to reject Him. Man chose to know right from wrong, succumbing to Satan's seduction to eat from the Tree of Knowledge of Good and Evil. Sin entered the world, and man was separated from fellowship with God. God had to punish man for his sin, so man was expelled from Eden, and his intimate fellowship with God was damaged and quickly deteriorated over the centuries as man constantly chose disobedience over loving God. As man grew more and more sinful, God got to the point where He regretted creating man.

> *The Lord saw that the wickedness of man was great in the earth, and that every intention of the thoughts of his heart was only evil continually. And the Lord regretted that he had made man on the earth, and it grieved him to his heart. So the Lord said, "I will blot out man whom I have created from the face of the land, man and animals and creeping things and birds of the heavens, for I am sorry that I have made them." But Noah found favor in the eyes of the Lord.*
> (Genesis 6:5-8)

Man had been exposed to sin, and like a cancer, it continued to consume him.

> *And Moses said to Aaron, "What did this people do to you that you have brought such a great sin upon them?" And Aaron said, "Let not the anger of my lord burn hot. You know the people, that they are set on evil. For they said to me, 'Make us gods who shall go before us. As for this Moses, the man who brought us up out of the land of Egypt, we do not know what has become of him.' So I said to them, 'Let any who have gold take it off.' So they gave it*

to me, and I threw it into the fire, and out came this calf." (Exodus 32:21-24)

Surely there is not a righteous man on earth who does good and never sins. (Ecclesiastes 7:20)

The heart is deceitful above all things, and desperately sick; who can understand it? "I the Lord search the heart and test the mind, to give every man according to his ways, according to the fruit of his deeds." (Jeremiah 17:9-10)

The picture is clear. Before receiving the grace of God, man is wicked and depraved compared to the righteousness of God. Since there was no way man could be righteous enough to be pleasing and acceptable to God, the source of this salvation had to be from God alone. However, the responsibility for the success of this plan depended on man's willingness to admit he is wicked, evil, and incapable of doing anything about it in his own strength and to repent accordingly. He needs humility. Once a man confesses and repents, asking God to direct his life moving forward, he receives forgiveness and salvation from God. Remember Jesus' words:

For God so loved the world, that he gave his only Son, that whoever believes in him should not perish but have eternal life. For God did not send his Son into the world to condemn the world, but in order that the world might be saved through him. Whoever believes in him is not condemned, but whoever does not believe is condemned already, because he has not believed in the name of the only Son of God. And this is the judgment: the light has come into the world, and people loved the darkness rather than the light because their works were evil. For everyone who does wicked things hates the light and does not come to the light, lest his works should be exposed. But whoever does what is true comes to the light, so that it may be clearly seen that his works have been carried out in God. (John 3:16-21)

Proud people hate the light because it exposes them for who they really are. So they reject the light.

STARTING POINT: THE GOSPEL OF SALVATION

> *You adulterous people! Do you not know that friendship with the world is enmity with God? Therefore whoever wishes to be a friend of the world makes himself an enemy of God. Or do you suppose it is to no purpose that the Scripture says, "He yearns jealously over the spirit that he has made to dwell in us"? But he gives more grace. Therefore it says, "God opposes the proud, but gives grace to the humble." Submit yourselves therefore to God. Resist the devil, and he will flee from you. Draw near to God, and he will draw near to you. Cleanse your hands, you sinners, and purify your hearts, you double-minded. Be wretched and mourn and weep. Let your laughter be turned to mourning and your joy to gloom. Humble yourselves before the Lord, and he will exalt you.*
> (James 4:4-10)

Only by humbling ourselves before God can we have any hope of being saved from eternal damnation. We are wicked and unworthy of salvation, period! The tragic thing is the wicked natural state of sinful man is not taught much these days. Instead, the gospel message is being reduced to something like this: "You are a good person who sins sometimes. This prevents you from living a fuller, richer life. But Jesus died for your sins so you can go to heaven. Invite Jesus into your heart today and you will go to heaven!"

This is humanism: the false belief that man in his nature is good and capable of making himself better by his own efforts. This is a gross insult to God and falls far short of true salvation. Salvation requires us to acknowledge that our sins are a grave affront to God, and we deserve eternal damnation for even one sin! This humanism is also an insult to the painful sacrifice Jesus paid for our sins. He gave up His life and took the righteous wrath of a holy God upon Himself, sparing us eternal damnation. If we do not recognize and confess our evil natural state, have we met the requirements for God's forgiveness? If a man does not confess his guilt, should a just judge be lenient?

The next time you witness an altar call, listen carefully to the message. If the primary message is based on inviting Jesus into your heart, it is probably humanism that appeals to our flesh. But if the message calls for confession and repentance, humbling ourselves before a righteous and holy God, if it clearly states that Jesus satisfied the wrath of God upon the cross and ends with a call for the Holy Spirit to direct your actions moving forward, you have heard the true gospel presented. The gospel should lead us to tears of brokenness. Our hearts should be broken over how we have sinned against the One who created us and shed His blood on our behalf.

Before salvation and regeneration by the grace of God's Spirit, man is evil, perpetually rebellious, and sinful. All God asks is that we sincerely confess that fact and repent, placing our complete faith and trust in Jesus Christ. Confession without repentance is meaningless. If we do not confess our hopelessly lost and sinful state, can we truly be saved? If we refuse to understand and accept who God is (righteous, just, and holy) and who we are (evil, wicked, and unable to get better on our own), we have chosen Journey #1: living an aimless life of strife that leads us to eternal hell.

We must believe and trust in who God is: righteous, just, and holy. We must accept that we are hopelessly sinful and lost, incapable of saving ourselves, and wholeheartedly confess and repent before God. If we confess this with complete sincerity, we have been saved from eternal damnation, and we have the true starting point of our journey to a life of happiness and eternal life with God.

Who is Man after Salvation and Being Born Again?

The simple answer from the Scriptures is that we are a new creation as the result of being saved through spiritual rebirth.

> *Therefore, if anyone is in Christ, he is a new creation.*
> *The old has passed away; behold, the new has come.*
> *All this is from God, who through Christ reconciled us*
> *to himself and gave us the ministry of reconciliation.*
> (2 Corinthians 5:17-18)

The born-again believer is reconciled with God. The gospel has been called "the Great Exchange" by some. Jesus, God in human form and sinless, became sin for us, and in exchange for our complete faith and trust in Him, we are new creations, considered righteous and guiltless before

God. This is an amazing testimony to a God who loves His creation so much that all He asks is that we sincerely confess our guilt before Him and repent of our desire to continue to sin against Him. After we do this in humility and sincerity, we are born again and receive the Holy Spirit of God as our guide and down payment on eternal life. But there is one serious challenge we must reconcile from the Scriptures. Jesus said:

> *Not everyone who says to me, "Lord, Lord," will enter the kingdom of heaven, but the one who does the will of my Father who is in heaven. On that day many will say to me, "Lord, Lord, did we not prophesy in your name, and cast out demons in your name, and do many mighty works in your name?" And then will I declare to them, "I never knew you; depart from me, you workers of lawlessness."*
> (Matthew 7:21-23)

To someone who is not a serious student of God's Word, these can be frightening verses. And sadly they are rarely discussed in many churches because they are not popular and do not appeal to the flesh of people who attend and pay tithes. But what a disservice we are doing to professing Christians, if we do not address these verses in the complete context of the Bible. They are a clarion warning against being lulled into a false sense of eternal security that we do not have unless we are born again.

The discussion has raged since the first-century church concerning the eternal security of salvation in the true believer. But this question is pointless unless we can first determine how the Bible identifies a true believer. I have the opportunity, because of my position as a talk show host, to interact with hundreds of people every year. I am alarmed at how many professing Christians cannot give a biblical answer to justify their claim of being a true believer. Just like the youth I mentioned at the beginning of this chapter, when pressed on why they believe they are truly saved, many of the answers are circular logic and self-contradictory. This explains exactly what Jesus warned about in Matthew 7:21-23: many who *think* they are saved will be separated from Him for eternity because they had a wrong definition of salvation. So let's take the time to study the Scriptures in context.

What Salvation Is Not

Salvation is not necessarily leading a sinless life.

Therefore, confess your sins to one another and pray for one another, that you may be healed. The prayer of a righteous person has great power as it is working. (James 5:16)

If we confess our sins, he is faithful and just to forgive us our sins and to cleanse us from all unrighteousness. If we say we have not sinned, we make him a liar, and his word is not in us. (1 John 1:9-10)

All wrongdoing is sin, but there is sin that does not lead to death. (1 John 5:17)

So whoever knows the right thing to do and fails to do it, for him it is sin. (James 4:17)

Salvation does not lend itself to a life that justifies our ongoing sinful behaviors.

What shall we say then? Are we to continue in sin that grace may abound? By no means! How can we who died to sin still live in it? (Romans 6:1-2)

Everyone who makes a practice of sinning also practices lawlessness; sin is lawlessness. You know that he appeared in order to take away sins, and in him there is no sin. No one who abides in him keeps on sinning; no one who keeps on sinning has either seen him or known him. Little children, let no one deceive you. Whoever practices righteousness is righteous, as he is righteous. Whoever makes a practice of sinning is of the devil, for the devil has been sinning from the beginning. The reason the Son of God appeared was to destroy the works of the devil. (1 John 3:4-8)

Without an understanding of the entire context of Scripture, we might be very confused right about now. So, salvation is not a sin-free life, but salvation is also not continuing to sin? Make up your mind! The Bible gives us the complete truth, as it always does:

> *For I do not understand my own actions. For I do not do what I want, but I do the very thing I hate. Now if I do what I do not want, I agree with the law, that it is good. So now it is no longer I who do it, but sin that dwells within me. For I know that nothing good dwells in me, that is, in my flesh. For I have the desire to do what is right, but not the ability to carry it out. For I do not do the good I want, but the evil I do not want is what I keep on doing. Now if I do what I do not want, it is no longer I who do it, but sin that dwells within me.* (Romans 7:15-20)

These are some of the most important verses of the entire Bible. Paul acknowledges that in spite of being saved by the grace of God and loving Him deeply, he continues to sin. You can almost hear the pain as he laments his ongoing sin. He points out something very important in verse 20: In spite of the grace of God, we still have a sinful nature within us. This sinful nature will tempt and torment us until the day we die. It always wants to bring out the old you – the one that loves to indulge in your sinful flesh. And unless we learn how to surrender to the Holy Spirit, that flesh will not decrease and may actually grow within us, even as believers. It will haunt us, rob us of joy and effectiveness, and cause us to struggle in our marriages, at work, and in our Christian fellowships. You will be a person who chooses Journey #2: living a life of mediocrity that may get you into heaven but with little temporal or eternal reward.

The sinful nature in us can be controlled and diminished by the grace of God if we cooperate with the Spirit instead of resisting Him. And even when we do occasionally give in to our sinful nature, there is hope:

> *My little children, I am writing these things to you so that you may not sin. But if anyone does sin, we have an advocate with the Father, Jesus Christ the righteous.* (1 John 2:1)

> *If we confess our sins, he is faithful and just to forgive us our sins and to cleanse us from all unrighteousness.* (1 John 1:9)

John tells us we have an advocate when we sin, and when we continue to sincerely confess our ongoing sins to God, He is faithful and just to forgive us our sins. But the Scriptures also say that the true believer should not have the desire to continue to sin. Our heart and mind should now view sin differently than we did before we received the grace of God. The sins we used to anticipate and enjoy should now sicken us, because we know the extreme offense they are to a righteous, just, and holy God. They should bother us when we remember the enormous price Jesus paid for our redemption. Our continuing sin should drive us to a godly sorrow, when we disobey the One who gave His life for us, renewing our commitment and zeal to love and obey Him in every area of our life. This is called repentance.

Some fall into a dangerous trap sprung by Satan, which drags them back under self-condemnation because they apply a human definition to repentance, replacing the definition God gave us in His Word.

> *From that time Jesus began to preach, saying, "Repent, for the kingdom of heaven is at hand." (Matthew 4:17)*

The word *repent* is the Greek word *metanoeo*: "to think differently." The incorrect human definition is that repentance is to stop sinning. When we accept this flawed definition and continue to do the very things for which we repented, we can get dragged back under condemnation by Satan's lies. We repent and keep doing the things we have said we will stop doing, getting more and more frustrated as we continue to lie to ourselves, and eventually we just give up. We even question if we were ever saved to begin with, revealing a lack of true faith in Jesus and what He accomplished on the cross. This wrong human definition of repentance can damage professing Christians.

It is important to use God's definitions for the words He speaks instead of applying wrong or misleading human definitions. No wrongly defined word is more critical than *repentance*. When we use the definition God has given us, we understand we are no longer condemned for our occasional sins when we confess and repent. When we apply the wrong human definition, we begin a spiral of confusion and doubt that leads us to a place of frustration, despair, and hopelessness.

So after conversion and ongoing sanctification, what does the life of a born-again believer look like?

- We love the Lord Jesus Christ more than anything – with all our heart, mind, soul, and strength.
- We try to obey all He has commanded us.
- We love other Christians as Christ loves us, unconditionally showing mercy, kindness, and forgiveness.
- We change our minds about our sin (repent): we grow to detest the sin we once loved and justified, and allow the Holy Spirit to convict us of our sins and lead us from temptation.
- Lastly, when we do sin against God or others, we confess and repent once again.

This is Journey #3: a life of peace, love, joy, temporal reward, and abundant eternal reward. Before we move on, are you prepared to make an informed decision about the journey you want to pursue? Have you come to belief and faith that God is holy, righteous, and just? That His justice demanded a punishment for our sins? That Jesus Christ, God in the flesh, is the only sacrifice acceptable to God for our sins? Do you believe complete faith and trust in Jesus Christ is the only way to have a righteous standing before God? Have you asked God to forgive you of your sins (confession) and changed your mind about your sins (repentance)?

> *Because, if you confess with your mouth that Jesus is Lord and believe in your heart that God raised him from the dead, you will be saved. For with the heart one believes and is justified, and with the mouth one confesses and is saved.* (Romans 10:9-10)

The decision to believe in your heart is not some flippant choice. The Greek word for *believe* is *pisteuo*: "to entrust; commit; completely persuaded; morally convicted." This transcends an intellectual belief that Jesus is the Son of God. James 2:19 tells us the demons believe that and they shudder. Believing in your heart means a complete commitment to the truth of who Jesus is, what He accomplished on the cross, what He will do when He returns in judgment, and what He teaches us is righteous for our benefit and the benefit of others.

If you have confessed and repented before God, you've been granted eternal life with Him; you're free from the eternal punishment of sin. Now you are free to choose to either live a life of mediocrity with little reward here and for eternity (Journey #2) or a life of peace, joy, love, and growth in Jesus Christ with abundant eternal reward (Journey #3). If you desire the latter, the Bible gives us the formula. It will not always be easy, but as your trust in God increases with each day, you will acquire the peace that surpasses human understanding and live a life that benefits yourself and others.

But you must know beyond the shadow of a doubt that your confession and repentance are sincere and that you have received the forgiveness and grace of God. After all, Jesus said many false converts would be rejected on judgment day, thinking they were saved, but being sent to eternal hell. So how can we know for sure we have received God's forgiveness and grace?

Proof of Our Salvation

> *For by grace you have been saved through faith. And this is not your own doing; it is the gift of God, not a result of works, so that no one may boast. For we are his workmanship, created in Christ Jesus for good works, which God prepared beforehand, that we should walk in them.*
> (Ephesians 2:8-10)

Perhaps no single word in the Bible is more crucial to understand than *grace*. According to Strong's Concordance, the Greek word for grace is *charis*: "favor; the divine influence on the heart and its reflection in the life, including gratitude." The human definition used has been reduced to "unmerited favor" in many churches today. And while we certainly do not deserve the grace of God, receiving without merit is *how* we receive grace, not solely what it is.

> *For the grace of God has appeared, bringing salvation*

> *for all people, training us to renounce ungodliness and worldly passions, and to live self-controlled, upright, and godly lives in the present age, waiting for our blessed hope, the appearing of the glory of our great God and Savior Jesus Christ, who gave himself for us to redeem us from all lawlessness and to purify for himself a people for his own possession who are zealous for good works. Declare these things; exhort and rebuke with all authority. Let no one disregard you.* (Titus 2:11-15)

Grace saves us *and* teaches us to deny sin and lead an increasingly holy life. The grace that saves us is not a different grace from the one that leads us to holiness. So the increasing fruit we bear as Christians is proof we have received the grace of God that we claim has saved us. We are not talking about a works-based salvation, but about the effects of God's grace that saves us – an increasingly holy life (sanctification). This sanctification is achieved by yielding our will to God's. We continue to turn away from our sinful nature and the desires of our flesh and live the life Jesus taught us to live. But this path to sanctification is a slow one where we will on occasion continue to choose sin over righteous living. When we do choose sin, we confess and repent once again. But God's grace forgives us of our sins, maintaining our righteous standing before Him, even as we occasionally choose to disobey Him.

> *But someone will say, "You have faith and I have works." Show me your faith apart from your works, and I will show you my faith by my works. You believe that God is one; you do well. Even the demons believe – and shudder! Do you want to be shown, you foolish person, that faith apart from works is useless? Was not Abraham our father justified by works when he offered up his son Isaac on the altar? You see that faith was active along with his works, and faith was completed by his works; and the Scripture was fulfilled that says, "Abraham believed God, and it was counted to him as righteousness" – and he was called a friend of God. You see that a person is justified by works and not by faith alone. And in the same way was not also Rahab the prostitute*

justified by works when she received the messengers and sent them out by another way? For as the body apart from the spirit is dead, so also faith apart from works is dead. (James 2:18-26)

James stated that our righteous works are the *effects* of the grace we received through faith in Jesus Christ. The Bible refers to this as fruit:

But now that you have been set free from sin and have become slaves of God, the fruit you get leads to sanctification and its end, eternal life. For the wages of sin is death, but the free gift of God is eternal life in Christ Jesus our Lord. (Romans 6:22-23)

And so, from the day we heard, we have not ceased to pray for you, asking that you may be filled with the knowledge of his will in all spiritual wisdom and understanding, so as to walk in a manner worthy of the Lord, fully pleasing to him, bearing fruit in every good work and increasing in the knowledge of God. (Colossians 1:9-10)

Now the works of the flesh are evident: sexual immorality, impurity, sensuality, idolatry, sorcery, enmity, strife, jealousy, fits of anger, rivalries, dissensions, divisions, envy, drunkenness, orgies, and things like these. I warn you, as I warned you before, that those who do such things will not inherit the kingdom of God. But the fruit of the Spirit is love, joy, peace, patience, kindness, goodness, faithfulness, gentleness, self-control; against such things there is no law. And those who belong to Christ Jesus have crucified the flesh with its passions and desires. (Galatians 5:19-24)

Judging the Fruit of Others

Later we will discuss the subject of Christians judging others, as there are correct and incorrect ways we are to do it. But for now, I want to give a word of caution regarding judging the fruit of other believers.

Can a newly planted apple tree be expected to bear as much fruit as a ten-year-old tree? It may not bear any fruit for three to six years.

But the more we fertilize, water, mulch, and care for the root system, the quicker it bears fruit. New Christians cannot be expected to bear as much fruit as more seasoned Christians. We must not discourage younger Christians if they bear less fruit of lower quality as they are maturing. We remember we were once young "trees," freshly planted with little fruit. As more mature Christians, we must come alongside our younger brethren and encourage them – teaching them and helping them mature at a rate faster than we did by teaching them the Word and sharing our experiences.

> *I therefore, a prisoner for the Lord, urge you to walk in a manner worthy of the calling to which you have been called, with all humility and gentleness, with patience, bearing with one another in love, eager to maintain the unity of the Spirit in the bond of peace.* (Ephesians 4:1-3)

We are to be humble, gentle, and patient toward the weaker Christian.

> *I charge you in the presence of God and of Christ Jesus, who is to judge the living and the dead, and by his appearing and his kingdom: preach the word; be ready in season and out of season; reprove, rebuke, and exhort, with complete patience and teaching. For the time is coming when people will not endure sound teaching, but having itching ears they will accumulate for themselves teachers to suit their own passions, and will turn away from listening to the truth and wander off into myths. As for you, always be sober-minded, endure suffering, do the work of an evangelist, fulfill your ministry.* (2 Timothy 4:1-5)

We keep younger believers from falling away from the truth by reproving, rebuking, and exhorting them with complete patience, realizing only God's grace can prevent us from falling for false teachings.

> *So whatever you wish that others would do to you, do also to them, for this is the Law and the Prophets.* (Matthew 7:12)

We are to treat younger believers as we wanted to be treated when we were younger believers. We realize we were once more naïve and bore limited fruit in our lives. Often new believers are so zealous in their newly found love of God that their excitement and passion can hinder their judgment. They can become either extremely legalistic or extremely freedom oriented. As we help them mature in the Word of God, we help them find the narrow path of truth in the Bible. We should not quench their newfound passion for Jesus and the gospel, but we should also patiently guide them if they look for truth in the wrong places or teachers.

Legalists look down on less mature Christians, raising the bar of salvation for them. The emergent does not hold the believer accountable for his sinful behaviors, stunting his growth. These are stumbling blocks and sins. A true disciple remembers his early journey and seeks to speak the truth in love, helping the younger believer develop a strong root system to bear much fruit.

Loving Others

> *But when the Pharisees heard that he had silenced the Sadducees, they gathered together. And one of them, a lawyer, asked him a question to test him. "Teacher, which is the great commandment in the Law?" And he said to him, "You shall love the Lord your God with all your heart and with all your soul and with all your mind. This is the great and first commandment. And a second is like it: You shall love your neighbor as yourself. On these two commandments depend all the Law and the Prophets."* (Matthew 22:34-40)
>
> *If anyone says, "I love God," and hates his brother, he is a liar; for he who does not love his brother whom he has seen cannot love God whom he has not seen. And this commandment we have from him: **whoever loves God must also love his brother**.* (1 John 4:20-21, emphasis added)

Loving others is a testimony to our salvation. Jesus said to love all men as we love ourselves. John says if we claim to love God but do not love our Christian brothers, we are liars.

Summary

True salvation begins with knowing who God is (holy, righteous, and just) and knowing who we are before salvation (hopelessly lost sinners incapable of ever becoming good in our own strength). Humility leads us to sincere confession and repentance. When we completely trust in who Jesus is and what He accomplished, we become born-again believers who receive the Holy Spirit and God's grace. This is the starting point of our journey to joy and eternal life.

God's grace saves us *and* teaches us to deny sin, and to pursue holy, righteous living by the power of the Holy Spirit in us. One proof of our salvation is that we increasingly bear fruit of righteousness and good works by the power of the Spirit. We love others as God loves us. When we sin and fail to love others, we confess and repent of our sinful actions. True believers confess and repent more, not less, as we are sanctified. God's grace continues to reveal sin that was hidden from us, leading to further confession, repentance, and more righteous behavior. The professing Christian who never feels the need for continuing confession and repentance either thinks he is perfect or is resisting the grace of God. Both of these will lead to ultimate disaster. The Christian who confesses and repents more frequently is the one growing in the grace of Jesus Christ. This contradicts our human thought process that tells us the less we need to confess, the more holy we are becoming. Actually, the opposite is true: increased frequency of heartfelt confession and repentance is proof we are being sanctified, which proves we were saved!

We are saved and born again when we abandon our human plan for salvation and in humility accept that only God's plan will work. This means we refuse to go on justifying our sins but, instead, continue to confess and repent when we do sin. Thus, we continue to grow by the grace of God.

If this is the journey you choose to take, you are pursuing a life of joy, peace, and happiness that leads to an eternity with great reward. You now know the starting point and the destination of your journey. Next, let's study our destination so we can plan our journey.

Key Points:

- The true gospel has been subtly replaced with humanist teachings, leading to many false converts in the church. Many who think they are going to heaven will be banished to eternal hell.

- Because the number of false converts has grown, the church has lost its influence on American culture and society, leading to growth in sin and rebellion against God by our nation.

- The true gospel not only saves us from hell but changes our lives dramatically.

- The grace of God saves us and teaches us to renounce ungodliness, which leads to lives that are increasingly holy and pleasing to God (Titus 2:11-15).

Chapter Three

THE PURSUIT OF HAPPINESS

Chapter objective: to know biblical and human definitions of happiness.

We now know where our journey begins: a righteous standing before God. Our next step is to define our desired destination. What does a life of happiness and an eternal life with abundant reward look like? How will we know we are headed toward our desired destination and when we have arrived? What exactly is happiness? It depends on the thought process you choose to define and pursue happiness.

Think back to when you were young, before the cares of adulthood became reality. Happiness was much simpler to define back then. It could be the final day of school with three months of summer fun ahead of us. It could be a family trip to see exciting sights or spending a week on a lake swimming, skiing, and fishing. It could be the excitement of getting our driver's license. As adults facing everyday challenges with work, family, and the world, we look back and realize that happiness seems to be a fleeting thing, here today and gone tomorrow. And as we pursued some things we thought would make us happy, we found out later they failed to deliver and in some instances became prisons: alcohol, drugs, or even careers.

When we were teens, we thought we'd be happy when we became

adults. We vowed we would never be like our parents, trapped in a life of mediocrity. Our lives would be full of excitement and happiness. There was a big world out there, and it was waiting at our fingertips as our vehicle for happiness. Well, that illusion came crashing down once we realized the tremendous responsibilities of adulthood.

I was a huge Star Trek fan when I was young, and I remember an episode where Spock, the stoic Vulcan, was tricked by a rival (Stahn) who stole the woman Spock was supposed to marry. Once Spock realized his fiancée was in on Stahn's plan, he gave up on his pursuit of the woman and said, "Stahn, she is yours. After a while you may find that *having* something is not nearly as pleasurable as *wanting* it. It is not logical, but it is often true."

We can relate to the words of Spock in how we pursued things we thought would make us happy. Maybe it's having that one woman, that great job, or that new home or fancy car. We jump from one worldly thing to the next, thinking they will bring happiness. And once we have that next greatest thing, we realize *having* is often not as pleasurable as *wanting*. The sad truth is a majority of adults in America aren't really happy at all. And many Christians are as disillusioned about the pursuit of happiness as unbelievers. Christians, who profess to believe in eternal life with God, seem just as confused about happiness as the rest of the world. This is because we have replaced God's definition of happiness with a flawed human definition that tells us we will never face problems.

Happiness can mean many different things to different people. The teen believes becoming an adult will make him happy. The rich man thinks more money will make him happy. The single woman thinks getting married will make her happy. And the worker approaching retirement thinks retiring will make him happy. But even when we attain these things, we aren't happy because our flesh will never have enough to make us content. A fleshly/animal thought process believes things of this world can lead to happiness. Our past experiences prove to us this is not truth, but because we've been trained to think like animals, we keep pursuing the same *cause* and expect different *effects* the next time. This seems to fit the unofficial definition of insanity: doing the same thing over and over but expecting a different outcome.

Many go through life pursuing happiness but never finding it. Fame is fleeting, and wealth becomes fool's gold to those who stockpile it. Like a person addicted to drugs, we need a greater high every time, but until it's too late, we don't realize the very things we use to become happy have enslaved and destroyed us. The Bible is clear that the things we desire will become our masters. Jesus said:

> *No one can serve two masters, for either he will hate the one and love the other, or he will be devoted to the one and despise the other. You cannot serve God and money.* (Matthew 6:24)

The majority of Americans and professing Christians pursue desires of the flesh, thinking they will make us happy. We spend more money on pornography than the rest of the world combined. We live in homes far bigger and more extravagant than we need. We accumulate massive amounts of public and private debt in pursuit of things we think will make our lives more comfortable now, even at the expense of our long-term security. We are addicted to things we think will make us happy, only to realize they make us less happy. This is because, as the Bible teaches us, the flesh is never satisfied.

> *Thus says the Lord: "Cursed is the man who trusts in man and makes flesh his strength, whose heart turns away from the Lord. He is like a shrub in the desert, and shall not see any good come. He shall dwell in the parched places of the wilderness, in an uninhabited salt land."* (Jeremiah 17:5-6)

Trusting in our flesh leads us away from, rather than toward, happiness and eternal life with God. The first thing we need to decide is what *is* our definition of happiness? Because whatever we set our heart's desires on will become our master. Will we set it on the world's definition of happiness (money, popularity, and fame)? Or will we pursue God's definition of happiness? The choice is simple: we choose either our flesh or the Spirit God has placed in us to lead us to what we think will make us happy.

Christians have the Bible to give us clear definitions and instructions on how to be truly happy. Always remember this: the Bible was written for our benefit. It teaches us how to find forgiveness with God, attain eternal life with Him, and live with joy in this world. So what does the Bible say about becoming happy?

The word for *happy* does not appear in the ESV New Testament but does appear in the KJV six times. The Greek word is *makarios*: "well-off, happy." The same word, *makarios*, is used throughout the New Testament in the ESV, defined the same way but translated as "blessed."

Blessed are those whose lawless deeds are forgiven, and whose sins are covered; blessed is the man against whom the Lord will not count his sin. (Romans 4:7-8)

Blessed is the man who remains steadfast under trial, for when he has stood the test he will receive the crown of life, which God has promised to those who love him. (James 1:12)

These verses give us the big picture of true and eternal happiness. Realizing God has forgiven our sins, keeping God's Word, and handling difficult circumstances well will lead us to true happiness – eternal life with God. Jesus went into greater detail, laying out our journey to happiness in the Beatitudes:

Seeing the crowds, he went up on the mountain, and when he sat down, his disciples came to him. And he opened his mouth and taught them, saying:

"Blessed are the poor in spirit, for theirs is the kingdom of heaven.

"Blessed are those who mourn, for they shall be comforted.

"Blessed are the meek, for they shall inherit the earth.

"Blessed are those who hunger and thirst for righteousness, for they shall be satisfied.

"Blessed are the merciful, for they shall receive mercy.

"Blessed are the pure in heart, for they shall see God.

> "Blessed are the peacemakers, for they
> shall be called sons of God.
>
> "Blessed are those who are persecuted for righteousness' sake,
> for theirs is the kingdom of heaven.
>
> "Blessed are you when others revile you and persecute you
> and utter all kinds of evil against you falsely on my account.
> Rejoice and be glad, for your reward is great in heaven,
> for so they persecuted the prophets who were before you."
> (Matthew 5:1-12)

The Beatitudes summarized how to be happy in this life *and* for eternity. Jesus begins by encouraging those who are *poor in spirit* and who *mourn*. So we begin to realize who God is (righteous, just, and holy) and who we are before saving grace (lost, condemned, and wretched). This is the starting point of our journey to earthly and eternal happiness.

Meek describes those who realize we are sinners in need of God's grace, dependent upon Him for our next breath and everything we need. We realize, in spite of salvation, we are in constant need of God's continuing grace because we continue to sin, and anything of lasting value we say or do is only a work of the Holy Spirit. We do not allow ourselves to become puffed up and prideful or dependent on this world.

Those who *hunger and thirst for righteousness* realize they are incapable of these attributes but desperately want and need them, so they seek them from the only true source: God. They want and need the righteousness of Christ more each day. Without it we know we will be empty and stagnant. We walk through the desert of life seeking the next water hole to quench us and keep us going: Jesus' righteousness.

Merciful refers to being compassionate. We forgive others because God forgives us of much more than any person could ever do against us. Forgiving others is one of the best ways to achieve joy. The saying "acid only hurts the container it is in" is so true. When we do not forgive others, it damages us much more than the other person. *Our* lives become unsettled and anxious. And when we are angry and unforgiving and cannot get even, those emotions come out eventually, and hurt someone we love who does not deserve our wrath. Then we are sinning, damaging our relationship with God and others. Forgiveness relieves us of stress and the need to get even. Remember what Jesus said happens if we are unwilling to forgive others:

> *For if you forgive others their trespasses, your heavenly Father will also forgive you, but if you do not forgive others their trespasses, neither will your Father forgive your trespasses.* (Matthew 6:14-15)

Forgiving others is proof you have been forgiven by God. Not forgiving others consistently is proof that you do not realize the depth of your sin against God and you believe what others have done to you is worse than your sins against Him. When we realize the serious consequences of what Jesus said here, we find it much easier to become a forgiving person. Forgiving others is for our benefit and happiness.

The *pure in heart* are people who are not double-minded; they know what they need and desire: to be made holy by God. They are not swayed back and forth between the desires of the flesh and the righteousness of God. Their heart's motives are pure and focused on loving God. They realize the more they stay focused on the things of God, the happier they will be.

Peacemakers are happy because they will be called sons of God. Being a peacemaker doesn't mean you attend anti-war demonstrations or never defend yourself against evil. It means we seek peace with one another as believers, basking in fellowship that helps one another grow in grace and fruit. We set aside arguments over non-essential doctrines that divide so many these days. We never compromise on salvation doctrines, but we do realize God sanctifies each believer uniquely. Instead of berating the younger Christian because he attends a conference with a "soft" teacher, you encourage him in his desire to grow in Christ. You are humble enough to admit you too were once a baby in the faith, needing milk. You help the young believer learn from your experiences. You desire to see the young believer develop a strong root system of correct doctrine and principles in the Bible, so he will grow to bear much fruit for God.

> *And the Lord's servant must not be quarrelsome but kind*

> *to everyone, able to teach, patiently enduring evil, correcting his opponents with gentleness. God may perhaps grant them repentance leading to a knowledge of the truth, and they may come to their senses and escape from the snare of the devil, after being captured by him to do his will.*
> (2 Timothy 2:24-26)

Verse 10 in the Beatitudes tells us to be happy when we are persecuted for Jesus' sake, because ours is the kingdom of heaven. Jesus warned us the world would hate us, because it first hated Him. So by undergoing scorn, criticism, and persecution, we partake in a small way in the persecution and hatred Jesus experienced while on earth, and we inherit eternal life with Him (salvation).

The final verses speak to heavenly reward. Jesus says you should actually be happy when people treat you unjustly, because your reward in heaven will be great. God will reward us for the wrong done to us and for our troubles in this world.

> *A lawyer asked him a question to test him. "Teacher, which is the great commandment in the Law?" And he said to him, "You shall love the Lord your God with all your heart and with all your soul and with all your mind. This is the great and first commandment. And a second is like it: You shall love your neighbor as yourself. On these two commandments depend all the Law and the Prophets."* (Matthew 22:36-40)

The Beatitudes perfectly summarize what Jesus taught in these verses, and living them out leads to true happiness, both now and for eternity. They give us a beautiful picture of happiness: Know who God is and who we are before salvation; confess and repent, becoming a child of God. Then prove you are a child of God: be humble, righteous, merciful, forgiving, loving, and pure in heart (motive), knowing God rewards us for eternity when we're treated unjustly in this life (delayed gratification). This is the complete gospel.

Jesus went on to teach us how to apply the Beatitudes in our daily life. The single greatest characteristic of the true believer is humility. Can humility make us happy?

So after he had washed their feet, and had taken his garments, and was set down again, he said unto them, Know ye what I have done to you? Ye call me Master and Lord: and ye say well; for so I am. If I then, your Lord and Master, have washed your feet; ye also ought to wash one another's feet. For I have given you an example, that ye should do as I have done to you. Verily, verily, I say unto you, the servant is not greater than his lord; neither he that is sent greater than he that sent him. If ye know these things, happy are ye if ye do them. (John 13:12-17 KJV)

Can we be happy when we give to others knowing they cannot repay us?

He said also to the man who had invited him, "When you give a dinner or a banquet, do not invite your friends or your brothers or your relatives or rich neighbors, lest they also invite you in return and you be repaid. But when you give a feast, invite the poor, the crippled, the lame, the blind, and you will be blessed, because they cannot repay you. For you will be repaid at the resurrection of the just." (Luke 14:12-14)

God rewards us when we give to others, expecting nothing in return (agape love). Later we will discuss the thought process to use to achieve happiness. First, I want to share a report from Mayo Clinic, one of the most respected medical research facilities in the world. It's the largest medical clinic in the world, staffed with more than 3,300 physicians, scientists, and researchers and spends more than $500 million a year in medical research. Researchers conducted an in-depth study on why some people are happy and others are not; the report was published in The Mayo Clinic Handbook for Happiness.[9] The results of this and other research were summarized in a Mayo Clinic article in 2015:

> Only a small percentage of the variation in people's reports of happiness can be explained by differences in their circumstances. It appears that the bulk of what determines happiness is due to personality and – more importantly

---

[9] The Mayo Clinic Handbook for Happiness: A 4-step Plan for Resilient Living. Cambridge, Mass.: Da Capo Press/Lifelong Books; 2015.

– thoughts and behaviors that can be changed. So, yes, you can learn how to be happy – or at least happier.

Although you may have thought, as many people do, that happiness comes from being born rich or beautiful or living a stress-free life, the reality is that people who have wealth, beauty or less stress are not happier on average than those who don't enjoy those things.

People who are happy seem to intuitively know that their happiness is the sum of their life choices, and their lives are built on the following pillars:

- Devoting time to family and friends
- Appreciating what they have
- Maintaining an optimistic outlook
- Feeling a sense of purpose
- Living in the moment[10]

Science knows *what* can make people happy, but it does not understand *how* we can accomplish it. The Beatitudes give us the *why/how* to be truly happy. Let's look at the Mayo Clinic pillars and compare them to the Word of God and its principles:

- Devoting time to family and friends (Christian fellowship)
- Appreciating what they have (thankful, not coveting)
- Maintaining an optimistic outlook (believe God's promises for believers)
- Feeling a sense of purpose (Great Commandment: love God and others)
- Living in the moment

But if God so clothes the grass of the field, which today is alive and tomorrow is thrown into the oven, will he not

---

10   http://www.mayoclinic.org/healthy-lifestyle/stress-management/in-depth/how-to-be-happy/art-20045714.

much more clothe you, O you of little faith? Therefore do not be anxious, saying, "What shall we eat?" or "What shall we drink?" or "What shall we wear?" For the Gentiles seek after all these things, and your heavenly Father knows that you need them all. But seek first the kingdom of God and his righteousness, and all these things will be added to you. Therefore do not be anxious about tomorrow, for tomorrow will be anxious for itself. Sufficient for the day is its own trouble. (Matthew 6:30-34)

Applying the biblical principles from the Word to the Mayo Clinic pillars, we can arrive at this definition of happiness: happiness is being in fellowship with believers who love God and each other, appreciating all God has provided, fully confident in His eternal promises.

The world will encourage you to focus on immediate benefits that you think will make you happy: wealth, fame, sex, and drugs/alcohol, while ignoring the big picture – the long-term and eternal effects of your choices. God tells us to focus on the big picture, the eternal reward set before us as His children, so the immediate circumstances will not cause us to worry or stumble. In fact, the Beatitudes teach us that the more bad things that happen to us in this world, the greater our eternal reward and benefit!

Summary

The world's definition of happiness is directly opposed to God's definition. The world teaches us to live in the here and now regardless of the long-term effects – what we call a fleshly/animal thought process. Satan and his minions try to distract us to take our eyes off Jesus. Like Peter, we begin to sink when we do not remain focused on Jesus and His teachings. God teaches us that the long-term effects of being a born-again believer will keep our immediate circumstances in proper perspective, not robbing us of happiness when life inevitably brings forth difficult circumstances. Jesus taught us that when we handle difficult circumstances well, we will be rewarded, both in this life time and for eternity. This is using a godly thought process: thinking eternal big picture.

Satan and his minions will focus you on the little picture: the here and now. God encourages us to focus on the big picture: eternity and the reward set before us. When we stay focused on Jesus, the bad things that happen to us in this life are not insurmountable mountains; they are little mole hills we can easily travel over, as we stay focused on big-picture happiness and reward.

Our destination is an earthly life of peace and joy, even when circumstances are difficult. As we handle difficult circumstances the way God teaches us, they bring us greater happiness and eternal reward. Not only do we want to arrive at this destination, we should want our family, friends, and neighbors to go with us. Teaching others God's definition of happiness points them to a life of joy and eternal reward with God.

We are now ready to study and learn the "road map" for the journey and destination that is ahead of us. Knowing, understanding, and following this road map will help assure us of a safe and timely journey to our destination. Not following it will lead to a longer trip or even prevent us from arriving at our planned destination. This road map is the Bible.

Chapter Four

OUR ETERNAL ROAD MAP TO HAPPINESS *GOD'S WORD*

Chapter objective: to discern between deception and truth.

We know our starting point, and we have chosen our desired destination: an earthly life of happiness, peace, and joy, leading to an eternal life with abundant reward. Next, we must study the road map that connects the beginning and destination of our journey. Any of us who have taken long trips in our automobiles know the potential obstacles:

- Failure to follow directions and taking a wrong road.
- Problems with our automobile breaking down.
- Fatigue and the need for rest to avoid a crash.
- Unexpected detours or traffic jams.

Let's apply a biblical example to each of these potential problems on our journey.

Failure to follow directions

This failure can occur when we choose human doctrine instead of biblical doctrine – when we ignore God's Word or do not understand it. Even the best of road maps are useless if we do not follow the objective directions.

Problems with our automobile breaking down

These problems can be related to our mind, heart, and conscience faltering from not being properly aligned with God. As a car needs to be maintained to run smoothly, our mind, heart, and conscience need regular service and care to know God's will.

Fatigue and the need to rest

Fatigue can be related to stressing ourselves out with worry, trying to accomplish things that only God can. This occurs when we rely on our human strength and understanding instead of the wisdom and power of the Holy Spirit.

Unexpected detours or traffic jams

Traffic jams can be related to problems in our life that are out of our control and just happen. When things get out of our control and we handle them the wrong way, they rob us of our happiness and delay our arrival. But if we handle obstacles correctly, we will stay focused on our destination.

Having a reliable road map and knowing how to read it will keep us on course so our journey is not delayed or ended prematurely. That road map is, of course, the Word of God. When we are able to interpret our road map correctly, it will even help us with the other three potential problems.

We live in a world of sound bites; we catch news in quick segments, and we trust whatever the talking heads tell us we should believe. Real friendships are being replaced by superficial Facebook "friends," where we can ignore deep relationships. We communicate on Twitter instead of sitting down and having meaningful conversations. And many treat the Bible like the evening news or Twitter: just skim it quickly looking for the bottom line. Because we are growing more and more self-centered, we look for biblical sound bites that we use to justify our fleshly desires. This is just one reason an honest but half-hearted attempt to follow biblical doctrine could actually result in human doctrine that takes us off course.

We know the Word of God is eternal truth in its entirety. So why do Christians argue over the Bible and cause division and strife? Because each one of us interprets certain biblical teachings differently; we don't read it in complete context and with correct principles of interpretation. We become confused and eventually just give up, and miss out on teachings of the Bible that, if understood and applied accurately and consistently, lead us to joy and happiness. An example is when Christians look at John 3:16-17 as *truth* but do not understand it in complete context. Jesus spoke:

> *For God so loved the world, that he gave his only Son, that whoever believes in him should not perish but have eternal life. For God did not send his Son into the world to condemn the world, but in order that the world might be saved through him.* (John 3:16-17)

If we stop right there and do not understand these verses in complete biblical context, we will believe a deception – that Jesus saved everyone when He died on the cross. This is called *universal salvation*. But when we read the verses that immediately follow, we get the truth. Jesus continued:

> *Whoever believes in him is not condemned, but whoever does not believe is condemned already, because he has not believed in the name of the only Son of God. And this is the judgment: the light has come into the world, and people loved the darkness rather than the light because their works were evil.* (John 3:18-19)

If we read John 3:16-17 out of context, we feed our flesh and think like animals: "Jesus died on the cross, so I am automatically going to heaven." But as the late Paul Harvey would say, the next two verses are "the rest of the story." Please take time to understand what I say next. It may unsettle you at first, but understanding this is critical for correctly interpreting the Word of God: a single verse in the Bible is not automatically truth on its own. One verse, or even a couple of verses, not understood in correct context, can be used to deceive us. Satan tried to deceive Jesus in the desert by quoting a single Scripture, but Jesus rebuked him by reciting Scripture in complete and correct context. If Satan used this deception on Jesus, do we really think he won't try the same tactic on us?

It is a fact that Jesus came to save the lost, not condemn them. But the truth is this: Jesus did come to bring salvation to the lost, but not everyone in the world will be saved. Later in this chapter, we will discuss the difference between a *fact* and *truth*. We arrive at truth by understanding that many teachings in the Word of God were given as "logical conjunctives," something we will study later in this chapter, but a brief explanation now will help you understand the difference between deception and truth.

A logical conjunctive is a statement that contains two components: a freedom/benefit and a restriction applied to that freedom or benefit. Truth is the narrow area where the two overlap. The *freedom* Jesus gave was that men could be saved from eternal damnation and reconciled to God. The *restriction* placed on that freedom is that they must confess, repent, and truly believe and trust in Him alone. Saying all men are saved because of verses 16 and 17 is deception. By using all four verses, we discover the narrow path of truth.

John 3:16-19 points to the first four principles, which I will share to help you correctly reach an objective interpretation of the Word of God, so you can follow it the way God intended. These principles speak to:

- Causality
- Non-contradiction
- The sometimes-subtle difference between a lie, deception, facts, and truth
- Using logical conjunctives to differentiate between biblical and human doctrines

Once we understand these principles, we will learn techniques to apply them to our lives that will not only benefit us, but also help others come to saving faith in Jesus Christ. Before we dive into these crucial principles, let's step back and take a big-picture view of the world, called our worldview.

We covered earlier that only 19% of self-professed, born-again believers profess a biblical worldview. Because Christians have not been taught how to read the Bible by using the principles we will share, many become confused about important teachings God gave us in His Word. We search the Bible for clues as to what God says in relation to our lives, piecing together bits of information we hope will give us the ultimate answer to the meaning of life. Let's relate this to reading a mystery novel.

In a well-written murder novel, the author leads us on a trail of twists and turns that can lead us to conflicting conclusions, wondering, "Who did it?" We finally reach the last chapter and discover it was the butler! Now, go back and read that same novel, already knowing the butler did it. Subtle clues and information the author shares throughout the book that point to the butler as the guilty party become apparent. We think, "Oh, so that's why the butler was late that one morning." or "That's why the butler said what he said at that meeting." Because we read the novel initially from a little-picture perspective, we could not see the big picture. Reading it a second time from a big-picture perspective, knowing the outcome, gives us fresh eyes to better understand why the author shared particular details at certain times.

We should use exactly the same approach in reading and understanding the Bible. When we know the conclusion to this great book, we are able to connect the dots and better know the intent of the author and the conclusion to which the book leads us. We understand the *why* and *how* of what God wrote. The conclusion of the Bible is this: that Jesus will return one day to judge all men, to determine their eternal destination, and to establish His everlasting kingdom where true believers will live with Him for eternity.

With this big-picture perspective in mind, let's look at four biblical principles that will help us understand and follow our road map to eternal life with God; this will allow us to really enjoy the journey.

Principle #1: Causality

Causality: "The relationship between something that happens or exists and the thing that causes it; the idea that something can cause another thing to happen or exist."

God established causality to govern His created universe and maintain order. Without it, we would have chaos, and man could never learn and improve upon things, because there would be no patterns indicating why things happen. With causality we experience something (effect) and find reasons and patterns to show why it occurs (source/cause). Understanding and applying causality is the beginning of rational thought.

Medical science looks at illnesses (effects) and figures out why these illnesses occur (cause). Once they identify the cause, they can recommend ways people can be healthier by avoiding the cause of the illness. An example is weight gain, which is usually an effect of a poor diet and lack of an exercise routine (cause). A person can try to treat the effects without addressing the cause, but the bad effects will return. People drink alcohol, use drugs, and take prescription medicine for depression, because they are unhappy and think doing these things will make them happy. But these actions can deepen our depression and become self-made prisons, because we treat effects instead of identifying and treating the cause, which can lead to a permanent cure. When we can identify the cause of our unhappiness, we can correct the root problem without deepening the hole we dig for ourselves.

When we understand causality in the Bible, we are able to understand why God does what He does.

> *Do not be deceived: God is not mocked, for whatever one sows, that will he also reap. For the one who sows to his own flesh will from the flesh reap corruption, but the one who sows to the Spirit will from the Spirit reap eternal life.* (Galatians 6:7-8)

Sowing is the cause and reaping is the effect. In fact, this verse tells us we are mocking God if we deny that causality exists. When we know *why* (cause) something happens, we can then accurately predict the effects (*what*) of that cause. Causality is such a widely accepted principle that it is used in every area of our lives. Denying and refusing to understand causality is denying rational thought itself. Even animals understand causality. When our cats hear our garage door open, they know "daddy" is home. Yet many Christians do not understand causality, and that damages how we interpret the Word of God.

> *For thus says the Lord: When seventy years are completed for Babylon, I will visit you, and I will fulfill to you my promise and bring you back to this place. For I know the plans I have for you, declares the Lord, plans for welfare and not for evil, to give you a future and a hope.* (Jeremiah 29:10-11)

These verses point out how important understanding causality is. Many Christians claim Jeremiah 29:11 as their "life verse" and believe it means God will never let them suffer. If they look at verse 11 as a cause, they become disillusioned when God disciplines them by allowing trials in their lives. But when we understand causality, we see that verse 11 is the effect of verse 10, which is the cause. God had to discipline Israel for their idolatry and disobedience but promised them when His discipline was over, He would restore and heal them. When we hold on to verse 11 as a promised effect of God's discipline, we see the value in it and can patiently await His promise. This helps us trust that God is always working for our benefit as His children, regardless of what we are going through.

> *And we know that for those who love God all things work together for good, for those who are called according to his purpose.* (Romans 8:28)

Causality helps us realize why God disciplines us and allows us to go through trials. First, we know the eventual effects are for our benefit, and second, when we understand He is teaching us something for our benefit instead of punishing us, we can learn the lesson quicker and shorten the severity of the discipline.

One of the serious problems we are experiencing in society today is over-medication, particularly in addressing depression. Some of the Christians I meet with are on anti-depressant medications. When we help them understand causality and how to interpret the Word of God correctly, many are able to eventually come off their medications – the very medications that can cause more confusion in their thought process. Misapplying causality is the reason we are in crisis regarding the growing depression prevalent in our society. For years the medical community has used this model:

Cause: Chemical imbalance

Effect: Bad thought process (depression)

However, in recent years, as we have learned more about how God designed our brains to work, a new model is emerging within medical thought[11]:

Cause: Bad thought process

Effect: Chemical imbalance

The very medications we take to help us become happy can destroy us. Watch a commercial for anti-depressants and listen to the side effects. We are being trained to think and live like animals, where we pile one medication upon another in our pursuit of happiness. One commercial for an anti-depressant says a side effect of using it could be deeper depression and suicidal thoughts. We are like Pavlov's dogs: they ring the bell and get our attention by convincing us we are depressed. We come running and ingest whatever they tell us will make us happy. When we actually get worse, we run back and take the next medication they tell us will make us better. The cycle continues until the brains of many Americans are almost destroyed and incapable of any rational thought process. Today, sixty-four million Americans are on some form of anti-depressant medication, often because they have a bad thought process. While medication may at times be necessary or useful, prolonged usage can be very damaging to the brain and body, and cannot deal with the cause of the problems we face. Only God's grace and Spirit can address the causes and bring about permanent healing.

The correctly interpreted Word of God is the only real prescription for true, lasting happiness. And understanding the cause and effect taught in the Bible is the first step toward happiness.

---
11 www.thebestbrainpossible.com; www.socialanxietyinstitute.org

Rejoice in the Lord always; again I will say, rejoice. Let your reasonableness be known to everyone. The Lord is at hand; do not be anxious about anything, but in everything by prayer and supplication with thanksgiving let your requests be made known to God. And the peace of God, which surpasses all understanding, will guard your hearts and your minds in Christ Jesus.

Finally, brothers, whatever is true, whatever is honorable, whatever is just, whatever is pure, whatever is lovely, whatever is commendable, if there is any excellence, if there is anything worthy of praise, think about these things. What you have learned and received and heard and seen in me – practice these things, and the God of peace will be with you. (Philippians 4:4-9)

Biblical cause: Think on things true, honorable, just, pure, lovely, and commendable.

Biblical effect: Peace of God will be with you, giving you joy no matter your circumstances.

Depression can be the result of people fearing the future because of their current circumstances. When Christians understand causality and correctly interpret the Word of God, we realize why the future is bright, regardless of our current circumstances. God's Word, correctly understood and followed, leads us to peace and keeps us from being depressed. We understand that He holds the future in His hands, and His plans will not be thwarted. We understand that God's cause is that His children live a life of peace and joy, spending eternity with Him forever away from sin, suffering, and death. And if we follow His teaching and instruction, we will reap the effects of that cause.

Knowing how the story ends affects how we live our part in that story. In 1997, two years before I came to saving faith in Jesus Christ, the Green Bay Packers were one of several "gods" I worshipped. In January of that season, they finally battled through decades of mediocrity and returned to the Super Bowl. Nancy and I watched the game with my parents, and when the New England Patriots scored a touchdown in the third quarter to narrow the Packers' lead, I leaned over to Nancy and said, "I haven't been this nervous since the birth of my children."

Eventually the Packers came back and won the game, and I was happy. But throughout the game, I was a nervous wreck, wondering what the final outcome would be.

I recorded the game and went back and watched it a week later. This time when New England narrowed the Packers' lead, I was completely calm, because I knew the eventual outcome. Understanding the Bible and the eventual outcome God has determined for His children helps us relax when things are not going our way, because we know the eventual outcome of our lives. Understanding causality is a key to correctly understanding and living the Word of God.

Causality Verses

> *And because you listen to these rules and keep and do them, the Lord your God will keep with you the covenant and the steadfast love that he swore to your fathers.* (Deuteronomy 7:12)

Cause: Obey God's rules

Effect: God will keep His covenant

> *And to Adam he said, "Because you have listened to the voice of your wife and have eaten of the tree of which I commanded you, 'You shall not eat of it,' cursed is the ground because of you; in pain you shall eat of it all the days of your life; thorns and thistles it shall bring forth for you; and you shall eat the plants of the field." (Genesis 3:17-18)*

Cause: Eating of the Tree of Knowledge of Good and Evil

Effect: Curses and pain

> *And he said, "What comes out of a person is what defiles him. For from within, out of the heart of man, come evil thoughts, sexual immorality, theft, murder, adultery, coveting, wickedness, deceit, sensuality, envy, slander, pride, foolishness. All these evil things come from within, and they defile a person." (Mark 7:20-23)*

Cause: The evil thoughts of the human heart

Effects: Evil actions

These last verses will be particularly important later when we study how God designed our brain and heart to work and how we can determine if our flesh or the Holy Spirit influences our actions. We will see that our heart is the ultimate cause of our actions. If our hearts are guided by the Holy Spirit, we will produce good fruit. If our heart is guided by our flesh, our fruit will be bad and poison us and others. One of the most effective lies Satan uses against us is to try to flip causality.

> *And the Lord said to Satan, "Have you considered my servant Job, that there is none like him on the earth, a blameless and upright man, who fears God and turns away from evil?" Then Satan answered the Lord and said, "Does Job fear God for no reason? Have you not put a hedge around him and his house and all that he has, on every side? You have blessed the work of his hands, and his possessions have increased in the land. But stretch out your hand and touch all that he has, and he will curse you to your face." (Job 1:8-11)*

Take the time to understand what Satan tried to do here:

God's Causality

Cause: Job is blameless and upright.

Effect: I have blessed the work of his hands.

Satan's flipping of Causality

Cause: God has blessed the work of Job's hands.

Effect: Job only loves and obeys God *because* he is blessed and protected.

Satan accused Job of conditional obedience to God and suggested that if God removed the blessings Job would curse God to His face. Satan will use some twisted causality flip against you to get you to curse or give up on God. Satan is sowing bad seeds in the prosperity gospel movement these days. He uses deceptive teachings to lead naive followers to believe their level of obedience can manipulate God into giving them health, wealth, and extravagance. If our economy crashes and the American dream is shaken, some of these naive followers will literally lose their minds and curse God. They will do exactly what Satan said Job would do when their health and wealth theology falls apart.

If we do not understand causality, we will struggle to interpret God's Word correctly. Slow down when you read God's Word and look for cause and effect in what God is teaching us. You will discover how understanding causality can help you to be happy. Here is a causality teaching we can count on:

Cause: Joy and security of knowing our eternal destination

Effect: Joy, no matter our circumstances, because we know how the story ends

Key Points on Causality

- Causality is used throughout the Bible.
- Every effect has a cause.
- What a man sows (cause) he will reap (effect).
- Jesus taught that a good cause bears good effects, and a bad cause bears bad effects.
- We get in trouble when we try to flip cause and effect. Flipping causality is a favorite lie Satan uses to separate us from God.

Important note: God is not governed or restricted by the laws and principles established in His universe. He is fully capable of doing supernatural things that defy what we call causality. He can take a bad cause and give it good effects (Romans 8:28). He caused a donkey to speak. Jesus healed people from terminal diseases and raised people from the dead. It is important we never try to put God in a box to limit His power or authority over everything He has created.

Also, we can have a good cause but not see good effects immediately. In fact, many times we do the right thing, but the effects seem negative at first. This is where we must be patient and trust God that He will make the eventual and eternal effects positive when we do the right cause.

Principle #2: Non-contradiction

Jesus said, *"Beware of false prophets, who come to you in sheep's clothing but inwardly are ravenous wolves"* (Matthew 7:15). If we do not understand non-contradiction, we are vulnerable to false teachers that will deceive us, which will cost us reward and perhaps even our eternal salvation.

> *I know that after my departure fierce wolves will come in among you, not sparing the flock; and from among your own selves will arise men speaking twisted things, to draw away the disciples after them.* (Acts 20:29-30)

> *But false prophets also arose among the people, just as there will be false teachers among you, who will secretly bring in destructive heresies, even denying the Master who bought them, bringing upon themselves swift destruction. And many will follow their sensuality, and because of them the way of truth will be blasphemed.* (2 Peter 2:1-2)

Contradictions don't actually exist, conflicts do. I can be both happy and sad (conflicted), but I cannot be both happy and *not* happy at the same time (contradiction). Something or someone cannot *be* something and *not be* something at the same time. I cannot both *believe* and *not believe* the same thing at the same time. Understanding the difference between contradiction and conflict is crucial to not being led astray by the many false teachers and false gospels we see today. A contradiction is something that claims to be true and false at the same time. (I am married to Nancy but not married to Nancy). A conflict is a disagreement over two competing opinions or stated facts. (I am a good husband who does not always do the right things.) The presence of a contradiction proves something is not right. I am either married to Nancy or not married to Nancy, and both statements cannot be true (contradiction). But I can be a good husband and not always do good things: that is a conflict.

"I'm telling you the truth: I always lie!" This is a statement of contradiction. But a person who values honesty can still lie on occasion. He might fear that telling the truth could harm him or others, so he wrestles with a conflict.

<u>A lack of contradiction doesn't necessarily prove something is truth, because we may not yet have all the information needed.</u> This can lead to circumstances that will hinder our journey: something we believed to be truth actually has a contradiction when we learn new information. At that point we find out if we are humble or proud. If we discover a contradiction in our beliefs and we are humble, we change our mind about the belief. But if we choose to ignore the contradiction and continue to believe something that has been proven to be contradictory, we are prideful, and we damage our brain in the long run.

Here is another example of the difference between a conflict and a contradiction:

The gospel of John records that Jesus turned water into wine at the wedding feast in Cana, but the other three gospels did not record this miracle. So we have a conflict, where we wonder why John recorded the event, while the other writers did not record it. This is not a contradiction. A contradiction would be if John stated, "Jesus turned water into wine at Cana," and another gospel said, "Jesus did *not* turn water into wine at Cana." We see that some of the miracles and teachings of Jesus were recorded in all four gospels, while others were in one gospel account but not another. So we are left with a certain level of mystery as to why some of the authors recorded some events that others chose to ignore in their writings. And of course, there are several plausible explanations for this.

> *Now there are also many other things that Jesus did. Were every one of them to be written, I suppose that the world itself could not contain the books that would be written.*
> (John 21:25)

Another explanation is that not every writer was present at every event or teaching of Jesus. The gospels are written on strict, reliable, eyewitness accounts, and the authors would never plagiarize or add to the writings, because they were well aware of who Jesus was and would not dare do such a thing.

Lastly, imagine if each of the four gospels said exactly the same things in the same order. What would skeptics say? "Well, these are obviously carefully concocted fables, because they all say the exact same thing! If they were genuine, the authors would have at least some details that differ from book to book!"

Because a truth is stated in one part of the Bible but not stated in other parts, it is not a contradiction. But if one book in the Bible states a truth that is directly refuted in another book of the Bible, we would have a contradiction. The Bible contains no contradictions, period. We wrestle with conflicts, because of our limited human understanding and wisdom, but nowhere does the Word of God ever contradict itself. But Christians who do not understand the difference between a conflict and a contradiction are easy prey for false teachers and enemies of the gospel.

For centuries well-intentioned Christians have disagreed over whether the gifts of the Holy Spirit are still given to believers, or if these gifts ended with the completion of Scripture. I have not found a verse in the Bible that gives a *definitive* answer one way or the other. If one was found, perhaps the arguments would cease. This is an example of a conflict we have within the Church, but it is not a contradiction found in the Bible.

A contradiction would be if one teaching in the Bible clearly said the gifts have ceased, while another verse says they continue. But no such verses exist. So men continue to wrestle with this conflict, some lacking the godly wisdom to know for certain.

Another conflict we wrestle with is God being sovereign and man having a free will to choose his thoughts and actions. Some believe God predestined some for salvation and others for condemnation, while others point to verses like Romans 10:9 that shows man has a responsibility in receiving forgiveness and eternal life. This is not a question about man achieving salvation by his own efforts; that is humanism. It is a question of how we reconcile God's sovereignty, grace, and knowing all things with man's call to confession, repentance, and complete faith in Jesus Christ to be given forgiveness and eternal life.

When we wrestle with issues such as these, it exposes our thought process. Will we react with prideful self-righteousness, believing we have God and His ways completely figured out? Or are we men and women of humility, who understand we cannot fully comprehend everything about God in this lifetime? There is nothing wrong with having a robust, respectful discussion about these doctrines, because we seek a greater understanding of the Word of God. <u>But when pride and self-righteousness enter the discussion, it ceases to glorify God.</u>

It is important to have a basic understanding of non-contradiction, as opposed to conflicting opinions and statements, for two reasons.

First, if we believe God contradicts Himself, then we believe God is capable of lying. God says in His Word that He cannot lie. So if we believe God is contradictory, then we really cannot believe anything He says in the Bible. But just because God said something in the Old Testament that Jesus didn't repeat in the New Testament does not make God contradictory. Jesus is the Word of God and God! Failure to understand non-contradiction has fueled the growth of the Emergent Church movement, leading millions of young professing Christians into heresy and eternal damnation, if they do not confess and repent. It has fueled the dangerous belief that since Jesus never *directly* said homosexuality is a sin, it is no longer a sin. This conclusion completely defies logic and rational thought.

Here is a human example: I meet you for the first time, and as we talk, I tell you I am married to Nancy. Six months later we meet again, and you ask me what is going on in my life. I tell you about my work and personal life, but do not say, "I am still married to Nancy." Does this mean I am no longer married to Nancy? If you believe so, you jumped to a wrong conclusion, believing that if I am still married to Nancy, I will state that every time we talk. This is the rationale behind movements like the Emergent Church. Emergents conclude, "Mike is no longer married to Nancy or he would have said so." This is the same illogical conclusion they reach when they state homosexuality is no longer a sin, because Jesus never overtly stated it was still a sin. Jesus never said pedophilia was a sin, so does that make it acceptable? Just because God spoke truth one time and did not reiterate that truth every time He spoke in the future, it doesn't mean it is no longer truth.

What we really have in the fact (not truth) of Jesus never directly stating homosexuality is a sin is a conflict in how we interpret the Scriptures. (We will discuss the difference between a fact and truth later in this chapter). But by understanding that God cannot contradict Himself and by reading the Word of God in a non-contradictory manner, we can easily resolve the conflict. People who cannot resolve conflict in a way that is beneficial are in a fleshly/animal thought process. They only see their perspective and refuse to consider another. They are prideful.

Understanding that God cannot contradict Himself is of vital importance as we see false prophets and teachers increasing in number. If Jesus had truly contradicted the Father, then Jesus is not God, who is the same yesterday, today, and forever. So the emergent believes that either Jesus is not God or that God cannot be trusted because He contradicts Himself.

The second reason it is important to understand non-contradiction is that our brain was designed by God to reject contradictions.

> *For all who have sinned without the law will also perish without the law, and all who have sinned under the law will be judged by the law. For it is not the hearers of the law who are righteous before God, but the doers of the law who will be justified. For when Gentiles, who do not have the law, by nature do what the law requires, they are a law to themselves, even though they do not have the law. They show that the work of the law is written on their hearts, while their conscience also bears witness, and their conflicting thoughts accuse or even excuse them on that day when, according to*

my gospel, God judges the secrets of men by Christ Jesus.
(Romans 2:12-16)

The word *conflicting* means "one directly opposed to the other" – a contradiction. Later we will study the human conscience and the crucial role it plays in our lives, either confirming or refuting the influence of the Holy Spirit in our lives. When our thoughts as believers attempt to contradict the influence of the Holy Spirit, and we ignore our conscience, we get ourselves into a lot of trouble and become double-minded as James wrote about. When emergents, who have a contradictory belief about homosexuality, are confronted with their contradiction but refuse to be humble and admit their error, what happens?

> *Indeed, all who desire to live a godly life in Christ Jesus will be persecuted,* **while evil people and impostors will go on from bad to worse, deceiving and being deceived**. *But as for you, continue in what you have learned and have firmly believed, knowing from whom you learned it and how from childhood you have been acquainted with the sacred writings, which are able to make you wise for salvation through faith in Christ Jesus. All Scripture is breathed out by God and profitable for teaching, for reproof, for correction, and for training in righteousness, that the man of God may be complete, equipped for every good work.* (2 Timothy 3:12-17, emphasis added)

Paul tells us evil people who live in increasing contradiction go from bad to worse. And He tells us how to prevent this from happening to us: the Word of God. In Romans, Paul said every man has a God-given conscience that knows right from wrong. Watch a little child's reaction when he lies or hits another child unjustly; you can see the guilt all over his face. Every man's God-given conscience knows lying, stealing, and murder are wrong. When we do these things, or justify that doing them is righteous, we damage our thought process and begin the process of searing our conscience. Left unchecked, we continue to contradict our consciences in disobedience to God.

> *Therefore God gave them up in the lusts of their hearts to*

impurity, to the dishonoring of their bodies among themselves, because they exchanged the truth about God for a lie and worshiped and served the creature rather than the Creator, who is blessed forever! Amen.

For this reason God gave them up to dishonorable passions. For their women exchanged natural relations for those that are contrary to nature; and the men likewise gave up natural relations with women and were consumed with passion for one another, men committing shameless acts with men and receiving in themselves the due penalty for their error.

And since they did not see fit to acknowledge God, God gave them up to a debased mind to do what ought not to be done. They were filled with all manner of unrighteousness, evil, covetousness, malice. They are full of envy, murder, strife, deceit, maliciousness. They are gossips, slanderers, haters of God, insolent, haughty, boastful, inventors of evil, disobedient to parents, foolish, faithless, heartless, ruthless. Though they know God's righteous decree that those who practice such things deserve to die, they not only do them but give approval to those who practice them. (Romans 1:24-32)

I call this process "flipping your conscience" with the potential result being the conscience is seared. A seared conscience can result in a person *feeling* that sin is right. But until the conscience of a person is seared, there is hope in Jesus Christ through the gospel of confession and repentance.

The conscience of the unsaved person testifies against their sin; it knows their actions objectively contradict God. When born-again believers continue to sin, does our conscience continue to testify against us? Yes, but the testimony against us is much greater. Additionally, the Holy Spirit in us also testifies against our sin. When we are born again, we receive a new heart and God's Spirit within us:

And I will give you a new heart, and a new spirit I will put within you. And I will remove the heart of stone from your flesh and give you a heart of flesh. And I will put my Spirit within you, and cause you to walk in my statutes and be careful to obey my rules. (Ezekiel 36:26-27)

When our thoughts and actions as believers contradict the new heart and Spirit God gives us, the Holy Spirit, our heart, and our conscience will continue to convict us and help us resolve the contradiction. However, if we train ourselves to ignore the conviction and not respond correctly, we not only pollute our heart and begin the process of flipping our conscience, but we also quench the Spirit by not listening to Him as He attempts to lead us towards the proper response to our sin. Eventually, this continual quenching of the Holy Spirit and feeding of our flesh leads to our fellowship with God being damaged, and we might forfeit earthly and eternal reward. If you find yourself feeling consistently anxious and unsettled, you are living in contradiction. Your sinful behaviors and fleshly thought process contradict the new heart and Spirit God has given you. You are being double-minded, and until you resolve the contradictions, you will remain unhappy, subject to life's inevitable ups and downs.

Here is an example of living in contradiction: I tell you it is wrong for you to lie to me, but I justify that it is OK for me to lie to you or others. My unconscious brain sees this as a contradiction, and it will cause me to become unsettled. God did not make our brains to accept contradictions, so they must be settled or the contradictions will continue to haunt us. When we try to justify a contradiction, we can become emotionally and physically ill. A growing number of Christians battle confusion and depression, because they cannot identify or settle contradictory beliefs and actions in their lives. Because they hold others to a different standard of righteousness than themselves, they are double-minded:

If any of you lacks wisdom, let him ask God, who gives generously to all without reproach, and it will be given him. But let him ask in faith, with no doubting, for the one who doubts is like a wave of the sea that is driven and tossed by the wind. For that person must not suppose that he will receive anything from the Lord; he is a double-minded man, unstable in all his ways. (James 1:5-8)

The word *double-minded* James uses is literally "double-spirited." He tells the believer that if what he says and does are split between the Spirit of God and the spirit of this world, he should not expect wisdom from God. His conscience knows he is contradictory between God's Spirit and his sinful human spirit, which damages himself and others. Progressive Christians, who do not understand the Bible in a non-contradictory way, are confused and cause confusion within the church. And unless we understand and share the Word of God in a non-contradictory manner, we fan the flames and spread contention within the body of Christ.

Summary

- God is a triune God: Father, Son, and Spirit, who cannot lie or contradict Himself. He is the same yesterday, today, and forever.
- God's Word, like Him, is non-contradictory and never changes. The New Testament fulfilled the Old Testament; it did not change it.
- If we believe God and His Word are contradictory, we can easily be swayed by false movements and teachers that are on the rise.
- Living with contradictory beliefs can make us emotionally and physically ill, because our brains were not made by God to embrace contradiction.
- If our conscience becomes seared and we continually justify good as evil and evil as good, we store up the wrath of God against us on judgment day.
- A key to joy is resolving contradictions by understanding the Word of God in complete context.

Principle #3: What is biblical truth?

Then Pilate said to him, "So you are a king?" Jesus answered,

> *"You say that I am a king. For this purpose I was born and for this purpose I have come into the world – to bear witness to the truth. Everyone who is of the truth listens to my voice." Pilate said to him, "What is truth?" After he had said this, he went back outside to the Jews and told them, "I find no guilt in him."* (John 18:37-38)

What is your definition of truth? Is it situational or eternal? Do you believe something can be truth today but not be truth tomorrow? Can truth be one thing to you and something different to me?

Why are people so easily deceived? Why did the German people willingly follow a man who would eventually rule them as a tyrant and bring their nation to the brink of total destruction? Why did the Russian people follow Josef Stalin, who would later murder tens of millions and enslave them under communism? Why do Americans continue to elect politicians who tell us one thing, yet do the opposite?

We fall for false teachers and tyrants because they say what we want to hear, but we do not take the time to understand why or how they will accomplish their plan in a way that benefits us. They appeal to our flesh by making brash statements that appeal to our anger or frustration. And unless we use an excellent thought process, we will fall for their passionate statements because we will react like animals, abandoning rational thought and big-picture thinking.

How many of the German or Russian people would have supported Hitler or Stalin if they knew what the eventual outcome would have been? If they had insisted that these despots explain exactly how their plan would unfold, these men would have been rejected before they consolidated power. Both of these men stated facts, or correct knowledge (the what): their people were suffering. But these men were never forced to tell *why* they were the best ones to solve the problems or *how* they intended to do it. They appealed to the fears of people, whipping them into a frenzy. In other words, they treated them like animals, instead of encouraging rational thought and discussion. This is exactly what we are seeing happen in America today. Unless Christians learn how to use a godly thought process, many will fall for clever deception.

Unless we understand and utilize the biblical model for truth, we will continue to fall for slick leaders who know how to appeal to our flesh by manipulating us to bypass <u>rational thought and logic</u>. In fact, this <u>is exactly what has been presented as education in public schools over the past several decades.</u> We have abandoned teaching logic through the classical education model and have replaced it with an agenda to condition students to blindly follow others without rational thought. Young people have been conditioned to react like animals, instead of considering the information presented by using understanding and wisdom. <u>They are being taught *what* to think instead of being taught *how* to think</u>. Remember this quote from Lenin? "Give me four years to teach the children, and the seed I have sown will never be uprooted."

Today, 53% of Americans under the age of thirty have a positive view of socialism. Unless we can help people understand how to discern between deception and truth, things will only grow worse. The Bible gives us the system to accomplish this.

Conflicting or contradictory definitions for words like *grace, sin,* and *repentance* have damaged the thought process of individuals and brought confusion and dissent into the church. There is no more important matter facing the Christian church today than correctly defining *truth*. Is truth objective or subjective? Is truth temporal or eternal? This issue must be addressed if the church is going to do what it is called to do: call men to salvation and sanctification through Jesus Christ alone. The ability to determine truth objectively in the face of feelings and emotions is what distinguishes people who get the full benefit of salvation and sanctification from those who may be saved but are hindered by humanism.

This information may seem unimportant or counterintuitive at first, because we have been subjected to indoctrination by the humanist systems of this world: government, public education, and media. Our ability to think has been eroded by these institutions that want to control us and treat us like animals.

Reader alert: It is important that you do not just quickly read this chapter and move on. I urge you to read this section slowly, and check it against the Bible before moving on to the remainder of this book.

Understanding and identifying the subtle differences between opinions, facts, deception, and truth is essential to salvation, sanctification, and to leading a life of joy through a godly thought process.

> *Do your best to present yourself to God as one approved, a worker who has no need to be ashamed, rightly handling the word of truth. But avoid irreverent babble, for it will lead people into more and more ungodliness, and their talk will spread like gangrene.* (2 Timothy 2:15-16)

Paul stated we ought to do our best to present ourselves to God as one approved. This information will help you to do just that. The word for *rightly handling* in the Greek was *orthotomeō*: "make a straight, precise surgical singular cut that is perpendicular to the horizon (to make a cut from above, which is God's view, straight down)." The *word of truth* refers to the Bible. Rightly handling the Scriptures means we take God's view on Scripture. We should think like God, which means we need to use a godly thought process, not a human thought process.

The word for *irreverent* in Greek was *bebēlos*: "counterfeit the threshold (entry) in order to misdirect the dwellers." This teaches us that using counterfeit definitions will lead people away from God. If you give a definition to a word that is not God's, you can misdirect others. One of the reasons Christians don't get the full benefit of sanctification and end up depressed is they choose to believe definitions that contradict God, and our conscience knows it, and the contradictions cause us to become confused and depressed.

The word for *babble* in Greek is *kenophōnia*: "fruitless discussion, empty sounds." This clearly spoke to wrong definitions for the right word. The right word is a fact, the *what* that appears to be from God. However, the definition for this right word is wrong because it has a wrong meaning or understanding (the why). God has one definition and one purpose for one word. If God wanted to say something else with a different meaning, then He would use a different word. We are looking for God's definitions.

Taken together, this passage states that in order to show ourselves approved to God we need to have His view on the words used in the Bible and use His definitions. Appearing to talk about the Bible, but using definitions based on human traditions, is misleading to both the worker and the students. Let's look at the crucial words we will need to define in order to understand God's definition for truth.

When I was ten years old, my favorite food was a stack of pancakes, and I could not imagine the day when I would love any food more. Today, a medium-rare steak is my favorite food. Was I lying when I said pancakes were my favorite food? No, I was stating truth as I understood it best at that particular time. I lacked the maturity to realize that someday I could change my mind about my favorite food.

The reality is I was stating a fact, because when I was ten, pancakes were my favorite food. The definition of *fact* is "a piece of information presented as having objective reality." A fact is reality, which we could also say is a right "what." The Bible didn't use the word *fact*. There is a Hebrew word and a Greek word for fact or data, and it never occurred in the Bible. God wasn't concerned with us merely stating facts. God's thoughts are higher than facts. Humans are completely focused on facts to the point that they define *truth* as "fact." Humanists are able to deceive people in this way. They define facts as truth. Since Jesus never directly stated homosexuality is a sin (a fact), they equate a fact with truth in their mind, despite the fact that other scriptures are clear that homosexuality is indeed a sin. They place their fact above God's truth.

Nothing is more essential to correctly understanding the Bible than understanding the difference between our human definition for truth and the Bible's definition for truth. At age ten, I did not have all the necessary information about food to state a truth that met the requirements of the biblical definition of truth about pancakes being my favorite food for the rest of my life. I was stating what I believed to be truth at the time with no intention of deception. But as more information became available to me, I made a decision that altered what I believed to be truth at that time.

Another word in both Hebrew (*kachash*) and Greek (*pseudomai*) depicts the opposite of fact; we can call it a wrong "what." Here are verses from both the Old and New Testament where these words were used:

> But Sarah denied it, saying, "I did not laugh," for she was afraid. He said, "No, but you did laugh." (Genesis 18:15)

So when God desired to show more convincingly to the heirs of the promise the unchangeable character of his purpose, he guaranteed it with an oath, so that by two unchangeable things, in which it is impossible for God to lie, we who have fled for refuge might have strong encouragement to hold fast to the hope set before us. (Hebrews 6:17-18)

The word for a wrong *what* is *lie*. In the Genesis passage, it was translated as "denied." The Hebrews passage stated God was unable to lie: something that was the opposite of fact or reality. In fact, the Greek word for *lie* can be broken into two words: *pseudo* and *mai*. The word *pseudo* is a lot like the definitions we saw for irreverent babble: "to mislead with something that appears to be right but is actually wrong." What is *mai* in Greek? It is the word *am*, which is fact or reality. To lie is to mislead with a fake "am." When Moses asked God whom should he say sent him, God's response was, "I AM."

A fact is something that appears correct in the present, but could be subject to change upon receiving more information. Now that we have the correct definition for fact, let's learn another crucial word. Up until 1543, the official stance of the Roman Catholic Church was that the sun orbited the earth. It stated this as a truth. But Nicolaus Copernicus theorized the exact opposite, and it was confirmed eight-nine years later by Galileo Galilei. The earth actually orbited the sun, directly opposing the doctrine of the Catholic Church. Both Copernicus and Galilei were threatened with excommunication and death for their alleged heresy.

Today we know these men were correct; they had a right *what*. The Catholic Church was incorrect; it had a wrong *what*. However, would we say the Catholic Church lied? If the Catholic Church did not intentionally state a falsehood (wrong *what*), then what word should we use? What the Catholic Church stated as truth was what we might define as an opinion: "a view or judgment formed about something, not necessarily based on fact or knowledge."

The Greek word for opinion is *gnome*. Here are two passages where it was translated as "my judgment":

Now concerning the betrothed, I have no command from the

Lord, but I give my judgment as one who by the Lord's mercy is trustworthy. (1 Corinthians 7:25)

And in this matter I give my judgment: this benefits you, who a year ago started not only to do this work but also to desire to do it. (2 Corinthians 8:10)

So, a fact is a right what. A lie is a wrong what, stated with the purpose of intentionally misleading people. An opinion is a what that is believed to be right, but may or may not be eternally right, because we do not yet have all the information necessary to determine if it will always be correct. For example, we could say, "When I was ten years old, my opinion was that pancakes would be my favorite food for the rest of my life." Why is it crucial that we are able to distinguish between fact, lie, and opinion?

The crisis we face in America has been advanced by progressive judges who try to interpret the Constitution using their personal views and understanding. In 1973, the Supreme Court imposed its own moral standards to erroneously determine that the Constitution allowed for a woman to kill her unborn child. In 2015, the Court used its own moral standards to erroneously rule that the Constitution imposed a definition of marriage contradictory to God's eternal definition. These progressive judges stated their opinions. The issue is that people confuse these opinions with facts and truth. The source of this confusion ultimately comes down to how the judges reached these *what* conclusions.

Medical science has now taken a step closer to Christian thought, and development photos from in the womb offer evidence of life at conception.[12] If the Supreme Court was humble, it would revisit its 1973 opinion because new information is now available that was not at that time. It would change its opinion because justices want to pursue truth. As Christians, we know life begins when God knits a child into the mother's womb. If the Supreme Court used even a human thought process, it would revisit its 1973 decision.

Progressives present opinions because they believe that the writers of the Constitution could not have anticipated issues such as abortion and

---

12 http://www.lifenews.com/2014/09/16/amazing-fetal-development-photos-confirm-human-life-begins-at-conception/

homosexuality. On the other hand, a strict constitutionist at the very least pursues facts because he believes the Constitution alone should be used to interpret itself.

We see the same corruption infecting the church. Progressive emergents use their own standards of human morality to reinterpret the Bible to advance humanism and subjective morality. They believe the Bible was written by men who could not anticipate life in the 21st century. They apply their human understanding, corrupted by the sinful nature, to interpret the Bible to appeal to the flesh, which results in opinions of men presented as if they are God's doctrine. The only debate is whether these people are stating lies or opinions. Are they deceivers or simply deceived? Clearly, truth is higher than fact and opinion.

Before we define truth, let's summarize the possible statements from my pancake story.

Fact: At ten years old, my favorite food was pancakes.

Opinion: At ten years old, I believed pancakes would always be my favorite food.

Lie: If today I stated I like pancakes more than a medium-rare sirloin steak, I would be lying.

Truth

How do we determine God's intentions for the words He used in the Bible? How do we determine truth? What is the definition for truth?

The way to show yourself approved to God is to determine the non-contradictory why and how for what the Bible stated. The Bible, interpreted and understood in a non-contradictory manner, is the only reliable source to interpret itself. When we use something other than the Bible to interpret it, we are humanists, relying on human understanding in place of God. What does the Bible say about truth?

Jesus said to him, "I am the way, and the truth, and the life. No one comes to the Father except through me. If you had known me, you would have known my Father also. From now on you do know him and have seen him." (John 14:6-7)

The word *truth* in Greek is *aletheia*: "what is true in any matter under consideration." This definition is crucial to understand. It tells us that real truth cannot be contradicted by new information. My belief that pancakes would always be my favorite food was contradicted by new information. In the future I tasted steak and liked it far more than pancakes. My belief was an opinion, an apparent truth, subject to change upon further understanding or experience.

The truth defined in the Bible is eternal, not subject to flawed human understanding or more information that comes later. Truth is a fact that is eternally right. Only one source can create truth. Truth comes from God alone, the One who knows everything that has existed or ever will exist.

Truth involves facts (correct whats) that will remain correct for eternity. Humanists believe they can state an eternally correct what that is contradictory to the Bible. However, this perspective proves the person is deceived. God has much more power over information than simply knowing the facts (the what):

> *Great is our Lord, and of great power: his understanding is infinite.* (Psalm 147:5 KJV)

God's understanding is infinite. In fact, look at what this passage says about knowledge:

> *Love never ends. As for prophecies, they will pass away; as for tongues, they will cease; as for knowledge, it will pass away.* (1 Corinthians 13:8)

Knowledge is finite! Man is misled when he values knowledge (what) over understanding (why). Humanists worship the knowledge of man instead of the One who has all understanding. Let's look at the definitions for three words that people wrongly use interchangeably.

- The word *knowledge* comes from the Greek root word *gnosis,* meaning "knowing, knowledge, science."
- The word *understanding* is from the Hebrew word *tabun,* meaning "extension of an argument, discretion, reason, and skillfulness."

- The word *wisdom* is from the Hebrew word *hakma,* meaning "wise in administration and prudent in affairs."

Knowledge is basic and even animals have some. Understanding can apply knowledge correctly, and wisdom is the correct administration of that knowledge and understanding. Clearly, understanding and wisdom are essential to real truth. Now we see the issue between humanism and biblical Christianity! Humans can use faulty understanding (the why) because of free will, so they can create an effect (what) and convince themselves it is truth. An example occurs when emergents deny God's righteous and just nature and state He is only love. Their wrong theology leads people to wrong knowledge (what) and understanding (why): because Jesus is only love to them (why), they believe we all go to heaven (what/effect).

When men try to remake God in their image, they state God is the master over knowledge (what). This self-justification erroneously considers humanity to be on equal footing with God because both God and man can possess knowledge (what). This arrogance prevents discussion of understanding and wisdom (why and how): the other necessary ingredients for truth.

The Bible states that God has infinite understanding (knows all the whys), and the effect is He can accurately state eternal knowledge (what). Biblical Christianity works with causality in a non-contradictory manner. Humanism attempts to reverse causality and ignore contradictions. Humanism treats effects as if they are causes and appeals to our sinful nature by only presenting these facts (whats).

Wisdom (the how) objectively proves a person's understanding (why) and knowledge (what). This is similar to the godly thought process.

Human wisdom based only on what a person knows and understands from within could never be eternal. However, humanists believe humans can work together to create solutions that will last forever. When someone's solution doesn't work, do they admit they were wrong or justify themselves by blaming others? Self-justification is easiest to see when the person doesn't explain his wisdom (how) or understanding (why).

God is able to create solutions that last eternally because, while God knows everything that exists, it is His infinite understanding that exhibits

His eternal wisdom. God owns the causes (how and why), while the knowledge (what) is only an effect to Him. However, you can recognize humanists by how much they are focused on effects (whats). Humanists worship the effects instead of the First Cause (God).

Animals have basic knowledge, but lack understanding or wisdom. They know the what but not the why/how.

> *Be not like a horse or a mule, without understanding, which must be curbed with bit and bridle, or it will not stay near you.* (Psalm 32:9)

God gave man a mind and conscious brain to understand the why in addition to knowledge (what). Man can understand facts and build upon them using cause and effect. The how is the principles and wisdom applied to knowledge and understanding. The Bible speaks of two types of wisdom: human or godly.

> *Where is the one who is wise? Where is the scribe? Where is the debater of this age? Has not God made foolish the wisdom of the world?* (1 Corinthians 1:20)

> *For the wisdom of this world is folly with God. For it is written, "He catches the wise in their craftiness," and again, "The Lord knows the thoughts of the wise, that they are futile."* (1 Corinthians 3:19-20)

<u>Human wisdom, humanism, is foolishness to God because humans don't have all understanding (why).</u>

> *Yet among the mature we do impart wisdom, although it is not a wisdom of this age or of the rulers of this age, who are doomed to pass away. But we impart a secret and hidden wisdom of God, which God decreed before the ages for our glory.* (1 Corinthians 2:6-7)

> *And because of him you are in Christ Jesus, who became to us wisdom from God, righteousness and sanctification and redemption, so that, as it is written, "Let the one who boasts, boast in the Lord."* (1 Corinthians 1:30-31)

Because of Jesus Christ and the Holy Spirit who indwells true believers, we have access to the wisdom of God. The Holy Spirit speaks a principle (how) with understanding (why). This is a godly thought process, which we will cover in depth later. Here is a brief summary:

- *What* is our knowledge that leads to a statement, belief, or action. (effect)
- *Why* is the motivation and understanding for that belief or action. (cause)
- *How* is the application of wisdom in our belief or action. (human or godly)
- A correct *what* by itself is the thought process of the flesh. Even animals have knowledge.
- A correct what and why is a human thought process. We know why we know what we know.
- A correct what, why, and how is a godly thought process. The man of God possesses correct knowledge (what), uses understanding (why) to improve upon things, and knows how to use godly wisdom to create eternal effects that benefit him and others.

A fact is something we believe to be right at the present, but we lack all the information necessary to claim it as truth, which is eternal regardless of any new information that comes forward. Truth is something that will always be correct, regardless of any new information or opinions presented.

Jesus Christ is the same yesterday and today and forever.
(Hebrews 13:8)

Anyone can make a statement (what) and present it as truth. Think back to my discussions with young people when I asked if they were Christians. They all answered yes and stated a fact: Jesus died on the cross. Remember, they could not give me a correct reason (why) or application (how) that would support their belief. Sadly, these professing Christians did not truly know God and His ways. If they did, they would have the understanding (why) and wisdom (how) to understand the true gospel. They knew a fact (Jesus died on the cross), but did not understand why He had to do it, or how it accomplished God's will for salvation. They are in a fleshly/animal thought process. Even Satan knows Jesus died on the cross for sins. When these students go off to college and study under humanist professors, many will be led away from their Christian faith because they are unable to defend their beliefs with a correct understanding and wisdom (why and how). Statistics show this is happening to almost 80 percent of young professing Christians. Because they believe a fact (what) but cannot give the why and how, they are easy prey for humanists. They know a fact but do not have real truth.

We can change our mind about a fact when we receive new information that brings greater understanding, but truth is eternal and not subject to changing conditions or new information. <u>The Bible gives us a way to identify eternal truth: correct knowledge, understanding, and wisdom (what, why, and how)</u>. If we confuse facts with truth, we can easily be deceived. Anyone can state anything and claim it is truth. What does the Bible say about taking any man at his word?

> *The brothers immediately sent Paul and Silas away by night to Berea, and when they arrived they went into the Jewish synagogue. Now these Jews were more noble than those in Thessalonica; they received the word with all eagerness, examining the Scriptures daily to see if these things were so.* (Acts 17:10-11)

The Bereans were nobler than the people of Thessalonica because they compared everything the apostles taught to the Word of God. They understood that any man could state a belief eloquently enough that it could deceive people. They knew everything professed as truth must be confirmed by the Scriptures.

> *Jesus said to him, "I am the way, and the truth, and the life. No one comes to the Father except through me."* (John 14:6)

Jesus also warned us that many false christs and prophets would come in the future to deceive people who do not use a godly thought process. He said:

> *Then if anyone says to you, "Look, here is the Christ!"*

> or "There he is!" do not believe it. For false christs and
> false prophets will arise and perform great signs and
> wonders, so as to lead astray, if possible, even the elect.
> (Matthew 24:23-24)

Did Jesus teach us how we could know they were false teachers? Yes, when Jesus returns, every eye will see him coming, and there will be much crying.

> Behold, he is coming with the clouds, and every eye will see
> him, even those who pierced him, and all tribes of the earth
> will wail on account of him. (Revelation 1:7)

If we do not know how to read the Word of God in a non-contradictory way, some single verses taken out of correct context can get us unsettled. Look at what Jesus said here:

> If I alone bear witness about myself, my testimony is not
> true. There is another who bears witness about me, and
> I know that the testimony that he bears about me is true.
> (John 5:31-32)

When I share these verses some Christians become confused or unsettled. But if we ignore what Jesus said, we miss an important principle He taught about how we could tell the difference between truth and clever deception that could destroy us for eternity. These verses teach us a crucial lesson on how we can remain faithful to God during this time of great falling away that we are warned about. Jesus gave us the biblical formula for discerning truth from deception. We need to look beyond what Jesus stated and understand way and how.

Jesus warned us not to believe what any person states, but to seek testimony to the truth that person claims to present. Jesus' testimony is proven true by an unimpeachable witness who cannot lie:

> And when Jesus was baptized, immediately he went up from
> the water, and behold, the heavens were opened to him, and
> he saw the Spirit of God descending like a dove and com-
> ing to rest on him; and behold, a voice from heaven said,
> "This is my beloved Son, with whom I am well pleased."
> (Matthew 3:16-17)

Jesus also performed many miracles to prove He was who He claimed. Let's analyze this situation. Jesus made a statement about Himself: *"I am the way, the truth and the life. No one comes to the father except through me."* Jesus stated a fact (what). But He also said his statement by itself was not proof that what He said was truth. Matthew 3:16-17 tells us why we can believe what He claimed is true: because God who cannot lie testified on His behalf. The many miracles Jesus performed (healing the sick, raising the dead, and forgiving sins) are how we can know He was who He claimed to be. His fruit backed up who He claimed to be.

Jesus said, "I can tell you who I am, but that alone does not make it truth." He stated a fact (what). He gave us a reason (wh*y*): the testimony of the Father and Spirit, supporting His claim to be the Son of God. And He portrayed His wisdom (how) that showed we could believe Him. The miracles He performed and the forgiving of sins together could only be done by God, so people should have known He is God.

The only other possible interpretation for Jesus' words was that His statement wouldn't have been truth because He stated an incorrect fact (what). Do you believe Jesus would have lied or been wrong? Jesus, like the Father, could only state correct facts (whats). Since a fact alone is not truth, we can see that truth goes beyond facts to include correct understanding and wisdom (why and how). This helps us define the last crucial word in this chapter: deception.

Truth can be seen as knowledge with correct understanding and wisdom (a right what with a right how and a right why). The Bible did not speak about facts. It spoke about truth, and truth is more than just facts. Look at this example: Would it be good to kneel before Jesus and say, "Hail, King of the Jews"? Answer this before reading the next passage.

> *And they stripped him and put a scarlet robe on him, and twisting together a crown of thorns, they put it on his head and put a reed in his right hand. And kneeling before him, they mocked him, saying, "Hail, King of the Jews!"*
> (Matthew 27:28-29)

These soldiers stated a fact (what), saying Jesus was the King of the Jews. However, their wisdom and understanding (how and why) were destructive. Their motive (why) and what they did after they made the statement (how) proved they were sinning.

Jesus said to the Jews, who included the scribes and Pharisees:

> You are of your father the devil, and your will is to do your father's desires. He was a murderer from the beginning, and does not stand in the truth, because there is no truth in him. When he lies, he speaks out of his own character, for he is a liar and the father of lies. (John 8:44)

The devil has no truth in him. The devil doesn't speak half-truths. It is either truth or it is not. When people say the devil spoke a half-truth, what they are actually saying, without realizing it, is the devil spoke a fact (what) with a wrong application (how) and wrong understanding (why). We covered this earlier: even Satan knows Jesus died on the cross for sins. Satan has knowledge, and that knowledge puffed him up in pride.

Satan knows facts (right whats), however, he does not state correct understanding (whys) or wisdom (hows) because he does not have understanding or wisdom. This is deception. Deception is a fact with wrong application and understanding (how and why).

The serpent said to the woman:

> "For God knows that when you eat of it your eyes will be opened, and you will be like God, knowing good and evil." So when the woman saw that the tree was good for food, and that it was a delight to the eyes, and that the tree was to be desired to make one wise, she took of its fruit and ate, and she also gave some to her husband who was with her, and he ate. Then the eyes of both were opened, and they knew that they were naked. And they sewed fig leaves together and made themselves loincloths. (Genesis 3:5-7)

The serpent stated two facts (whats): their eyes would be opened, and they would know good and evil. The serpent implied faulty wisdom and understanding (wrong how and why) to Adam and Eve: you will be like God and God wants you to be like Him. However, the actual why and how were not right: They were seeking to live in their own strength (why) by breaking fellowship with God (how).

In most television shows with teens, one character is the deceiver. The character states a fact (what) to someone and lets that person supply his or her own applications and understanding (how and why). "Look, your girlfriend just came out of that car, and so did your best friend." This was a fact. The deceiver is hoping the person will supply a jealous understanding and conclude his girlfriend and best friend are cheating on him.

False teachers and humanists use the same tactic. They will state a fact (what) and allow people in a fleshly thought process to supply their own incorrect understanding and wisdom (why and how). Since deceived people think according to the flesh, they do not possess correct understanding and wisdom, so they end up deceived by their own pride. This is why having the right definition for truth is crucial. If a person believes the definition of truth is reality, they are saying, truth is a fact (what). When the enemy approaches this person with a fact (what) and no wisdom or understanding (how/why), the person believes this information; this is actually deception.

We aren't easily deceived by lies today because much information is available. What deceives us is someone stating a right what without a right how and why – a fact without correct application or understanding. Our sinful nature supplies flawed understanding and wisdom (why and how) that justifies ourselves. There is another reason it is easier for us to believe deception instead of truth.

Thought Processes

Solomon asked for wisdom from God to justly lead God's people. God gave him wisdom and the effects of wisdom (wealth and a long life) because Solomon asked only for the cause and wanted this cause to benefit others. Immediately after Solomon got this wisdom from God, the following situation occurred:

> *Then two prostitutes came to the king and stood before him. The one woman said, "Oh, my lord, this woman and I live in the same house, and I gave birth to a child while she was*

> *in the house. Then on the third day after I gave birth, this woman also gave birth. And we were alone. There was no one else with us in the house; only we two were in the house. And this woman's son died in the night, because she lay on him. And she arose at midnight and took my son from beside me, while your servant slept, and laid him at her breast, and laid her dead son at my breast. When I rose in the morning to nurse my child, behold, he was dead. But when I looked at him closely in the morning, behold, he was not the child that I had borne." But the other woman said, "No, the living child is mine, and the dead child is yours." The first said, "No, the dead child is yours, and the living child is mine." Thus they spoke before the king.* (1 Kings 3:16-22)

Solomon needed to resolve this issue. If he used an evil thought process, he might kill both women and the child. If he used an animal/fleshly thought process, he would let the two women fight it out. If he used a human thought process, he would interview the people who knew both women and those who had been at their babies' deliveries. He would have made the best decision he could with the current facts available.

The evil thought process results in being 100 percent sure the right decision wasn't made. The animal thought process would have resulted in a 50 percent chance of being right. While the human thought process would have felt like a continual journey toward being 100 percent right, as more facts were accumulated, he would still not be 100 percent sure the right decision was made. (Someone could have lied or been bribed.) Years later the child could develop a physical feature only one of the mothers possessed, so we would have to readjust the decision. What did Solomon do as a result of having this thought process (wisdom) from God?

> *Then the king said, "The one says, 'This is my son that is alive, and your son is dead'; and the other says, 'No; but your son is dead, and my son is the living one.'" And the king said, "Bring me a sword." So a sword was brought before the king. And the king said, "Divide the living child in two, and give half to the one and half to the other."* (1 Kings 3:23-25)

What? That doesn't sound right! Solomon stated something the *opposite* of what we would naturally do! What Solomon stated looked wrong to everyone. What happened next?

> *Then the woman whose son was alive said to the king, because her heart yearned for her son, "Oh, my lord, give her the living child, and by no means put him to death." But the other said, "He shall be neither mine nor yours; divide him." Then the king answered and said, "Give the living child to the first woman, and by no means put him to death; she is his mother."* (1 Kings 3:26-27)

The true mother wanted to spare the child while the other woman said to kill him. What did both women do? They exposed their thought processes. Solomon's thought process from God focused on exposing the thought processes of these women, not on finding out the answer via his human thought process. Solomon didn't try to solve this directly, as if it was something he could intentionally grasp. He gave up control and waited for the causes to expose themselves. Both women shared their thought process, which allowed Solomon to get this decision right. However, the best part of this story is the last verse in the chapter, and most people miss it completely. Do you know what happened next?

> *And all Israel heard of the judgment that the king had rendered, and they stood in awe of the king, because they perceived that the wisdom of God was in him to do justice.*
> (1 Kings 3:28)

Everyone in Israel recognized this decision came from God and not from Solomon. A godly thought process might result in people thinking, "No offense, you are a smart person, but there is no way you came up with that solution. That had to be from some truth outside of you." Should we be upset when we get this same response from people? Here is what Jesus said:

> *In the same way, let your light shine before others, so that they may see your good works and give glory to your Father who is in heaven.* (Matthew 5:16)

Your deeds should be so incredibly good people realize they couldn't possibly come from you and would have to come from God Himself. The Greek word for *glory* is Strong's #1392 *doxazo*: "to esteem, honor, praise." Basically, it means "to think well of." *Glory* is a thought process word.

Jesus told us to let the wisdom that could only come from God make decisions through us, to the point people would think well of God. What does it really mean if you want affirmation for things you've done? A godly thought process is sometimes the opposite of every other thought process. People think a godly thought process is the one that immediately makes the most sense. That is the characteristic of a human thought process. Even our government realizes this.

When you apply for a patent, the first question is: "What is the nature of your invention?" The second is: "Would a person skilled in the art be able to come up with this idea?" If a person who is skilled in his own strength (human thought process) could naturally reach the same conclusion, you don't get a patent. Your idea has to be the opposite of what an expert would have thought of by using a human thought process.

A person could attach a horse to a cart. Someone else could attach two horses to pull a cart. While this is more complicated than one horse, the idea is not patentable. Another person could attach four horses, then eight horses. Then someone could attach no horses: an automobile. The automobile is the opposite idea from the direction everyone else is going. At first, it looks wrong, but then it is obvious it is a better idea.

One mark of a godly thought process is when people might respond with, "That doesn't sound right," and their second thought is "Oh, I get it." This was the response people had to Solomon's decision. The issue is that truth often appears to be the opposite of what we think is right. Real truth is often contradictory to our human understanding, and sometimes initially it just doesn't feel right. Jesus was confronted with a fact one time that was intended to present a challenge to His ministry:

> *The scribes and the Pharisees brought a woman who had been caught in adultery, and placing her in the midst they said to him, "Teacher, this woman has been caught in the act of adultery. Now in the Law Moses commanded us to stone such women. So what do you say?" This they said to test him, that they might have some charge to bring against him. Jesus*

> *bent down and wrote with his finger on the ground. And as they continued to ask him, he stood up and said to them, "Let him who is without sin among you be the first to throw a stone at her."* (John 8:3-7)

Jesus had compassion for sinners and wanted them to know redemption was available through Him. The Pharisees stated a fact: Moses did command that adulteresses could be stoned. If Jesus yelled, "You can't stone her," He would have denied the Law and contradicted God, but He used godly wisdom to disarm the Pharisees. In their human knowledge, the Pharisees thought they had finally trapped Jesus, thinking he would say either, "Don't stone her" or "You're right, stone her!" He gave them a theoretical biblical application (how): the person without sin should throw the first stone. But if one of them had, they would have been guilty of the exact thing of which they falsely accused Jesus: blasphemy by claiming to be God. If they had said they were sinless, they would be claiming to be God.

A person in an animal thought process becomes upset at truth because it appears to be the opposite of reality. While the Pharisees are a great example of this, we have already covered another in the example of the Roman Catholic Church belief that the sun revolved around the earth. The church was so convinced that its belief (opinion) was eternal truth that it threatened to kill anyone who brought forward new information that contradicted its belief. Leaders were the very heretics they claimed to be standing against! But Copernicus and Galilei presented new understanding that proved the Catholic Church was wrong.

<u>A person in a human thought process has two possible responses. The prideful person will immediately dismiss the truth by contradicting it with human wisdom; this is self-justification.</u> But the humble person considers another perspective and then uses his or her thought process to understand all the steps of truth.

<u>Humility is the key.</u> <u>We must admit that, unlike God, we may not have all the information required to state eternal truth in our human understanding.</u> Think of your spiritual growth as a Christian. You probably have a different interpretation of some biblical doctrines than you once held. You were humble enough to admit you did not know

everything. You were willing to submit to the eternal truth of God in His written Word to change your mind about certain beliefs you thought were truth at one time. Let's summarize this section:

- A fact is a right *what*.
- A lie is a wrong *what*, meant to mislead.
- An opinion is a *what* that is believed to be right, but may or may not actually be a fact.
- Deception is a right *what* with a wrong *why* and wrong *how*.
- Truth is a right *what* with a right *why* and a right *how*. No new information can change truth.

God's nature prevents Him from stating a lie (wrong what). The reason He states wisdom and knowledge (right how and a right what) is that He has infinite understanding (why). His knowledge (what) with understanding (why) and wisdom (how) is truth. Truth only comes from God. People in a fleshly or prideful human thought process attempt to be immediately comfortable by stating facts (whats) as if they were the truth. These people are unable to state correct understanding or application (whys or hows). They may end up in the lake of fire because they cannot discern between facts, deception, lies, and truth.

<u>A person in a humble human thought process is able to consider he is wrong (sinner), receive salvation, and gain the ability to have a godly thought process via the Holy Spirit.</u> However, if he does not understand the difference between a fact and truth, his journey is more difficult because he is deceived by things that sound right, but actually cause problems in his journey. He may be saved but not receive all the benefits of sanctification. He finds life far more difficult than it would be if he followed God's plan.

The person experiencing the benefits of sanctification is the one continually killing his flesh by following truth from the Spirit of Truth. This truth is uncomfortable because it is the opposite of our human nature.

Discerning Between Truth and Deception

<u>The world cleverly deceives us with statements that sound right but ultimately damage our belief system, values, and thought process</u>. Let's use a recent example of how this deception works:

In 2008, Barack Obama ran for President on a platform of "hope and change." Because the majority of Americans operate from a fleshly thought process, he was elected; people knew the system wasn't working (what). But did anyone bother to ask why the system was broken or how it could be fixed? The majority of Americans, including more than half of all professing Christians voted for a what, not knowing the answer to these two questions.

But it gets even worse. Four years later, after five trillion more dollars in debt, a disastrous national healthcare program, and learning we had elected a man who wanted to expand abortions and approve homosexual marriage, a higher percentage of professing Christians voted for him in 2012! This is proof that humanism is destroying our thought process by teaching us to think and react like animals. Even though in 2008 Obama stated he was pro-life, believed marriage was between one man and one woman, and pledged to reduce the national debt, more people, including professing Christians, voted for him after he was proven to be a deceiver.

Barack Obama stated a fact (what) without giving us a correct understanding or application (why or how). And because many were in a fleshly thought process, it sounded perfectly rational and profitable to them: the flesh appeals to the flesh. He stated a fact (what) in 2008: "I believe marriage is reserved for one man and one woman." His application (how) quickly showed he deceived Christians by promoting and endorsing legislation supporting homosexual marriage. His how proved his real understanding (why): his heart (cause) is deceitful, even though he claims to be a Christian.

Now, one might counter with, "Well maybe he just changed his views once elected. Isn't a person allowed to change his mind?" This is a valid observation. However, when you take the time to read Obama's stated public views before 2008, you see he has always supported homosexual marriage and abortion. So he did not change his mind; he blatantly lied to deceive others, an evil thought process.

His prior views on abortion and homosexual marriage were clearly covered by media, yet almost half of all professing Christians voted for him anyway because they were in an animal thought process themselves. They wanted what they wanted and stopped thinking when they heard "hope and change." Clearly, these people didn't determine what God wanted, or they would have understood the why and how. Any informed Christian knew Barack Obama was lying in 2008; more knew in 2012 that he was a deceiver who directly opposed the will of God, and they voted for him anyway. Unless Christians learn how to use a godly thought process, our nation will get worse and worse until the wrath of God comes down upon us.

We know evil is growing, and we should expect it from the world. However, the Christian church is supposed to oppose humanism and evil. Instead, our churches have remained mostly silent, not wanting to be political but allowing their members to incorrectly read the road map that is the Word of God. In fact, a growing number of Christian churches and denominations now approve of homosexual marriage, proving they do not truly understand how to interpret the Bible correctly.

Humanism has been infecting the church gradually over the past forty to fifty years. One of its most effective tools has been the Emergent Church movement, which preaches relative morality, feelings over truth, and the lie of universal salvation for all men. The Emergent movement has turned many Christian youth against the absolute truth of God's Word and falsely painted a picture of God that is all love and no justice. Research shows that more than half of all youth who grew up in the church have abandoned it in favor of seeking God on their own terms.

The Emergent movement has established a firm stronghold in many churches and denominations as manifested through several human doctrine effects:

- Less preaching from the Bible and more from life experiences.

- Less teaching about sin and an unhealthy emphasis on extreme grace.
- Less teaching of denying self and surrendering to God's will and more emphasis on church growth (quantity at the expense of quality).

Because Christian thought has been attacked and degraded by humanism, we have been unable to effectively point out the danger and consequences of Christians falling for emergent doctrine. Just like the world, emergents have hijacked words, applying human definitions to words God used in His Word:

- Sin has become a subjective personal opinion instead of an objective measure given by God.
- Grace has become a license to sin and believe whatever you think is right (Gnosticism).
- Love has become unconditional acceptance of the belief systems of others, even though they contradict the Word of God. We literally "love people into hell."

Matt. 7

Unless we effectively counter the Emergent movement, it will draw millions of professing Christians into Gnosticism and eternal separation from God through human doctrine. But when we learn and teach others how to use a godly thought process, we can protect ourselves and help others stay anchored in the Christian faith. Let's explore some human doctrine beliefs contained within this new emergence that is subtly deceiving many professing Christians.

Emergent Church Movement

The Emergent movement wants to reach people through social justice and love rather than condemnation by attracting them to a kinder, gentler form of Christianity. The movement rejects absolute truth and many biblical doctrines, encouraging people to seek truth within themselves rather than from a two-thousand-year-old book (their words, not mine).

The Emergent movement's correct fact (what): the church as a whole is ineffective in sharing the gospel and making disciples of Jesus. (We must be intellectually honest and admit they are right about this.)

Its self-stated reason (why): the church has become self-centered, driven by money, and self-righteous in condemning certain sins while overlooking sin within its own camp.

Its incorrect application (how): abandoning biblical doctrine and teaching, and thinking we need a "new Christianity" based on personal feelings instead of absolute truth. The correct application (how) is avoiding self-righteousness with the opposite focus: a return to the fundamentals of biblical doctrine, resulting in believers loving, and when necessary, confronting each other.

Remember that truth holds up in the end, but deception does not. Many of the Emergent leaders have come out denying the substitutionary atonement of sins by the death of Jesus Christ – the cornerstone of biblical Christianity. So their application (how) over time has revealed that their stated understanding (why) was actually deception. Their initial message does appeal to our human thought process. Their knowledge (what) sounds like truth unless we use a godly thought process, which causes us to determine the why and how. If we do not know how to get ourselves and others into a godly thought process, many will miss the narrow path to eternal salvation. So at its best the Emergent Church movement appeals to a human thought process, but over time it proves to be an animal or evil thought process. People who are deceived and not corrected get worse and worse:

> *Indeed, all who desire to live a godly life in Christ Jesus will be persecuted, while evil people and impostors will go on from bad to worse, deceiving and being deceived.*
> (2 Timothy 3:12-13)

The Emergent movement has birthed a whole series of deceptions, infiltrating the thought process and conscience of professing Christians and many churches.

Social Justice Movement

The social justice movement claims its roots are Christian and based on what Jesus taught us about helping the poor. It uses a human thought process while presenting itself as a godly thought process: the exact thing Jesus chastised the Pharisees for doing – teaching man-made doctrine as biblical doctrine.

Correct knowledge (what): be kind to and provide for the poor.

Correct understanding (why): to show the love and compassion of Jesus Christ.

Incorrect application (how): lacking the gospel of salvation but using human institutions (taxes to the government) instead of the church of believers to help the poor. The church is able through observation, prayer, and discernment to help people who cannot provide for themselves in spite of their sincere efforts. Government disperses funds without accountability and never shares the gospel of salvation that will help people for eternity. Giving money without the truth of the gospel hurts people for eternity; it does not help them.

Chrislam Movement

With the rise of Islamic terrorism around the world, our government, media, and public education systems go out of their way to excuse terrorism as a handful of radicals who are not real Muslims. There is a movement called Chrislam, which presents the lie that Muslims and Christians worship the same God. This is easily refuted if you know the Bible and the fundamental beliefs of Islam:

> *Beloved, do not believe every spirit, but test the spirits to see whether they are from God, for many false prophets have gone out into the world. By this you know the Spirit of God: every spirit that confesses that Jesus Christ has come in the flesh is from God, and every spirit that does not confess Jesus is not from God. This is the spirit of the antichrist, which you heard was coming and now is in the world already.*
> (1 John 4:1-3)

Islam denies that Jesus Christ is God in the flesh and states that Jesus did not die on the cross. But these false movements never let a little thing like biblical truth get in the way of their humanist agenda.

Their incorrect knowledge (what): Christians and Muslims worship the same God. This is idolatry, an evil thought process.

Their incorrect understanding (why): Islam is an Abrahamic faith, tracing its roots back to Ishmael.

Islam was invented in the seventh century by Muhammed when nomadic Arab tribes worshipped more than six hundred false gods, one of which was Allah. Muhammed stated in the Quran, "There is only one god, Allah, and his prophet Muhammed." As usual with the most deceptive movements, its followers latch on to a fact they present as truth. They point out that the Arabic word *Allah* can mean "god." This is a fact, but even a brief reading of the Quran shows us that Allah of the Quran is not God in the Bible. Also, the Bible uses the word *god* to refer to Satan (2 Corinthians 4:4). Allah denies that Jesus is his son. Allah calls himself the great deceiver and encourages his followers to lie; God cannot lie and never wants His children to lie. And unlike the Bible, the Quran is full of wild contradictions.

Chrislam's incorrect knowledge and understanding (what and why), along with the fact that the Quran tells Muslims to kill Christians and Jews, shows Chrislam is an evil thought process.

Christian Universalism

Christian Universalists claim that since love is God's nature and chief characteristic, a loving God would never let anyone go to eternal hell. Some claim that Jesus replaced the mean old God of the Old Testament with unconditional love and forgiveness. This is refuted repeatedly in the Bible:

> *In the beginning was the Word, and the Word was with God, and the Word was God. He was in the beginning with God. All things were made through him, and without him was not any thing made that was made.* (John 1:1-3)

> *Jesus Christ is the same yesterday and today and forever.* (Hebrews 13:8)

Jesus said:

> *Do not think that I have come to abolish the Law or the Prophets; I have not come to abolish them but to fulfill them. For truly, I say to you, until heaven and earth pass away,*

not an iota, not a dot, will pass from the Law until all is accomplished. (Matthew 5:17-18)

Universalist's incorrect knowledge (what): everyone goes to heaven, which is clearly refuted in the Bible.

Universalist's incorrect understanding (why): God's love alone assures every man of salvation.

Jesus repeatedly warned people that if they did not confess, repent, and place their complete trust in Him, they would spend eternity in hell. He also said many would end up there. So the incorrect knowledge (what) of this movement proves they are in a fleshly/animal thought process at best.

These are some of the major false movements attacking and destroying Christian thought in our churches. There are other false doctrines that, while not eternal salvation issues, cause fighting and breaking of fellowship within the body of Christ. We will address some of these in our next section on logical Biblical Conjunctives: The Narrow Path of Truth.

Summary

What we believe, say, or do is an effect. **Why** (cause/motive) we believe, say, or do things comes from the condition of our heart and conscience and whether the Spirit of Truth influences it or our flesh. **How** we say or do things is either flawed human wisdom or eternal godly wisdom. A person's wisdom (how) will usually expose their true motivation (why).

- A wrong fact (what) that is clearly refuted by the Bible is a lie. It is an evil thought process.

- A correct fact (what) with wrong or no understanding (why) consistent with the Bible is deception (fleshly/animal thought process).

- A correct fact and understanding (what and why) with wrong wisdom (how) is human wisdom (human thought process).

- Correct knowledge, understanding, and wisdom (what,

why, and eternal how) is godly wisdom (godly thought process).

The best way to confront something you believe might be a false teaching is to ask the person to give you their reason (why) for what they believe. If their reason lines up with the correctly interpreted Word of God, ask them their application (how) to determine if it is human or godly wisdom. As we have seen, some of these movements are from either an evil, fleshly/animal or human thought process. A human thought process can become a godly thought process by helping the person's application (how) line up with God's principles and methods.

This chart makes a good reference as you study thought processes:

				EVIL
What	Knowledge only	Fact	Effect	Animal (flesh) thought process
Why	Understanding	Reason	Cause	Human thought process
How	Wisdom	Decision	Principle	Godly thought process

The ability to detect the difference between the four thought processes is crucial for avoiding deception and helping others come to saving faith in Christ. When we can read, understand, and teach the Bible using non-contradiction and understand the thought process of ourselves and others, we can guard our heart and train our human conscience to understand right from wrong and help others do the same. We will be protected from the great deception and falling away Jesus warned us about.

Principle #4: Logical Conjunctives – The Narrow Path of Truth

Identifying and understanding logical conjunctives in the Bible helps us discern truth from deception and separate human and biblical doctrines. Many important biblical doctrines are conjunctives: sin, grace, forgiveness, salvation, and repentance.

What is a Logical Conjunctive?

A logical conjunctive is the place where a biblical freedom/benefit and a biblical restriction to that freedom/benefit overlap to identify truth and produce positive effects. Many of the doctrines of the Bible are logical conjunctives to keep us on the narrow path to happiness and eternal life. But when we try to apply the freedom side of the conjunctive without restriction, we can become a Gnostic/emergent. When we try to apply the restriction side to others without the freedom, we can become a Judaizer/legalist. These were the two false movements Paul continually fought and disarmed using the correctly interpreted Word of God. Both miss the narrow path of truth.

God dealt with His people using conjunctives. Even some of God's Old Testament covenants with His people were stated as conjunctives, giving the people a freedom/benefit with a limitation/restriction.

> *Israel has sinned; they have transgressed my covenant that I commanded them; they have taken some of the devoted things; they have stolen and lied and put them among their own belongings. Therefore the people of Israel cannot stand before their enemies. They turn their backs before their enemies, because they have become devoted for destruction. I will be with you no more, unless you destroy the devoted things from among you.* (Joshua 7:11-12)

> *So the anger of the Lord was kindled against Israel, and he said, "Because this people have transgressed my covenant that I commanded their fathers and have not obeyed my voice, I will no longer drive out before them any of the nations that Joshua left when he died, in order to test Israel by them, whether they will take care to walk in the way of the Lord as their fathers did, or not."* (Judges 2:20-22)

These covenants initiated by God came with conditions: If the people obeyed God (restriction), He would protect and bless them (benefit); if not, He would suspend His covenant with them until they repented. But in spite of men continuing to break covenant with God, He sent Jesus Christ to establish an everlasting covenant with His people:

> *Therefore he is the mediator of a new covenant, so that those who are called may receive the promised eternal inheritance, since a death has occurred that redeems them from the transgressions committed under the first covenant.* (Hebrews 9:15)

Salvation through the blood of Jesus Christ seals the promise of forgiveness of sins for true believers. But how does the Bible say we are saved by the sacrifice of Jesus? Through a logical conjunctive – benefit restriction. Forgiveness of sin: confess, repent, and faith in Christ alone.

If we do not walk in the logical conjunctive regarding salvation, we will fail to find the narrow gate. Jesus said:

> *Enter by the narrow gate. For the gate is wide and the way is easy that leads to destruction, and those who enter by it are many. For the gate is narrow and the way is hard that leads to life, and those who find it are few.* (Matthew 7:13-14)

On one side of the narrow gate are the Judaizers/legalists who believe their righteous deeds earn them heaven. On the other side are the Gnostics/emergents who believe sin no longer matters, and God's love alone gets us into heaven. Jesus said *the way is hard that leads to life*, but that bothers Americans and many Christians who have been pampered, spoiled, and coddled materialistically and spiritually.

Both extreme legalists and extreme emergents risk eternal damnation. The legalist will raise the bar on salvation for the individual, exceeding the teachings of the gospel, just like the Pharisees. We are saved by admitting our sins against a holy, righteous God (confession), repenting (think differently about sinning), and completely trusting in who Jesus is and what He accomplished on the cross. We are born again and receive the Holy Spirit; the proof of our salvation is a life increasingly holy and pleasing to God. But this is accomplished at a unique pace through each believer. The legalist tends to use his level of sanctification as the new bar of salvation for others. If he is convicted to not drink or watch television, you are also forbidden from doing those things. Anytime we add more restrictions on the gospel of salvation, we will be judged the same way Jesus judged the Pharisees:

> *Woe to you, scribes and Pharisees, hypocrites! For you travel across sea and land to make a single proselyte, and when he becomes a proselyte, you make him twice as much a child of hell as yourselves.* (Matthew 23:15)

Emergents risk eternal damnation on the other side of the spectrum. By discounting the Word of God and biblical doctrines and principles, they cause others to stumble into sin and disobedience.

> *For if we go on sinning deliberately after receiving the knowledge of the truth, there no longer remains a sacrifice for sins* (Hebrews 10:26)

When emergents teach others that things God clearly identifies as sins are permissible, they might be leading naive people into eternal damnation along with themselves. Do you remember what Jesus taught just before the narrow gate verse? He said:

> *So whatever you wish that others would do to you, do also to them, for this is the Law and the Prophets.* (Matthew 7:12)

This is another logical conjunctive. When we learn to read the Bible in a non-contradictory way, we start to see many doctrines and principles that fit the narrow gate warning Jesus gave us. <u>Jesus said the gate to eternal life is narrow and few find it, but this is counter to what is taught in many churches today, where salvation has been reduced to saying a quick prayer and inviting Jesus into your heart, giving many a false sense of eternal security.</u>

Legalists put unbiblical restrictions on others to prove they are saved. Emergents say there are no rules or restrictions about right or wrong. Both are unbiblical human teachings presented as truth, causing many to stumble and fall.

Let's look at more conjunctives that keep us walking through the narrow gate: forgiveness and judging others.

> *For if you forgive others their trespasses, your heavenly Father will also forgive you, but if you do not forgive others their trespasses, neither will your Father forgive your trespasses.* (Matthew 6:14-15)

We are forgiven (benefit) when we forgive others (restriction).

Judge not, that you be not judged. For with the judgment you pronounce you will be judged, and with the measure you use it will be measured to you. (Matthew 7:1-2)

If you want to judge others (freedom), you will be judged by the same measure (restriction). The New Testament has two different Greek words for *judge*. This particular word is *krino*: "to try, convict and punish," referring to judging the eternal soul of another, which we are not qualified to do. The other word for *judge*, *anakrino*, means "to discern," which we will discuss later as we address the correct and incorrect ways Christians are to judge others.

Other conjunctives found in Scripture:

But I say to you, Love your enemies and pray for those who persecute you, so that you may be sons of your Father who is in heaven. (Matthew 5:44)

Son of our heavenly Father (benefit): love your enemies and pray for them (restriction).

Whoever loves his life loses it, and whoever hates his life in this world will keep it for eternal life. (John 12:25)

Eternal life (benefit): hate the life of this world (restriction).

But seek first the kingdom of God and his righteousness, and all these things will be added to you. (Matthew 6:33)

Earthly needs will be met (benefit) if we seek God's righteousness (restriction).

Because, if you confess with your mouth that Jesus is Lord and believe in your heart that God raised him from the dead, you will be saved. (Romans 10:9)

Salvation (benefit): confess and believe in your heart (restriction).

Do not, for the sake of food, destroy the work of God. Everything is indeed clean, but it is wrong for anyone to make another stumble by what he eats. It is good not to eat meat or drink wine or do anything that causes your brother to stumble. The faith that you have, keep between yourself and God. Blessed is the one who has no reason to pass judgment on himself for what he approves. But whoever has doubts is condemned if he eats, because the eating is not from faith. For whatever does not proceed from faith is sin. (Romans 14:20-23)

Partake in food and drink (freedom): do not cause another Christian to stumble by your freedom (restriction).

"All things are lawful for me," but not all things are helpful. "All things are lawful for me," but I will not be dominated by anything. (1 Corinthians 6:12)

All things are lawful (freedom): make sure they are profitable and do not dominate you (restriction).

So, my brothers, earnestly desire to prophesy, and do not forbid speaking in tongues. But all things should be done decently and in order. (1 Corinthians 14:39-40)

Allow spiritual gifts (freedom): done with decency and order (restriction).

For you were called to freedom, brothers. Only do not use your freedom as an opportunity for the flesh, but through love serve one another. (Galatians 5:13)

We are free from the law (freedom); do not indulge the flesh (restriction).

Rather, speaking the truth in love, we are to grow up in every way into him who is the head, into Christ, from whom the whole body, joined and held together by every joint with which it is equipped, when each part is working properly, makes the body grow so that it builds itself up in love. (Ephesians 4:15-16)

Speak the truth (freedom) in love for the benefit of others (restriction).

Now as the church submits to Christ, so also wives should submit in everything to their husbands.

Husbands, love your wives, as Christ loved the church and gave himself up for her, that he might sanctify her, having cleansed her by the washing of water with the word, so that he might present the church to himself in splendor, without spot or wrinkle or any such thing, that she might be holy and without blemish. (Ephesians 5:24-27)

Wives submit to husbands (husband's benefit); love your wife as Jesus loved the church – as a sacrifice (husband's restriction).

Preach the word; be ready in season and out of season; reprove, rebuke, and exhort, with complete patience and teaching. (2 Timothy 4:2)

Reprove, rebuke and correct (freedom) with complete patience (restriction).

For the grace of God has appeared, bringing salvation for all people, training us to renounce ungodliness and worldly passions, and to live self-controlled, upright, and godly lives in the present age. (Titus 2:11-12)

God's grace saves us (benefit) and it teaches us to live self-controlled, upright lives (restriction).

> *What good is it, my brothers, if someone says he has faith but does not have works? Can that faith save him? If a brother or sister is poorly clothed and lacking in daily food, and one of you says to them, "Go in peace, be warmed and filled," without giving them the things needed for the body, what good is that? So also faith by itself, if it does not have works, is dead.* (James 2:14-17)

> We are saved by genuine faith (benefit); faith without righteous works is not genuine faith (restriction).

Logical biblical conjunctives lead us to the narrow path of truth. Legalists tend to preach the restrictions in the Word of God, while emergents tout the freedoms and benefits without the restrictions. Both miss the narrow path of truth and are in danger of missing out on eternal life. Understanding logical conjunctives in the Bible is an excellent way to guard yourself against subtle false teachings that can delay or end your journey to happiness and eternal life.

Summary

Unless we can correctly interpret the Word of God, we will be delayed or lost on our journey to happiness and eternal life. Four crucial principles to correctly reading our road map are:

1. Understanding causality.
2. Interpreting the Bible in a non-contradictory way. (Let the Bible interpret itself.)
3. Discerning between lies, deception, opinions, facts, and truth by using a godly thought process.
4. Recognizing logical conjunctives in the Bible that show us the narrow path of truth. Distinguishing between human and biblical doctrines.

Only one road map – the Bible – will lead us to the destination we desire. But unless we understand how to correctly read the Bible, we can be convinced to take a wrong road that will lead us to the wrong destination. Understanding causality, non-contradiction, and the way to determine godly truth from human deception is critical.

Next we will look at how sin and humanism have deteriorated our brain and thought process. Understanding the problem can lead us to the solution – cooperating with the work the Holy Spirit wants to do in and through us, which produces sanctification.

Chapter Five

HUMANISM'S CORRUPTION OF OUR THOUGHT PROCESS

Chapter objective: to understand our sanctification through God's design of our brain, heart, and conscience and the work of the Holy Spirit.

For though we walk in the flesh, we are not waging war according to the flesh. For the weapons of our warfare are not of the flesh but have divine power to destroy strongholds. We destroy arguments and every lofty opinion raised against the knowledge of God, and take every thought captive to obey Christ. (2 Corinthians 10:3-5)

Few areas of modern society have been infected more with humanist thought than the field of psychology, which is the study of how the human mind works. Without getting into an intense historical overview, psychologists like Freud and Jung perverted this scientific field with an atheistic, humanist perspective that man is good at his nature and capable of becoming even better through his own efforts.

The Bible is clear that before salvation all men are wicked and evil in their nature when compared to the righteousness of God. As we look at how our brain and mind work, we recognize that it is only by God's

Spirit, grace, and His Word that any man is capable of getting better over the long run. Humanist psychology can only put Band-Aids on puncture wounds, which gives man a false sense of improvement. This actually damages man instead of helping him.

When God created man and all creation, He said it was good, but sin entered the world through Adam, and everything started to deteriorate. I am attempting to show just how damaged our brain, mind, and thought process has become and how repair is possible through the Holy Spirit and Word of God.

Let me be very clear on something: we cannot save ourselves nor can we in our own human strength sanctify ourselves. But we can choose, because of free will, to either cooperate with or resist the work the Holy Spirit wants to do in our lives to sanctify us. This chapter will help us understand how we can cooperate with the Holy Spirit by knowing how God designed our brain, heart, and conscience to work and how our sinful nature has damaged our thought process. When we understand how our brain, heart, and conscience work, we are able to better understand our thought process and cooperate with the Holy Spirit to take our thoughts captive in obedience to Jesus Christ. Taking our thoughts captive is cooperating with the Holy Spirit in His desire to sanctify us.

The information in this chapter will be technical but resist the temptation to gloss over it because it is crucial from this aspect: knowing the difference between who you are and what you do is essential to leading a life of joy and reaching our eternal destination. When we confuse who we are with what we do, we are easy targets for Satan's lies. Just as he twisted causality to accuse Job of being unrighteous, he will use the same tactic on us. The apostle Paul recognized this critical difference. Let's look at Scriptures that help us differentiate who we are from what we do:

> *For I do not understand my own actions. For I do not do what I want, but I do the very thing I hate. Now if I do what I do not want, I agree with the law, that it is good. So now it is no longer I who do it, but sin that dwells within me. For I know that nothing good dwells in me, that is, in my flesh. For I have the desire to do what is right, but not the ability to*

> *carry it out. For I do not do the good I want, but the evil I do not want is what I keep on doing. Now if I do what I do not want, it is no longer I who do it, but sin that dwells within me. So I find it to be a law that when I want to do right, evil lies close at hand. For I delight in the law of God, in my inner being, but I see in my members another law waging war against the law of my mind and making me captive to the law of sin that dwells in my members.* (Romans 7:15-23)

Paul is saying he truly desires to live a sin-free life, but his sinful nature still occasionally leads him to sin. Paul talks about the battle between himself as a new creation that loves and desires to obey God and the sinful nature of his flesh. Paul *is* a new creation; but what he *does* is not always consistent with his new nature. As Christians we must understand this difference. Paul goes on to say:

> *Wretched man that I am! Who will deliver me from this body of death? Thanks be to God through Jesus Christ our Lord! So then, I myself serve the law of God with my mind, but with my flesh I serve the law of sin. There is therefore now no condemnation for those who are in Christ Jesus.* (Romans 7:24-8:1)

The truly born-again believer, in spite of his continuing sin, is spared the wrath of God and is no longer under the condemnation of sin. Paul seems to speak of a civil war going on in believers between the mind and the flesh. He also draws a distinction between who we are and what we do. We *are* people saved by the grace of God who *may* occasionally give in to our sinful nature, but when it happens it causes much anguish because the last thing we want to do is fail our Lord.

> *For those who live according to the flesh set their minds on the things of the flesh, but those who live according to the Spirit set their minds on the things of the Spirit. For to set the mind on the flesh is death, but to set the mind on the Spirit is life and peace. For the mind that is set on the flesh is hostile to God, for it does not submit to God's law; indeed, it cannot. Those who are in the flesh cannot please God. You,*

> *however, are not in the flesh but in the Spirit, if in fact the Spirit of God dwells in you. Anyone who does not have the Spirit of Christ does not belong to him. But if Christ is in you, although the body is dead because of sin, the Spirit is life because of righteousness.* (Romans 8:5-10)

Where is your mind set – on the flesh or on the Spirit of God? Do you believe the grace of God is a continuing license to sin? If so, then your mind is set on the flesh. But even the most mature of Christians will continue to commit sins on occasion, so how are we to determine the difference between the saint who continues to sin at times and the false convert, who lives in a cheap form of grace? Paul gave us the answer: it depends where your mind is set. The thought process we use will determine just how easy or difficult our journey will be. The Bible tells us that by the power of the Holy Spirit, we can improve our thought process:

> *The natural person does not accept the things of the Spirit of God, for they are folly to him, and he is not able to understand them because they are spiritually discerned. The spiritual person judges all things, but is himself to be judged by no one. "For who has understood the mind of the Lord so as to instruct him?" But we have the mind of Christ.*
> (1 Corinthians 2:14-16)

The Holy Spirit gives true believers the ability to improve our thought process and see things more in line with how God sees them. But our brain, heart, and conscience have been damaged by a lifetime of sin and harmful life commandments (something we were taught and have erroneously accepted as truth). Let's take a look at how God designed them to function properly and how we can cooperate with the Holy Spirit to become more aligned with God's will for our lives by taking our thoughts captive to obedience to Christ.

The information here has been verified by credible medical science and is sometimes used in psychology.[13] Humanist psychology believes man in his own strength can get better. In reality, it is only by the grace and Spirit of God that we can overcome sin and lead a life of joy. We must understand the damage in our brain, heart, and conscience and

---
13   http://www.ncbi.nlm.nih.gov/pmc/articles/PMC2440575/

not resist the work the Holy Spirit wants to do in us as believers, if we are going to lead lives of joy.

> *See that no one repays anyone evil for evil, but always seek to do good to one another and to everyone. Rejoice always, pray without ceasing, give thanks in all circumstances; for this is the will of God in Christ Jesus for you. Do not quench the Spirit.* (1 Thessalonians 5:15-19)

This information will help us cooperate with, instead of quench, the Holy Spirit.

The Human Brain

I have found it helps some people to see the brain as the "hardware" that God uses to run the "software" of our thought process (thinking and reasoning). While there are many discrete parts of the brain, we only need to look at this information with a big-picture perspective. To begin with, humans have a conscious and unconscious brain. Animals have only an unconscious brain. Here is the difference:

The unconscious brain. The unconscious brain is stimulated by the five external senses: sight, touch, smell, hearing, and taste. It takes in information from these five external stimuli and looks for patterns that fit or agree with past information it has received and filed. It always looks backwards, not forward. If a new stimulus fits the acquired pattern, the unconscious brain sees it as appropriate. If it receives a stimulus that opposes a learned pattern, it sees the new stimulus as contradictory and rejects the new information because God designed the unconscious brain to be non-contradictory.

Here is an example that might help: Let's say you were raised in a solid Christian family with parents who taught you to value honesty above all other things. Your father also taught you to obey your boss at work when he asks you to do something. For years you were conditioned that honesty and obedience were good and profitable, while lying and disobedience were bad and would lead to punishment.

Then one day you start a new job selling widgets. In your training you are told that sometimes you will need to lie to potential customers to get them to buy your widgets. Your unconscious brain had settled on a pattern of: being truthful and obeying lead to reward and lying and disobedience lead to punishment. But now it has been given a new "life command": that lying is profitable and telling the truth is unprofitable. You now have a contradiction you need to settle one way or the other or you will become increasingly confused and unsettled. You either need to quit your job and continue to believe that honesty is profitable, or you must obey your employer and lie to be successful in your new job. If you do not choose one or the other, you will experience confusion as you try to segment your life into compartments: honesty and lying. This contradiction damages our brains. We become confused about what is right or wrong and find ourselves under stress, trying to live two lives.

Think of the unconscious brain as instinctive, going by what feels appropriate, even if it is not moral. It looks for stimuli that fit a consistent past pattern, and when it receives a new command that contradicts how it has been trained, it becomes very unsettled. This is how animals behave. A new dog can be trained to be a pet and/or an attack dog. When we hear stories of dogs suddenly attacking their owners, we know some sort of stimulus occurred that triggered a reaction that fits the pattern established in the unconscious brain through training. The dog was trained as a pet for the owners, but as an attack dog against enemies. A stimulus caused the dog to attack the owner as an enemy, even though the owner did nothing wrong.

The unconscious brain automatically takes in information through the five senses faster than you are able to comprehend and reacts to the stimulus without conscious thought or action.

The conscious brain. In contrast to the unconscious brain, the conscious brain can look forward, imagine, and act through complex thought and reasoning, where the unconscious brain looks backwards at patterns and beliefs and then acts instinctively. This conscious brain has different characteristics and roles than the unconscious brain, including:

- Selected stimulus: the conscious brain can only take in one stimulus at a time by choice.
- Words: half of the conscious brain consists of words and definitions.

- Emotions: every word has an associated emotion. For example, you have different emotions when a person says, "ice cream," than when they say, "dead fish."

- Knowledge and understanding: the conscious brain works with facts and knowledge (whats) and understanding (whys). The unconscious brain only works with knowledge (whats).

- Imagination and memory: the conscious brain has the ability to imagine and remember.

- Morality: lying occurs in the conscious brain by choosing a cause in contradiction with reality.

- The conscious brain naturally works to take the easiest route (comfort) and only sees its own point of view. Sin and death have caused it to deteriorate over time.

The unconscious brain works automatically, resulting in a lack of true free will. The conscious brain is where choices are made, and imagining and remembering occur. A dog cannot intentionally think about what he will do next week. We are able to imagine because we have a conscious brain. This ability to have choice also means we can lie with our conscious brain. The unconscious brain cannot lie; it works on facts and reality. The unconscious brain is concerned with right and wrong as it relates to patterns. The conscious brain can ignore patterns and intentionally do something that is not a fact and not in agreement with reality.

Another way to look at this is the unconscious brain only concerns itself with the what. We call this knowledge. The conscious brain functions on understanding, which is the why. The ability to understand (alter the why) allows the conscious brain to state a fact (what) different from reality, such as lying or deceiving.

Here is a personal example: The largest fish I ever caught was a thirty-three-inch northern pike. I was excited and started telling my friends all about the experience. But over time, the positive reaction I received from others when I told the story diminished. Well, miraculously, that thirty-three-inch pike slowly grew to a forty-inch pike as I retold the story. But as my imagination started to change the story, I was uneasy in telling the revised story with the bigger fish, because while I was consciously stating the fish was forty inches, my unconscious brain knew reality. The fish I caught was thirty-three inches, not the forty-inch measurement I was telling others. I consciously chose to lie, but my unconscious brain knew reality and made me feel tense every time I told the enhanced story. Once I returned to telling the truth, I felt settled again in telling my story.

Tension

The difference between the conscious and unconscious brain is our greatest source of internal strife and tension. Understanding and resolving this tension is an effective way to improve your thought process:

- Your unconscious brain does not know what you are thinking in your conscious brain until it is expressed in what you say or do (external stimulus).

- Your unconscious brain keeps an accurate record of everything you've ever said or done in chronological order. It becomes very unsettled when it hears you say something that contradicts what it sees as reality.

Research shows tension between the conscious and unconscious brain, due to this difference in information, causes the body to produce chemicals that are toxic to the body. One researcher even claims a majority of the physical illnesses we experience can be traced to this disconnect between our conscious and unconscious brains – to our thought process.[14] The ensuing chapters will look at ways we can reduce this internal tension. Let's revisit the example we used about the person being told to lie in their new job.

Since the conscious brain works on understanding, this means it has a sixth potential stimulus that can influence it: *understanding* to process information that seems to contradict what we previously learned so we can grow. In the example above with the man getting a new job,

---

14   https://www.psychologytoday.com/blog/prime-your-gray-cells/201108/happy-brain-happy-life

we treated him as if all he had was an unconscious brain. However, he could have used his conscious brain to think through the contradiction and look for another perspective. He could ask not to work with the specific product or ask for a different job within the company, so he would have a different boss. Or he could avoid both contradictions by quitting.

He could take the time through understanding to weigh his options and consider his decision, whereas if he acts instinctively out of his unconscious brain, he simply reacts. Since the pattern his unconscious brain has accepted and filed is "be honest *and* obedient," he is now faced with a contradiction he must settle because his new boss is telling him, "lie *and* obey." If he does not settle this contradiction, he will be a mess at work and in his personal life. If he tries with his conscious brain to justify that lying is good, his unconscious brain will cause him to be unsettled.

So in addition to the five external stimuli identified, the conscious brain has a sixth potential stimulus that can influence it: understanding. We can process information that seems to contradict what we have previously learned, and we can grow.

The unconscious brain acts based on the past and external stimuli only: sight, touch, smell, hearing, and taste.

The conscious brain of every human can process information using understanding to consider other perspectives and solve problems. This information relates to every human being; but what about the born-again Christian? In addition to the five external stimuli and understanding by which every man can be influenced, the born-again believer has a seventh stimulus that can affect his choices: the Holy Spirit that indwells the believer and influences our thoughts that lead to our words and actions.

The Bible often relates behavior to our thought processes. Acting directly out of our unconscious brain can be seen as a fleshly or animal thought process: we do what we are programmed to do by our external stimuli, which is the world. Acting out of our conscious brain by using human understanding as the stimulus can be seen as a human thought process. Acting out of our conscious brain by letting the Holy Spirit be the stimulus can be seen as a godly thought process. This is taking our thoughts captive:

> *We destroy arguments and every lofty opinion raised against the knowledge of God, and take every thought captive to obey Christ.* (2 Corinthians 10:5)

Which Brain Do We Choose to Use?

Humans can choose whether to let their unconscious or conscious brain dictate their actions. At times we can and do use our unconscious brain to act instinctively. An example is tying your shoes. This will help you understand how your unconscious brain watches and learns from actions coming from your conscious brain and develops a pattern. When you were learning to tie your shoes, it took a lot of practice. You had to consciously focus on which way to hold the laces and how to intertwine them in each step. Eventually you mastered the art, and your unconscious brain filed away how to tie your shoes. Now we never even think when we tie our shoes because it is an unconscious brain function.

Quarterbacks practice in their conscious brains, learning plays and watching where potential pass receivers run their routes. The team practices until each team member knows his assignment on a given play. They repeat the correctly run play every practice until each player's unconscious brain has memorized his assignment, which makes it automatic when that play is sent into a game. In the NFL a quarterback has on average 2.3 seconds to throw the ball once he has received it, before he is hit by an opposing pass rusher. If a quarterback used his conscious brain to look at each receiver (up to five on any given play) and think about whether he should throw that receiver the ball or not, he could never process all of his progression reads (sequential choices of where to throw the ball) before getting hit by the defensive player. So his unconscious brain quickly takes him through his "reads," and he throws the ball to the first open receiver. His unconscious brain has been trained to progress through his options quickly and throw the ball to the first open receiver.

Allowing our unconscious brain to take over and do regular tasks is sometimes profitable. But because the unconscious brain always reacts from patterns received and filed from previous experiences, there is a danger in many situations to use it to react without allowing our conscious brain to use understanding. When it has been programmed that something bad is considered right, using our unconscious brain to simply react can be destructive to us and others.

When Paul shared in Romans 7 that he continued to behave in a way contradictory to the Spirit of God and identified the cause as the sinful nature, he identified patterns established through sin and choices made and filed in the unconscious brain. While we become a new creation through salvation, sanctification is a process of allowing God's grace and the Holy Spirit to establish a new pattern of righteous behavior and patterns in us where we repeatedly do God's will instead of the desires of our flesh. Which of us has not read Romans 7 and cried out, "That's me!"? We try our best to reject sin and do what is right and pleasing to God, only to find ourselves once again confessing and asking God for forgiveness. This is because before salvation, we established a pattern of sin in our unconscious brain through our sinful nature.

The conscious brain, where understanding and the Holy Spirit can influence us, is the key to reprogramming the unconscious brain toward righteous behaviors by establishing a new pattern in the unconscious brain. This is sanctification, which is for our benefit, and it only occurs when we let the Holy Spirit influence the previously patterned belief system in our unconscious brain, which has been damaged by our sinful nature. As our unconscious brain hears us state our new will out loud (I choose to obey God for my benefit) and sees us act in a godly manner more consistently, a new pattern starts to be formed in our unconscious brain that becomes fitting as we face more and more choices.

Let's summarize what we have learned so far before moving on to the next part of the brain:

Unconscious Brain

- Responds to five external stimuli: sight, touch, taste, hearing, and smell.

- Reacts to patterns established within it over years of learning and experience.

- Cannot handle a contradiction.

- Focuses on past experience and external events, while the conscious brain can use understanding to imagine and anticipate the future.

- Does not know what the conscious brain is thinking until it hears or sees an effect from our conscious brain (stating something out loud, writing something down, or taking an action).

Conscious Brain

- Every person has a sixth stimulus available to initiate action – understanding. The true believer has a seventh stimulus – the Holy Spirit. Either of these can be utilized to make conscious choices that will form new patterns within the unconscious brain with time and repetition.

- The conscious brain can justify a contradiction through lying. Unlike the unconscious brain, it has a free will to act independent of prior training.

- Allowing the Holy Spirit to override the sinful nature in our unconscious brain and form a new pattern of response leading to an increasing pattern of righteous behavior is sanctification.

Nucleus Basalis

Sometimes reacting out of the unconscious brain makes sense, like with tying your shoes. But if we make a habit of acting unconsciously, we are in essence slaves to our previously established beliefs. So it is important that we engage our conscious brain where we can use understanding and access the influence of the Holy Spirit.

Determining which brain we choose to act from depends on a small one-way "door" called the nucleus basalis. If you and I are eating dinner in a restaurant, my unconscious brain could take in every conversation occurring and file them away. My conscious brain only takes in one conversation. I can choose to focus on you with my conscious brain or choose to focus on any conversation or event around me.

The part of the brain that determines what enters my conscious brain is the nucleus basalis. It can be seen as the doorway to the conscious brain. The decision to open the nucleus basalis and focus it on a stimulus is like operating the steering wheel of an automobile. Let's look at each step.

First, we have to choose to open the nucleus basalis, because it can remain closed to the external world. If it is closed, then all we can do is act according to our unconscious brain in response to external events. This is how people can be seen as animals to some people. They spend most of their time with their nucleus basalis closed to the external world.

While intentionally focusing is the most obvious method to open the nucleus basalis, other things can also open it. For example, surprises open it. When you are walking down a hall and a person suddenly jumps out at you, your nucleus basalis immediately opens and focuses on the source of the surprise. New information can open it, and it can feel like a surprise. Your son could tell a story about hanging out with his friends that you've heard many times when he suddenly shares a part of the story you didn't know. When this new information is shared, your nucleus basalis opens, and your conscious brain is engaged.

A great way to open the nucleus basalis of a person is to ask a question that causes them to think instead of giving a knee-jerk response. This forces them to use understanding in the conscious brain. Later we will discuss how to use great questions to expose and improve the thought process of ourselves and others.

Once we choose to open the nucleus basalis, the second step is to focus it on a stimulus. We can choose to point it to the external stimuli, internally toward our human understanding, or ideally to the Holy Spirit. If we point it toward and engage our human understanding, we use a human thought process. If we point it toward the Holy Spirit and the Word of God to direct us, we use a godly thought process.

Ideally, we want to focus the nucleus basalis on the stimulus until it is completely understood. This measures a person's attention span. One problem people have is they choose to open their nucleus basalis, but they don't keep it focused on the same stimulus for very long. Their thought patterns are scattered, and they seem incapable of focusing on problems and seeking solutions. Look how news stories are covered by the media. Regular news stories are rarely covered in great depth anymore. The media, focused only on ratings, has people jumping from one news story to the next, which grabs our attention and prevents us from thinking deeply on any one story. Like Pavlov's dogs responding to a bell, we instinctively respond out of reflex. Deep, rational thought is dying.

Over the last twenty years, millions of young people have been put on medication for issues diagnosed as Attention Deficit Disorder (ADD). A 2014 report stated that 6.4 million children had been officially diagnosed as suffering from ADD and were on serious mind-altering medications.[15] The Center for Disease Control (CDC) is calling for *more* widespread testing and medication application. The primary drugs used to combat ADD are Ritalin and Adderall: both have been linked to side effects including addiction, increased anxiety, and psychosis.

One must consider the possibility that this is intentional. People who lack the ability for rational thought can be easily controlled. When you look at how young people are kept busy with activities, video games, and social media, it is no wonder many seem incapable of understanding complex issues. As I write this book, Bernie Sanders, an avowed Socialist, is capturing the fancy of young people in our nation, presenting simplistic solutions for complex problems, appealing to our flesh and discounting deep, rational thought.

Key Points:

- The nucleus basalis is the part of the brain that determines what enters the conscious brain.
- The nucleus basalis is opened by choice, surprise, new information, or a question.

---

15   http://www.healthline.com/health/adhd/facts-statistics-infographic

- The nucleus basalis can be focused either internally or externally.

When we decide to act upon a thought, we are introduced to the next player in our brain.

The Amygdalae

The amygdalae, two almond-shaped, compact clusters of brain neurons, work with other parts of the brain to produce chemicals that supply energy for the ensuing action. They can be seen as a library that stores the individual's perspective to feelings and emotions on everything it has ever experienced.

The amygdalae take in all the information and make a decision based on previous experiences to determine if the body has the right amount of energy to act. This is like a web search engine: the brain identifies characteristics of the particular situation currently faced (location, smells, people present), and a search is done in the amygdalae to consider which previous experience best fits the current situation. Next, the amygdalae consider the lessons learned from those previous experiences to determine which of four types of responses it will contribute to the pending decision:

- **Fitting:** The amygdalae could determine the brain has accessed the correct amount of energy for the situation and is settled, requiring little energy involvement from them. (Notice the next three responses involve the amygdalae altering the decision made by the brain.)

- **Flight:** The amygdalae could determine from a previous situation the body is in danger, and it would be best to flee. At this point, they take over and request the necessary energy to avoid the situation as well as looking for the quickest way to flee the situation. (The adult who avoids a location where he was bullied.)

- **Fight:** The amygdalae could determine from a previous situation the body is in danger and needs to fight, because they either believe it can win the fight, cannot flee the fight, or detest the other being so much they don't care about the danger involved. They take over and request the energy needed to attack, as well as determine how to attack. (The bullied youth who has finally had enough.)

- **Freeze:** The amygdalae could determine from a previous situation the body is in danger, and it would be best to fight and flee. The contradictory decisions from the same stimulus results in the body freezing up. (This is the deer-in-the-headlights phenomenon.)[16]

Key Point: The amygdalae can make a decision and direct movement (after the brain has made a decision) based on the intensity of the emotions and feelings from previous single experiences, not understanding the results could be different this time.

When the amygdalae take over by directing the actions (flight or fight), the result can be destructive. When it is, this is the evil thought process. The person is in an animal thought process, and then one event occurs that causes the person to seemingly lose their mind and become destructive. Ferguson, Missouri, is a perfect example. The people were in an animal thought process (without conscious brain involvement) when one event caused wide-scale destruction. Their amygdalae were firing, and the chemicals that were released resulted in temporary physical actions.

Do not be overcome by evil, but overcome evil with good.
(Romans 12:21)

Jesus said:

But I say to you, do not resist the one who is evil. But if anyone slaps you on the right cheek, turn to him the other also.
(Matthew 5:39)

These chemicals tend to be reabsorbed in a matter of seconds. This is why people say, "Count to ten before you act." The best way to respond to a person who is in a destructive thought process is to not do anything. But if you must talk, speak as soft, positively, and slowly as possible,

---

16   https://www.britannica.com/topic/fight-or-flight-response

taking plenty of pauses. The goal is to distract the person in the evil thought process and wait for them to reabsorb the chemicals.

How do people stay in an evil thought process? They avoid becoming conscious and focus on lashing out at others; others will then retaliate and help them get more chemicals into their system. They surround themselves with people who will keep them firing, which we call mob mentality. Here is a primary example of mob mentality from Scripture:

> *Now the chief priests and the elders persuaded the crowd to ask for Barabbas and destroy Jesus. The governor again said to them, "Which of the two do you want me to release for you? And they said, "Barabbas." Pilate said to them, "Then what shall I do with Jesus who is called Christ?" They all said, "Let him be crucified!" And he said, "Why, what evil has he done?" But they shouted all the more, "Let him be crucified!" So when Pilate saw that he was gaining nothing, but rather that a riot was beginning, he took water and washed his hands before the crowd, saying, "I am innocent of this man's blood; see to it yourselves." (Matthew 27:20-24)*

The key point to remember is the amygdalae direct movement *after* the brain has made a decision, based on the intensity of emotions and feelings from previous single experiences. Once the information has made it through the amygdalae, there is one more crucial stop before it results in external actions.

The Heart

The heart is the last step in both the unconscious brain (fleshly/animal thought process) and conscious brain (human thought process) before action is taken. This has been known for centuries, confirming what the Bible taught thousands of years ago.

> *But what comes out of the mouth proceeds from the heart, and this defiles a person. For out of the heart come evil thoughts, murder, adultery, sexual immorality, theft, false witness, slander. (Matthew 15:18-19)*

Your heart has its own independent nervous system consisting of more than thirty thousand neurons. Your body creates a chemical in response to every thought that makes it through the amygdalae. The heart checks all of these chemicals. The heart can respond and make decisions based on intuition and feelings. In fact, the heart can respond with the production of atrial natriuretic peptide (ANP), a hormone regulating many brain functions and, like the amygdalae, can motivate behavior.[17]

The heart takes in all the information like the amygdalae, makes a decision, and can alter the decision previously made by the brain and/or the amygdalae. At this point the external actions (effects) are seen. However, the heart serves another purpose that has only recently been confirmed. The heart can make its own decisions, have its own opinions, and attempt to influence the brain.[18] This can be seen as the heart arguing with the brain. The heart checks the accuracy and integrity of our thought process and makes a case against the brain if the requested action is inconsistent with experiences. Contradictory thoughts stress the heart. When the heart argues with the conscious brain decision, the individual's mind/soul must cast the deciding vote between the head and the heart.

The Greek word used for "heart" in the New Testament is Strong's #2588 *kardia*, which means "that organ in the body which is the center of the circulation of the blood, and hence was regarded as the seat of physical life" and "denotes the center of all physical and spiritual life." The heart is the center of this process because what is placed in the heart is the effect of what has been chosen, and the subsequent actions that are taken are an effect of what has been placed in the heart. The Word of God has much to say about the heart:

> *The Lord saw that the wickedness of man was great in the earth, and that every intention of the thoughts of his heart was only evil continually. And the Lord regretted that he had made man on the earth, and it grieved him to his heart.* (Genesis 6:5-6)
>
> *The heart is deceitful above all things, and desperately sick; who can understand it? I the Lord search the heart and test*

---

[17] http://www.ncbi.nlm.nih.gov/
[18] https://www.heartmath.org/research/science-of-the-heart/heart-brain-communication/

> *the mind, to give every man according to his ways, according to the fruit of his deeds.* (Jeremiah 17:9-10)
>
> *For from within, out of the heart of man, come evil thoughts, sexual immorality, theft, murder, adultery, coveting, wickedness, deceit, sensuality, envy, slander, pride, foolishness. All these evil things come from within, and they defile a person.* (Mark 7:21-23)

The heart of a man is the gatekeeper before our words and deeds are performed. The Scriptures clearly state that the heart of sinful man is only capable of bad things.

> *And I will give you a new heart, and a new spirit I will put within you. And I will remove the heart of stone from your flesh and give you a heart of flesh. And I will put my Spirit within you, and cause you to walk in my statutes and be careful to obey my rules. You shall dwell in the land that I gave to your fathers, and you shall be my people, and I will be your God.* (Ezekiel 36:26-28)

This is what God does when a sinner confesses, repents, and throws himself on the mercy and sacrifice of Jesus Christ. The new heart from God gives us the ability to take our thoughts captive before sin comes out from us, where the old heart would fight to confirm our previous bad behavior. But this new heart is not immune to the effects of our sinful nature and must be guarded and nurtured by God's Word and Spirit. But by God's gift of grace, we are now actually able to do things that are holy and pleasing to God.

How Does Our Brain and Heart Track Temptation?

A man sees a beautiful woman that is not his wife. He focuses on her (opens the nucleus basalis) and his conscious brain begins to imagine the possibilities. The unbeliever has only human understanding to use to consider another perspective – why he should not act out on his imagination. All this time his amygdalae are urging him through chemical and electrical energy to act out on the temptation, because it seems right and is what he has chosen to do in past similar situations.

If the temptation is not taken captive in my conscious brain, I am faced with a desire to act out on the temptation (sin). If I am an unregenerate sinner (unsaved), my deceitful and wicked human heart confirms the sin I want to perform is normal and fits the pattern in my unconscious brain. I fall into the trap of continuing to sin, and that pattern of sin, which seems right in my unconscious brain, is reinforced when it sees me carry out the sinful act. My sinful nature is strengthened.

How does this scenario play out in the born-again believer? Once a temptation begins in my conscious brain, I can choose to allow the Holy Spirit to take the thought captive until I lose the energy to sin. We can focus on the Holy Spirit and God's Word until the amygdalae "run out of bullets." If I decide to give in to the temptation, I have one more avenue of escape – the new heart God has given me as a true believer. This new heart is the gatekeeper that urges me to reconsider before I do something damaging to me or others.

The action comes next: obedience to God or sin. My choice either reinforces the pattern in my unconscious brain or starts to develop a new pattern, which it will look for as fitting in the future. If I choose to obey God and not sin, I can state my will aloud like this: "I choose to say no to sexual immorality, obeying God and honoring my wife, because that will make me happier in the long run." Done consistently over time, this helps to rewrite the pattern in my unconscious brain. Eventually, once it sees me making the right decision, a new pattern emerges, saying no to sexual sin because I will be happier in the long run. Additionally, the amygdalae start to see a new fitting pattern emerge and provide less and less chemical and electrical energy to urge me to sin.

The new heart God gives to believers confirms that the decision made is consistent with the Holy Spirit and confirms the choice as righteous. This new heart is strengthened every time we choose righteous behavior by the power of the Holy Spirit. Talk to someone who overcame addiction to alcohol or drugs, and their story will track with this model. At first, saying no to their addiction seems impossible. But each time they refuse to partake, it becomes easier. Over time a new pattern of refusing the addiction becomes fitting in the unconscious brain, and the person can refuse to partake in the future.

The Human Conscience

The human conscience is where the final thought process battle takes place. The new heart God gives us loves Him and wants to take good actions. The conscience works either with or against the new heart given to the believer. It either confirms the good our new heart wants to do or resists it and influences it to return to the sinful patterns we knew before we received our new heart. When our conscience becomes aligned with the Holy Spirit, we become conformed to the image of Jesus Christ.

After becoming a believer and receiving the Holy Spirit, our lives should begin to change radically. Sinful things we once enjoyed should be increasingly distasteful and undesirable to us. But the longer you lived before salvation and the depths of sin you practiced before receiving grace, make this transformation to holiness a difficult journey. Our conscience has been influenced by the sinful nature and wrong teachings we received from people we look up to and respect (parents, teachers, friends, and even pastors). Our corrupted conscience stands in the way of the righteous intentions of the new heart God gave us. Our new heart loves God and wants to serve Him and love others as He loves us. Our conscience, influenced by our sinful nature, may want to continue to live according to our flesh. The condition of our conscience is evidence of our sanctification process, which leads to happiness and eternal reward. If our conscience confirms the new heart God gave us, it is proof we are being sanctified. When God breathed life into Adam, He gave him a spirit. In fact, the Hebrew word for *spirit* in the Old Testament is *ruah*: "wind, breath."

> *And they came, everyone whose heart stirred him, and everyone whose spirit moved him, and brought the Lord's contribution to be used for the tent of meeting, and for all its service, and for the holy garments.* (Exodus 35:21)

Our spirit and heart should work together for good. The Hebrew word for *heart* is *leb*: "the feelings, will and intellect; the center of physical and spiritual life." We covered this earlier but it is worth another look.

Before the flood:

> *The Lord saw that the wickedness of man was great in the*

earth, and that every intention of the thoughts of his heart was only evil continually. And the Lord regretted that he had made man on the earth, and it grieved him to his heart. (Genesis 6:5-6)

After the law of Moses was given:

The heart is deceitful above all things, and desperately sick; who can understand it? I the Lord search the heart and test the mind, to give every man according to his ways, according to the fruit of his deeds. (Jeremiah 17:9-10)

What must we do in our human heart to be saved?

Because, if you confess with your mouth that Jesus is Lord and believe in your heart that God raised him from the dead, you will be saved. For with the heart one believes and is justified, and with the mouth one confesses and is saved. (Romans 10:9-10)

When we are saved and born again:

And I will give you a new heart, and a new spirit I will put within you. And I will remove the heart of stone from your flesh and give you a heart of flesh. And I will put my Spirit within you, and cause you to walk in my statutes and be careful to obey my rules. (Ezekiel 36:26-27)

What are the effects of the new heart God has given us?

*The aim of our charge is love that issues from a **pure heart and a good conscience** and a sincere faith. Certain persons, by swerving from these, have wandered away into vain discussion, desiring to be teachers of the law, without understanding either what they are saying or the things about which they make confident assertions.* (1 Timothy 1:5-7, emphasis added)

The new heart God has given us works in tandem with our conscience developed from a sincere faith. Our new heart loves God and wants to please Him, but it is subject to the influence of our conscience, man's barometer of right and wrong. That conscience has been degraded by years of sin and wrong teachings.

In the New Testament, the Greek word for *conscience* is *syneidesis*: "moral consciousness; the soul as distinguishing between what is morally good and bad, prompting to do the former and shun the latter, commending one, condemning the other." Our conscience is part of our human soul, given to all men at birth to give them a sense of right and wrong.

> *For when Gentiles, who do not have the law, by nature do what the law requires, they are a law to themselves, even though they do not have the law. They show that the work of the law is written on their hearts, while their conscience also bears witness, and their conflicting thoughts accuse or even excuse them on that day when, according to my gospel, God judges the secrets of men by Christ Jesus.* (Romans 2:14-16)

The conscience of the unbeliever is more influenced by the flesh the longer he remains an unbeliever. The sinful nature of man has a greater and greater influence on the conscience to the point that eventually a fallen man's conscience could be seared and incapable of rescue.

> *And since they did not see fit to acknowledge God, God gave them up to a debased mind to do what ought not to be done. They were filled with all manner of unrighteousness, evil, covetousness, malice. They are full of envy, murder, strife, deceit, maliciousness. They are gossips, slanderers, haters of God, insolent, haughty, boastful, inventors of evil, disobedient to parents, foolish, faithless, heartless, ruthless. Though they know God's righteous decree that those who practice such things deserve to die, they not only do them but give approval to those who practice them.* (Romans 1:28-32)

The passage refers to *inventors of evil*. Justifying abortion and homosexual marriage are two examples of how the Christian conscience in America is being seared. Paul's message is that once the human conscience has been influenced by the flesh to the point that it now sees evil as good and good as evil, God gives up on them and turns them over to an evil thought process to do unspeakably evil things. A professing Christian who insists that abortion and homosexual marriage is righteous in God's eyes after they have been confronted with the truth of the Bible is at risk of a seared conscience.

The conscience plays a crucial role in our eternal destination. It either begins conforming to the truth of the Word and Spirit, confirming that we have been saved, or it refutes our professed salvation. It also plays a critical role in a believer experiencing real joy. The quicker our conscience is aligned with the Holy Spirit, the more we conform to God's will and make good choices that lead to true happiness. If we continue to allow our flesh and sinful nature to influence our conscience, we are out of spiritual alignment with God and void of true joy and peace.

Let's look again at Ezekiel 36:26-27, where God says He will give us a new heart as believers:

> *And I will give you a new heart, and a new spirit I will put within you. And I will remove the heart of stone from your flesh and give you a heart of flesh. And I will put my Spirit within you, and cause you to walk in my statutes and be careful to obey my rules.*

Notice something very important here: God removes our heart of stone and replaces it with a new heart, but His Spirit does not instantly heal the spirit in us. Our spirit needs to be regenerated through sanctification by His Spirit.

> *Draw near to God, and he will draw near to you. Cleanse your hands, you sinners, and purify your hearts, you double-minded.* (James 4:8)

The words *double-minded* literally mean "double-spirited." The Spirit of God competes with our wicked human spirit, developed from years of justifying our sin. If we submit to the wicked spirit within us, we will lean toward unrighteous action that feeds our flesh. If we submit to the Holy Spirit, our conscience is conformed to affirm righteous actions that prove we love God and others. We are being sanctified.

There are two important verses in the Bible we can reference to understand how the truth of God's Word convicts the conscience of man:

> *For as the rain and the snow come down from heaven and do not return there but water the earth, making it bring forth and sprout, giving seed to the sower and bread to the eater, so shall my word be that goes out from my mouth; it shall not return to me empty, but it shall accomplish that which I purpose, and shall succeed in the thing for which I sent it.* (Isaiah 55:10-11)

> *For the word of God is living and active, sharper than any two-edged sword, piercing to the division of soul and of spirit, of joints and of marrow, and discerning the thoughts and intentions of the heart.* (Hebrews 4:12)

God's Word always accomplishes something important: it either convicts man of his sin, which leads to confession, repentance, and salvation, or it will be used to condemn the man who rejects it. In the verse from Hebrews, we see that God's Word divides the soul and spirit and discerns the thoughts and intentions of the heart. The Word of God influences our conscience, which leads it to a correct assessment of right or wrong and results in the conscience aligning with the new heart God gives to born-again believers.

When we are born again, we receive a new pure heart from God that desires to love and obey Him. Our conscience, which for years has justified our sin and received harmful teachings contradictory to the Word of God, resists change and fights the new heart God has given us. It wants to convince us that feeding our flesh is a good thing. The new heart battles our damaged conscience (Romans 7). If we continue to allow our damaged conscience to override our new heart by justifying our sins as right, our new heart becomes damaged and corrupted. The new heart is influenced by the corrupted conscience, which leads to wrongful actions and our behaving in a way contradictory to the Word of God, even as believers.

But when the new heart overrides our corrupted conscience by directing us to obey God's Word, a new pattern of right or wrong is established in our conscience. The heart and conscience begin to agree with one another, which leads us to feel good when we obey what God has taught us.

> *For if the blood of goats and bulls, and the sprinkling of defiled persons with the ashes of a heifer, sanctify for the purification of the flesh, how much more will the blood of Christ, who through the eternal Spirit offered himself without blemish to God, purify our conscience from dead works to serve the living God.* (Hebrews 9:13-14)

> *For our boast is this, the testimony of our conscience, that we behaved in the world with simplicity and godly sincerity, not by earthly wisdom but by the grace of God, and supremely so toward you.* (2 Corinthians 1:12)

> *As I urged you when I was going to Macedonia, remain at Ephesus so that you may charge certain persons not to teach any different doctrine, nor to devote themselves to myths and endless genealogies, which promote speculations rather than the stewardship from God that is by faith. The aim of our charge is love that issues from a pure heart and a good conscience and a sincere faith. Certain persons, by swerving from these, have wandered away into vain discussion.* (1 Timothy 1:3-6)

We can choose to act instinctively out of our unconscious brain or open our nucleus basalis to think and act out of our conscious brain, where our human understanding and the Holy Spirit can influence our thoughts that lead to action. Whether we choose to act out of our unconscious or conscious brain, the actions we take are seen by the unconscious brain. This new action either confirms the sinful pattern established in the unconscious or starts to build a new righteous pattern in it. Our conscience is the gatekeeper of our unconscious brain. If it has been damaged by our sinful nature, it will resist and damage the new heart God has given us. Every time our new heart wins, the conscience becomes conformed to our new heart and the Spirit God has placed in us. Guilt is the emotion God gives us that the conscience uses to convict us of wrong thoughts and actions.

God designed our brain, heart, and conscience to work in this way. The following graphic gives an overview of what we have discussed concerning our thought process and taking it captive to Christ. More charts and information are available for viewing and downloading at www.michaeldlemay.com.

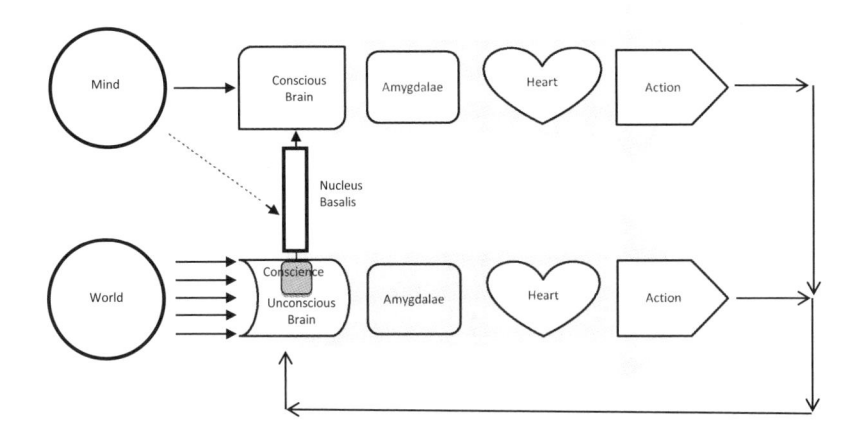

```
[Mind] → [Conscious Brain] → [Amygdalae] → [Heart] → [Action] →
                ↑
         [Nucleus Basalis]
                ↑
[World] → [Conscience / Unconscious Brain] → [Amygdalae] → [Heart] → [Action] →
```

Many people I work with find it helpful to use this diagram to track their thought process and temptation. Sin is often the result of a quick decision made in haste to satisfy our flesh. Memorizing and using this diagram to track the temptation and your thought process can help slow you down so you do not act impulsively and give in to temptations.

Next, we will look at some of the ways our brain, heart, and conscience have been damaged and how the Spirit and Word of God can help us repair the damage. This will help us reject sin, live with more peace and joy, and help others come to saving faith in Jesus Christ.

Chapter Six

IMPROVING OUR THOUGHT PROCESS

Chapter objective: to learn how to fight deception and take responsibility.

Comedian Flip Wilson rose to popularity in the 1960s with a skit where, whenever he would do something wrong and get caught, he would scream, "The devil made me do it!" While funny at the time, little did we know there was something prophetic in Wilson's comedy routine. America has become a nation where people claim little to no responsibility for their actions and are always looking for someone to blame for their problems. Humanist philosophy has succeeded in perpetrating the "victim card" as an excuse for every difficult situation. It has also succeeded in poisoning the minds of our younger people to the point where many of them actually believe their gender is fluid, changing from day to day. Increasingly, people take no responsibility for their thoughts or actions.

The last chapter discussed how God designed our brain, heart, and conscience to work. When sin entered the world, death and deterioration followed, and our sinful nature has caused problems in our thought process. But the Word of God and the power of the Holy Spirit can reverse the damage and help us use a godly thought process in spite of the damage done by sin. In this chapter we will look at some of this damage and at how, by the power of the Word and the Holy Spirit, we can live a life of joy as we turn our backs on sin and pursue righteous living in Christ Jesus.

> *If you love me, you will keep my commandments. And I will ask the Father, and he will give you another Helper, to be with you forever, even the Spirit of truth, whom the world cannot receive, because it neither sees him nor knows him. You know him, for he dwells with you and will be in you.* (John 14:15-17)

> *But the Helper, the Holy Spirit, whom the Father will send in my name, he will teach you all things and bring to your remembrance all that I have said to you.* (John 14:26)

The Holy Spirit and the Word of God can repair the damage done in our brain and conscience. Believers' unconscious and conscious brains can still operate as God designed them, and we have the Holy Spirit to influence our thoughts and repair the damage done through sin and faulty "life commandments," which we will discuss later. He is the stimulus that leads us to obey and love God and love others as God loves us.

> *The aim of our charge is love that issues from a pure heart and a good conscience and a sincere faith. Certain persons, by swerving from these, have wandered away into vain discussion, desiring to be teachers of the law, without understanding either what they are saying or the things about which they make confident assertions.* (1 Timothy 1:5-7)

We received God's Spirit when we were born again. It clashes with our human spirit that has been degraded by sin and wrong teachings. Our conscience, where this battle takes place, is either being conformed to God's Spirit or resists it and damages the new heart God has given us. The Holy Spirit wants to work on our conscience and make sure it is properly wired and dependable in warning us of pending danger. A properly wired conscience warns us when we are considering decisions that will hinder our journey to joy and eternal life.

Understanding the Role of Our Conscience

> *But what comes out of the mouth proceeds from the heart, and this defiles a person. For out of the heart come evil thoughts, murder, adultery, sexual immorality, theft, false witness, slander. These are what defile a person. But to eat with unwashed hands does not defile anyone.* (Matthew 15:18-20)

> *Let us draw near with a true heart in full assurance of faith, with our hearts sprinkled clean from an evil conscience and our bodies washed with pure water.* (Hebrews 10:22)

When a thought reaches our heart internally because of a decision we made, the new heart God has given us will oppose the temptation to sin, because this new heart desires to glorify God and not sin. Then up in our mind/soul, we must decide between the head (sinful thought) and our new heart (wants to be righteous).

This next section has a huge impact in understanding our thought process and our ability to take it captive to Christ. The conscience can actually be involved twice in our thought process.

> *If any of you lacks wisdom, let him ask God, who gives generously to all without reproach, and it will be given him. But let him ask in faith, with no doubting, for the one who doubts is like a wave of the sea that is driven and tossed by the wind. For that person must not suppose that he will receive anything from the Lord; he is a double-minded man, unstable in all his ways.* (James 1:5-8)

Double-minded in Greek is *dipsychos:* "two-spirited." Remember, God said He gives us a new spirit, but does not automatically fix our damaged human spirit. Since our new heart wants to love and obey God, this battle between these competing spirits is in our conscience. The conscience first acts similarly to the heart when a decision is filtered through it; it looks at a decision to determine if it is consistent or contradictory with the established pattern of the conscience. If our conscience is seriously damaged, it wants to confirm the sin we are considering is fitting. Here the conscience fights the new heart God has given us, and if it wins, it damages our new heart.

But remember, unless the conscience is seared (Romans 1), some good may still proceed from it. If we choose sin, our conscience can still influence after we sin with a feeling of guilt. So the conscience intercedes twice in influencing our decisions and subsequent behaviors: before and after we sin. And even though it may confirm bad decisions as appropriate initially, once it sees the resulting action, it still gives us a feeling of guilt and warns us of serious future damage.

In the next chapter, we will discuss the importance of meaningful Christian fellowship. One way I have found to check the condition of my conscience is through fellowship. When we are confronted by a fellow Christian over something we say or do that opposes the Word of God, our response says a lot about the condition of our conscience. If we try to justify the sin or excuse it in any way, it may be a sign that our conscience is damaged. But feeling remorse and godly sorrow over our sin and in humility acknowledging our wrong action are good signs that our conscience is aligning with the Holy Spirit.

Increasing feelings of guilt are a good sign that your conscience is aligning with the Holy Spirit. When things that never used to bother you start to bother you, the Holy Spirit is probably working on your conscience. In my case, I used very crude language before I became a believer. And even after becoming a Christian, I could still use crude language too often. Over time I felt increasing guilt over my choice of words: the Holy Spirit was aligning my conscience to conformity with the Word of God. Initially, pride would lead me to discount the concerns of anyone who confronted me. But, as the Holy Spirit continued to align my conscience with the will of God, I repented of my language and asked fellow believers to continue to hold me accountable for the words I used. Increasing humility is a sign of your conscience being aligned with the Holy Spirit.

Humility leads us to accept that, but for the grace of God, we would still be the worst sinner we know. It gives us a desire to be confronted with our wrong behaviors by fellow believers so we can become better aligned with God's will for our lives. Humility helps us realize just how dependent we are on God.

Humility leads to brokenness. Brokenness occurs when we give up on our plan to get us to our destination and take direction from God. We realize there is only one plan and path to our destination: God's plan.

Humility also helps us realize that no man in his own efforts can guarantee excellent outcomes, no matter how diligently we work toward them. Understanding this is the only way for the believer to have great peace and comfort. If we believe we can control all the outcomes, the undue pressure we put on ourselves and the distractions that overwhelm us can be damaging or destructive. Unrealistic expectations (thinking we can control every outcome) actually prevent our ability to have joy and love others. However, humility and brokenness result in us only trying to control what we can (our choices and behavior) and staying in the moment. When we focus on the correct cause – the Great Commandment of loving God and others – we can achieve peace, because we trust God with the temporal and eternal effects.

> *Therefore do not be anxious, saying, 'What shall we eat?' or 'What shall we drink?' or 'What shall we wear?' For the Gentiles seek after all these things, and your heavenly Father knows that you need them all.* (Matthew 6:31-32)

Jesus warned us not to focus on temporal effects. He then gave us the cause (what to focus on):

> *But seek first the kingdom of God and his righteousness, and all these things will be added to you.* (Matthew 6:33)

God takes care of the effects when we focus on seeking Him as the cause of our lives. He promises that all effects – even those that seem unpleasant at the time – are for our benefit:

> *And we know that for those who love God all things work together for good, for those who are called according to his purpose. For those whom he foreknew he also predestined to be conformed to the image of his Son, in order that he might be the firstborn among many brothers. And those whom he predestined he also called, and those whom he called he*

also justified, and those whom he justified he also glorified.
(Romans 8:28-30)

By using a godly thought process and being humble, we realize God controls every lasting effect.

Do not lay up for yourselves treasures on earth, where moth and rust destroy and where thieves break in and steal, but lay up for yourselves treasures in heaven, where neither moth nor rust destroys and where thieves do not break in and steal. For where your treasure is, there your heart will be also. (Matthew 6:19-21)

A fleshly/animal thought process unjustly takes things from others in this lifetime. A human thought process stores up wealth in this life to be comfortable, but it will not carry over to eternity. The godly thought process teaches us that by being generous to others, we love others as Jesus commanded and we are storing up eternal treasures in heaven that will last forever.

We destroy arguments and every lofty opinion raised against the knowledge of God, and take every thought captive to obey Christ. (2 Corinthians 10:5)

Using a godly thought process involves slowing our thought process down and not acting impulsively. We no longer rely on the five stimuli that animals depend on, and we forego human understanding, which is always short-term and ultimately self-serving. Instead, we think big picture and are future oriented.

When a believer trains himself to ignore his conscience, his life can become very miserable. The Holy Spirit, along with the new heart God has given us, will testify against our damaged conscience. And every time we choose to ignore the Holy Spirit, our conscience gets more and more damaged until it confirms wrong behavior as acceptable.

People who do not have a guilty conscience, yet continue to habitually sin, bring their professed salvation into question. They've deceived themselves, because if they truly had the Holy Spirit, He would be trying to fix the faulty wiring of the conscience. Left unresolved, the conscience can become seared to the point it wears down so badly that it starts to confirm sin as righteous. Many progressive Christians who support universal salvation, abortion, and homosexuality are headed in this direction. They truly believe their beliefs and actions are righteous because their conscience is becoming seared. They begin a downward spiral:

> *Indeed, all who desire to live a godly life in Christ Jesus will be persecuted, while evil people and impostors will go on from bad to worse, deceiving and being deceived.* (2 Timothy 3:12-13)

Believers will be tempted and occasionally sin. But if our conscience is conformed to the Spirit of God, it will warn us before we act. The Spirit will confirm the belief of our new heart to act righteously and turn away from sin. If our conscience has been badly damaged before we were born again, it might still want to resist the new heart God gave us and encourage us to sin. But even if it does, God's Spirit works in us to give us guilt once we choose to sin. Guilt is a gift from God we call the conviction of the Holy Spirit.

The final internal battle before we take an action is this: will I choose to let my damaged conscience infect my new heart? Or will I choose righteous actions that allow God's Spirit to start repairing my damaged conscience? If we choose to let the Holy Spirit heal our damaged conscience, it becomes stronger and more aligned with God. But if we choose to listen to our damaged conscience and sin, we damage it further and damage the new heart God has given us. We still might reach our destination of heaven, but the journey will be filled with anxiety and problems.

> *So I always take pains to have a clear conscience toward both God and man.* (Acts 24:16)

> *For our boast is this, the testimony of our conscience, that we behaved in the world with simplicity and godly sincerity, not by earthly wisdom but by the grace of God, and supremely so toward you.* (2 Corinthians 1:12)

> *Now who is there to harm you if you are zealous for what is good? But even if you should suffer for righteousness' sake,*

you will be blessed. Have no fear of them, nor be troubled, but in your hearts honor Christ the Lord as holy, always being prepared to make a defense to anyone who asks you for a reason for the hope that is in you; yet do it with gentleness and respect, having a good conscience, so that, when you are slandered, those who revile your good behavior in Christ may be put to shame. For it is better to suffer for doing good, if that should be God's will, than for doing evil. (1 Peter 3:13-17)

A conscience that testifies to and agrees with our new heart is proof of increasing sanctification. The final decision in the battle between our mind, heart, and conscience is seen through our resulting actions and filed in our unconscious brain, the place our conscience and sinful nature reside. It will look for patterns to act upon in the future. If we continue to sin, we fall into the pattern of justifying our sinful behavior. This is very important to understand: taking our thoughts captive is an attempt to change the patterns established in our unconscious brain and conscience.

If the unconscious brain receives a new set of patterns and beliefs consistent with biblical principles, it will be prepared to reject stimuli that can eventually enter our conscious brain. Remember, the unconscious brain works on the principle of non-contradiction, so if it sees something that is against the established pattern, it wants to reject it immediately. But once an unhealthy stimulus enters our conscious brain by focusing on it, we imagine the possibilities, and the battle against temptation and sin are on once again.

Since we are not yet perfected, sometimes an unhealthy stimulus will grab our attention and get into our conscious brain. But if our conscience becomes aligned with the Spirit of God, it gives us two lines of defense when this happens. First, our purified conscience will now confirm the desires of our new heart to resist acting out on the conscious decision. This is the first way we can effectively take our thoughts captive. But if we ignore our new heart and conscience and do sin, our conscience gives us a very strong emotion of guilt: conviction of the Holy Spirit.

This is sanctification: an increased ability to turn away from temptation, accompanied by increased guilt if we choose to sin.

When we habitually choose sin, dismissing the conviction of the Holy Spirit, we quench the Holy Spirit and diminish His continuing influence on us.

> *See that no one repays anyone evil for evil, but always seek to do good to one another and to everyone. Rejoice always, pray without ceasing, give thanks in all circumstances; for this is the will of God in Christ Jesus for you. Do not quench the Spirit.* (1 Thessalonians 5:15-19)

When we quench the Holy Spirit, we live in a growing state of contradiction: doing that which we know we should not do, to paraphrase Paul in Romans 7. At best, we live a life of stress, lacking joy and peace. At worst, our damaged conscience damages our new heart and grows stronger in its resistance of the Holy Spirit. In this case, we are the seeds in Jesus' parable that sprout up quickly, but wither under the pressure of the world.

> *Other seeds fell on rocky ground, where they did not have much soil, and immediately they sprang up, since they had no depth of soil, but when the sun rose they were scorched. And since they had no root, they withered away.* (Matthew 13:5-6)

Allowing the Holy Spirit to rewire our conscience is crucial. But other parts of our brain have also been damaged from our sinful state. Let's look at some common problems we face on the journey to sanctification.

Unconscious Brain Damage

Remember, the unconscious brain works from learned patterns, reacting rather than truly thinking. The majority of damage in it comes from having wrong definitions for words. If these words have strong emotions attached to them, simply hearing them can cause us anxiety and lead to damaging consequences.

When I was thirteen, a group of us were playing football while our fathers stood around talking. I heard my father say something to one of his friends that would damage my unconscious brain and thought process for nearly forty years. He said, "I heard the definition of the perfect woman is a lady in public and a whore in the bedroom." At that age I could not care less about girls, so I never consciously thought about what my father said. But my unconscious brain heard it and stored it as the beginning of patterned beliefs in my life. For the next forty years, I unconsciously viewed women that way.

This is an example of unconscious brain damage: I had a wrong definition for *woman* and every time I saw an attractive woman, I would unconsciously look at her as only a sexual object for my pleasure. But God's grace flowing through my wife helped me to identify and start fixing the damage. She lovingly confronted me one day and told me that at times she felt I viewed her as an object for my pleasure, rather than a partner to love and cherish. At first I was shocked, in unbelief and denial until I asked God to search my heart. The Holy Spirit confirmed what Nancy said, and I began to pray and work on redefining *woman* in my unconscious brain. Today I see my wife as a beautiful gift and partner God has given me, and I see other women in one of two ways: as either sisters in Christ or lost sinners in need of His forgiveness.

One couple we have been helping came to us because the wife was confused and depressed about her life, and their marriage was falling apart. After years of stressful marriage, the husband was about to just give up because his wife was a spiritual and emotional wreck. They had been to several churches looking for help but finding none. The woman had been on anti-depressants for twenty years, and her thoughts were scattered. As we met and got to hear her story, we uncovered severe damage in her unconscious brain.

She was convinced that she was a sincere believer, but she was angry at God and herself because she was not bearing fruit and was still on medication. She also kept going back and focusing on her sins rather than the forgiveness and grace of God. Her husband kept telling her she needed to accept that Jesus took her sins upon Himself. She would state she knew that but would continually put herself back under condemnation, because she did not feel the peace of God in her life and was convinced that being on medication of any kind was idolatry.

I recognized she was suffering from damage in her unconscious brain the first time we met. I asked her about her earthly father, and she shared that he had sexually abused her, told her she was worthless, and eventually abandoned her. I wrote those things on the white board and then said, "Close your eyes and relax. I am going to say something, and I want you to tell me the first words that come to you: God is your heavenly Father; how do you describe Him?"

Without hesitation she opened her eyes and pointed to what I had written on the board about her earthly father.

So I asked, "Do you believe that your heavenly Father will abuse you, tell you that you are worthless, and abandon you?"

Without hesitation she answered, "Yes!"

The only definition of *father* she knew was from her traumatic experiences with her earthly father, and she unconsciously applied that definition to God. I told her that until she could accept and believe the correct definition of *father*, she should refer to God as her king or protector or provider – anything but father. We worked with her for several weeks to break the word *father* into two different definitions: bad father and good father. Since her unconscious brain, which had the wrong definition of father, only responds to the five external stimuli (hearing, sight, smell, taste, touch), we had her write down and speak out loud, "God my heavenly Father is a good father, not at all like my bad earthly father. My good heavenly Father will never abuse me or tell me I'm worthless and will never abandon me." Within a few weeks, her unconscious brain had a new definition of God: a loving Father who will never abuse or abandon me and cherishes me. This was accomplished by stating her new belief out loud repeatedly, until her unconscious brain saw this new definition of God the Father as fitting.

A key to repairing unconscious brain damage is by using understanding and the Holy Spirit to influence your conscious brain to believe a new definition of a word that the unconscious brain has assigned with a wrong definition. Since the unconscious brain only reacts to the five external stimuli, this new definition must be stated out loud repeatedly, particularly whenever you start thinking about that word.

Almost every word we use will have a different definition when it is qualified further. God showed this woman that there is a huge difference between a bad father and a good father. As we continued to meet with her, further damage in her unconscious brain became evident due to another incorrectly defined word. She was better, but there was still no breakthrough. Something else was holding her back from receiving the forgiveness and joy of Jesus' sacrifice for her on the cross. She still did not feel forgiven.

Nancy asked if she believed Jesus died on the cross so God could forgive our sins. She said yes, but not for *her* sins. We asked her what her definition of *repent* was. She said, "To stop sinning, and I obviously haven't really repented because I keep on sinning, so God couldn't have forgiven me."

I showed her that her definition of *repent* was different from the definition in the Bible. *Repent* means to "change your mind and look at something differently." She wrongly believed that to repent would result in instant holiness. We showed her that true repentance meant we look differently at our sinful behavior, hating it instead of continuing to enjoy it. Eventually this leads to a change in behavior, but this is usually a process of growth, not an instant purification.

This lovely woman truly hated her ongoing sin. But because she wrongly believed God was a father who would abuse and abandon her and that *repent* meant to never sin again, she was unable to accept the love and forgiveness of God, leading to major depression and misery.

> *Search me, O God, and know my heart! Try me and know*
> *my thoughts! And see if there be any grievous way in me,*
> *and lead me in the way everlasting!* (Psalm 139:23-24)

I told her to open up to God and pray these verses out loud over the next week, to ask God to reveal what He sees in your heart, the center of our spiritual life. I told her to state her will out loud to God: "God please help me see myself as you see me!" I asked her to focus on doing this throughout the week, until she thought God had answered her sincere prayer.

Six days later she phoned me, crying like a little child. God had revealed to her what He saw: that she had never sincerely confessed and repented of her sin and trusted in Jesus, and she was trying to be righteous on her own. She cried out, "I know now I am not a born-again Christian!"

I told her to cry out to God right now and confess, repent of her pride, and trust in who Jesus Christ is and what He accomplished on the cross. Tell God you want Him to control your life from this day forward, instead of trying to do it yourself. She cried out to God with as much sincerity as any person I have ever witnessed.

She came in the next day and looked much different. The look of fear and confusion had been replaced with a greater calmness. She finally started the journey to temporal and eternal joy. This nice woman had severe unconscious brain damage based on a couple very wrong definitions. But God revealed the contradictions within her unconscious brain and gave her the correct definition of who He is as our Father and that repentance is not perfection where we never sin again, but a change of mind and heart about our sin. It leads to changed behavior, as we are sanctified, and a growing hatred for the things of the flesh we once desired. She and her husband continue to meet with Nancy and me, and we are blessed by seeing her come out of bondage and grow in the knowledge and grace of Jesus Christ.

Unconscious brain damage almost always results when the unconscious brain has a wrong definition for important words. By allowing the Holy Spirit and the Word of God to give us the new, correct definition that God uses in His Word, this damage can be repaired. If we accept a flawed human definition as right, instead of the definitions God gives us, we damage our brain. We will delay or even end our journey to earthly joy and eternal reward.

Repairing damage in the unconscious brain always begins by using our conscious brain to consider other perspectives through understanding, and in the case of true believers, by allowing the Holy Spirit and the Word of God to change unhealthy patterns in our unconscious brain.

Amygdalae Damage

The amygdalae provide the correct amount of energy to move us forward into action. When I was fourteen, three of us went bowling on a Saturday morning. We were slapped around by a couple of bullies who didn't like us for some reason. This action was repeated for each of the next three weeks. My unconscious brain now equated a bowling alley with a physical threat.

For the next twenty years, every time I went to a bowling alley, I felt unsettled, looking around in an uneasy manner. My amygdalae alerted me to potential danger, since that was how I viewed a bowling alley in my unconscious brain – a place of danger. The amygdalae, just like the unconscious brain, do not think. They simply want to react to the pattern established from previous experiences.

Eventually, I used human understanding in my conscious brain to consider other perspectives on what my unconscious brain and amygdalae wanted to act out on when I went to a bowling alley. I used understanding to give myself two separate and different perspectives from the pattern entrenched in my unconscious brain. First, I was now much bigger and more muscular, so if I felt threatened, there was a very good chance the bullies would regret approaching me this time. Second, I reasoned that over the past twenty years, they might have grown to be responsible men who were no longer bullies.

By focusing my conscious brain on other perspectives, I was able to lose my patterned fear of going to bowling alleys and started to enjoy my time there. But this was at a time before I became a Christian, so I did not have that seventh stimulus available to guide my thoughts: the Holy Spirit. If I had encountered those bullies again, I may have sought revenge for the mental pain they had inflicted on me for those twenty years. My human pride and desire for revenge could have led me to confront them and kick the snot out of them. Now that I have the Holy Spirit, I would approach them and use our difficult past to talk and share the gospel with them. If I discovered they had become true believers, I would have gained more Christian fellowship! So the outcome would be a win/win.

One way to repair damage in the amygdalae, when they fire as you remember past trauma, is to consider a different outcome the next time you are in a similar situation. This is what I did with my bowling alley incident. I continually reminded myself that if I met up with those bullies again, the outcome could be very different this time. Either I would be able to defend myself if needed, or perhaps they had matured and changed, regretting their past behaviors. So every time I prepared to go to a bowling alley, I would rehearse those new potential outcomes, calming down my amygdalae. I trained them to look at the potential new scenarios as fitting, consciously controlling the fight, flight or freeze options.

Conscious Brain Damage

We have seen that repairing damage in our unconscious brain and amygdalae always starts with using our conscious brain to present perspectives that differ from the patterns established in these other parts of our brain. We choose to consciously think instead of reacting irrationally. Therefore, the better the shape our conscious brain is in, the quicker we can repair the damage in the other parts of our brain.

Since a healthy conscious brain is critical to fixing problems in our unconscious brain and amygdalae, this knowledge is critical to embracing and using a godly thought process that leads to sanctification. If we do not understand how to use this information, we will continue to spin our wheels, getting nowhere fast.

Have you ever noticed that certain words can cause you or others to trigger? A person can seem just fine, and then a word or action causes them to become erratic or mad in an instant. This information will help you understand why. Your conscious brain is made up of dendrites (from the Greek word for *tree*). These dendrites look like trees, and each trunk represents a word, and each branch represents a connecting word.

For example, the "red tree" in your conscious brain is accessed when you think of the word *red* and may have the following branches: "stop," "fire engine," "blood," or "roses." Each branch would lead to a different tree with the same connecting word. The roses branch on the red tree would be connected to the red branch on the roses tree.

The red tree in the middle has a roses branch connected to the red branch on the roses tree, and a blood branch connected to the red branch on the blood tree. In addition, each connecting word has an associated emotion. For example, the emotion associated with the blood branch on the red tree may be strongly negative (frown face), while the emotion associated with the roses branch on the red tree may be strongly positive (smiley face). This may look like this:

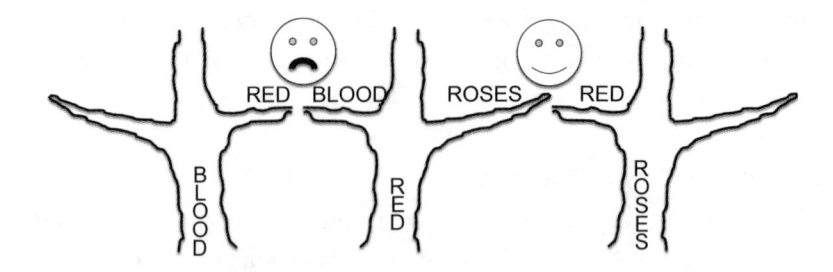

The conscious brain is equally made up of words and emotions, so let's look at how thoughts are formed.

Full Thought

The simplest unit in the conscious brain is known as a full thought. A full thought consists of three components:

1. Stimulus
2. Connecting thought
3. Associated emotion[19]

The stimulus can come through the five senses. I may see the color red. My mind opens my nucleus basalis to this stimulus and begins to focus on the red dendrite. For this example, let's say the branches in question are stop and roses.

My conscious brain wants to operate according to the shortest and quickest path, so it will naturally take the lowest and thickest branch, which may be stop because I have the most experience with red being connected to stop. Here is an example of what this may look like:

---

19 http://www.dobney.com/Research/sensory_emotion.htm

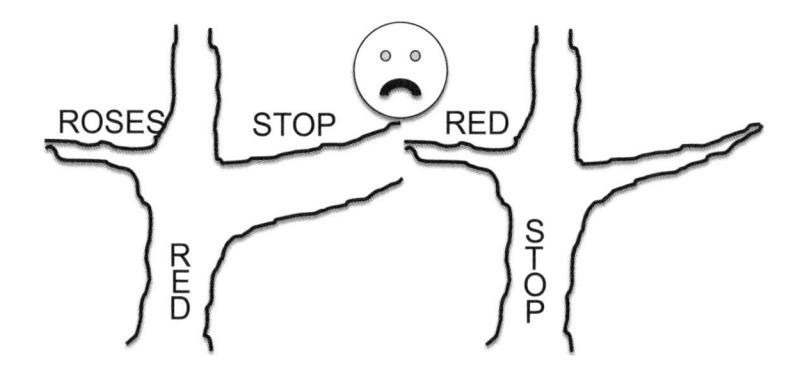

Notice, the stop branch on the red dendrite is thicker than the roses branch. The conscious brain will naturally want to take the path of stop when it gets the stimulus red through the five external senses. Word association tests work on this principle. People are told to say the first word they think of when they hear the stimulus to determine which branch is lowest and thickest in the person's brain. In this way the test can determine if the person's brain is wired towards negative or positive emotions.

As the electrical signal makes the leap from the stop branch on the red tree to the red branch on the stop tree, an associated emotion is triggered. I like to categorize these in five levels: strongly negative, negative, neutral, positive, and strongly positive. In this case, the emotion is negative (frown face).

The full thought consists of:

1. Stimulus (hearing red)

2. Connecting thought (stop)

3. Associated emotion (negative)

Another way to state the full thought is: I heard someone say, "red," and I felt negatively because I thought of stop. This is known as a thought loop. Notice, the causal chain is actually: stimulus, connecting thought, and associated emotion. I actually experienced the emotion as an effect of my dendrite branch choice. However, emotions travel faster than words inside the human body. What we experience within us is this order: stimulus, associated emotion, connecting thought. We feel like the stimulus occurred, and then we felt an emotion before we identified the connecting thought.

The stronger the emotion, the quicker we experience it. This is why when it comes to strongly negative emotions, people will say you made them feel something with your words. Actually, all you did was provide the stimulus. They chose the emotion when they chose the branch. We are responsible for our emotional responses, not others.

Our mind makes the choice to allow the brain to take the shortest path, but the mind can also choose other branches. In our example, the mind could have chosen the roses branch instead of the stop branch. You may know a person who has many negative branches that are lowest and thickest. No matter what stimulus you provide, he finds a way to state something negative. If you told him not to state something negative when you provide the next stimulus, he would naturally want to choose the lowest and thickest negative branch. However, his mind could check this selection and stop the choice. The mind would then look for a branch that was not negative. When he selected that branch, he would feel the emotion from that choice and not the emotion from the first choice he would have naturally made but didn't. How long it takes the person to choose an alternative can indicate the amount of damage in the conscious brain.

An analogy for this process will help us understand. We have many trees filled with squirrels in our backyard. They run up the trunk of a tree, select a branch, run to the end and jump to a branch on another tree, run to the trunk, and then run to the ground of this second tree. This squirrel did the same process that we have been calling a full thought. The process began at the base of one tree and ended up at the base of another tree. The squirrel made measurable progress. This is a thought loop.

In our analogy, the squirrel is the mind and the trees are the dendrites of the conscious brain. The key to making progress in your thoughts is to go from one dendrite to another and get back to the ground. When you get to the ground and complete a thought loop, you send the information to the amygdalae. In our example, I see the color red. I think *stop*, feel a negative emotion, and then send this full thought to the amygdalae, which sends it to the heart, which results in me stopping and taking action. An example from the Bible shows a thought being formed.

And he said, "I heard the sound of you in the garden, and I was afraid, because I was naked, and I hid myself."
(Genesis 3:10)

1. Stimulus: Adam heard the sound of God in the garden.

2. Connecting fact: I am naked.

3. Associated emotion: he was afraid.

Adam understood his thought process, identifying all of this as the cause of his action: *I hid myself.*

Complex Thought

What if the squirrel were to continue to a third tree rather than come to the ground on the trunk of the second tree? The place it ended up would be what we call a complex thought. A complex thought consists of more than one thought loop. In our example, while I'm driving a truck I may see *red*, think *stop* and *feel* a negative emotion, but rather than send this thought loop to my amygdalae, I can use this as a stimulus to create another thought loop.

The connecting thought may be *crash*, as in, *if I don't stop, I can have an accident.* The resulting emotion may be strongly negative, and the action I take is to slam on the brakes instead of gently pressing on them. Here is what it may look like:

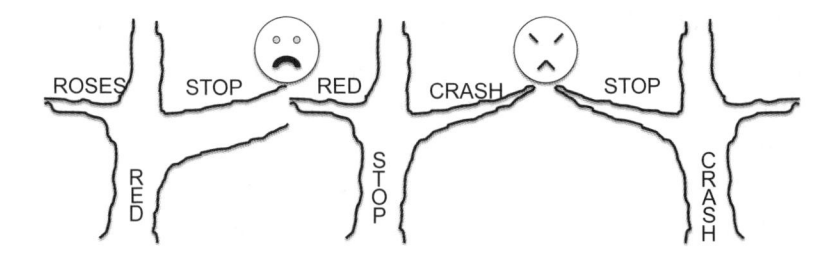

The "squirrel" began at the trunk of the red tree, made the jump to the stop tree, and instead of coming to the ground made the jump to the crash tree. In the same way, my mind began at the red dendrite when I saw red and didn't take action until I came to the crash dendrite.

This helps explain how some innocent sounding words can create such an emotional response or action from people; those words are a trigger! Someone hears or sees red, and they go right to crash, causing a violent word or behavior. In this way we can use word association techniques to try to understand how people think and respond.

> *We destroy arguments and every lofty opinion raised against the knowledge of God, and take every thought captive to obey Christ.* (2 Corinthians 10:5)

Taking every thought captive means we understand the stimulus and the decision we make when it comes to the connecting fact. Our actions will either obey Christ or keep looping and obey our flesh.

Key Points:

- A complete thought consists of a stimulus, connecting thought, and associated emotion.
- Another term for complete thought is a thought loop.
- A complex thought is a complete thought made up of two or more thought loops.

Repairing the Conscious Brain

Hopefully this information will help you deal with damaging thoughts you have and allow you to help others in a similar manner. Remember, only by God's grace and Spirit can we take our thoughts captive and find healing from deep emotional and spiritual wounds. But we can help ourselves and others to stop "looping" and slow down the destructive damage being done.

By restoring our conscious brain to excellent working condition, we can use it to repair our unconscious brain and amygdalae. We learn to slow down our thought process before we start looping, causing further reinforcement of damaging patterns. Believers have access to the Holy Spirit for the stimulus of our thoughts and actions in our conscious brains. By focusing on God and His Word, we can begin to repair our thought process, which frees us from past triggers and progresses sanctification and happiness.

Have you ever faced a serious problem that could have life-changing negative ramifications? Have you noticed that the more you think of the potential negative consequences, the more you worry, and the more stress you feel, and then you respond by either sleeping less, eating more, or engaging in other potentially harmful actions? This is usually the result of obsessing about the situation where we get stuck in a loop and begin to fear the worst-case scenario. We wear ourselves out obsessing about something that may not even happen or not be in our control, which damages ourselves. What would conscious brain damage look like?

Each negative thought loop produces a greater negative emotion sent to the amygdalae and results in a series of increasingly destructive thoughts or actions. However, this progression could end at any time because each loop is a decision. Remember, we saw amygdalae damage cause a sudden intensely destructive response. It's as if the person went from the first tree in the conscious brain damage example immediately to the last tree. In my example of the bullies in the bowling alley, this would mean if I saw them again, I would immediately trigger a fight or flight response.

In the movie *Citizen Kane*, the main character's wife leaves him after a conversation in their bedroom. Once she leaves, he attempts to deal with her suitcase, gets frustrated, and throws it out the door. That was one thought loop. What ensues is a series of thought loops, and with each loop he exhibits a more destructive action. He seems to be out of control, completely destroying the bedroom, when the next thought loop begins with him picking up a snow globe. He immediately stops, says a word with a tear in his eye, puts the snow globe in his pocket, and calmly walks out of the bedroom. The snow globe began a thought loop that did not have a negative emotion, so the destructive cycle immediately ended.

This example shows how to stop the destruction but not how to repair the damage. How would we repair the damage in the conscious brain? The damage in the conscious brain is due to the strong negative emotion tied to a set of facts. One way to repair this damage is to lessen the strong negative emotion tied to the connecting fact, so it can be intentionally addressed. Telling your story well to someone who is good at hearing a story does this.

Every fact in your conscious brain has an emotion tied to it: strong negative, mild negative, neutral, mild positive, or strong positive. When you tell a story involving a traumatic fact, the emotion tied to it can change as an effect of telling the story. If a person has a strong positive emotion and they tell the story to someone who mirrors back a strong positive emotion, the fact will now be tied to an even stronger positive emotion. This is like telling a funny story that gets funnier each time you tell it. The reason it gets funnier is the story is tied to the original funny feeling as well as the funny responses you got from others.

Christian fellowship plays a critical role in helping each other embrace a godly thought process. If I am sharing an experience with strong negative emotions because of what happened, you can mirror it back to me with a less negative emotion. You can use the Bible to assure me that God is not surprised by what happens, He cares for me, and just because something negative happened once, it does not mean a similar situation will always yield the same negative effects. You can help me focus on the big picture – eternal life with God that makes my earthly circumstances less important in the big picture.

Think back to times when you thought your world was caving in around you. Perhaps someone you loved left you; maybe you lost your job and wondered how you would provide for those dependent on you. Yet here you are today, still alive and not in as bad a place as you feared at the time. God has been there and saw us through what we thought was the worst of times.

An old Jewish idiom says, "Walk into the future backwards, looking behind not ahead. We don't know the future anyway, but when we walk into it looking backwards, we can see the times that God got us through tough times." In other words, we concentrate on God, not on our current circumstances. We understand the one who adopted us as

His children through Jesus Christ truly cares about us and will protect us if we trust Him.

When I was in my early twenties, I had a fiancée whom I loved leave me. I shared my story with my best friend who was also having woman problems. We would sit in our favorite bar several times a week, and as the alcohol affected us, we would cry in each other's beer and share our stories. We both thought we would never be loved again. Every time we shared our stories, our emotions would become stronger and more negative. We thought we were being there for each other, but in reality we were feeding into each other an increasingly negative set of emotions and damaging our thought processes, which made us become more and more depressed every time we relived and shared our stories.

My emotional state became so damaged that at age of twenty-three, I held my .357 Magnum handgun to my head with the trigger cocked and considered ending my life. But God, who knows all things, knew I would confess of my sins and become His adopted child twenty-two years later. He protected me, although at the time I had no idea He was the one influencing me to slow down and consider another perspective.

I contrast that with life now as a Christian. When I face challenging times and my thought process starts to deteriorate, I seek fellowship with Christians who understand thought processes. Instead of crying in each other's beer, we encourage one another with the Word of God and share times when we thought our world was caving in around us. We remind each other that God will never abandon us. God was and always is faithful, providing what we need to move on and grow in the knowledge and grace of Christ. We help each other have a godly thought process instead of a fleshly thought process. We focus on the love, grace, mercy, and provision of God and take a big-picture view of our lives instead of obsessing on the small picture here and now. We walk into the future backward, choosing to look back on all the times God has been faithful instead of obsessing on future what ifs that may be out of our control.

In order to help repair the damage in someone else's conscious brain, we need to hear their story and mirror back a less negative emotion. This will cause the person to have a less negative emotion attached to the story, which will make it easier for them to tell the story again. With each telling of the story, the emotion ought to get less negative. The goal is not to help them have a positive emotion; that may not be possible. For example, a woman shouldn't ever feel good about being raped. However, the negative emotion she has should become less negative, so it doesn't result in more destruction or isolation.

How does this relate to our lives as believers? When we face a situation with potentially strong negative consequences, we can rehearse the story and realize the truths in God's Word. He has promised us He will never abandon us; He knows our anxious thoughts and will always provide what we need (not necessarily what we want or think we need). As our faith in God grows, we look back on other situations in our lives when we thought the worst case scenario was going to play out and realize things did not turn out as bad as we thought they would.

> *Therefore do not be anxious, saying, 'What shall we eat?' or 'What shall we drink?' or 'What shall we wear?' For the Gentiles seek after all these things, and your heavenly Father knows that you need them all. But seek first the kingdom of God and his righteousness, and all these things will be added to you. Therefore do not be anxious about tomorrow, for tomorrow will be anxious for itself. Sufficient for the day is its own trouble.* (Matthew 6:31-34)

When you are trying to help an unbeliever, help him think back to other times when he was faced with fear or uncertainty about the future: losing a job; losing a girlfriend, or similar situation. He probably felt his world was caving in around him and imagined the worst case scenario, yet here he is today, still alive. Help him to understand that when we are stuck in a bad thought process, we imagine the worst case scenarios that often do not even happen, and we bring tremendous stress and worry upon ourselves, sometimes doing permanent damage and reinforcing a destructive thought process.

This situation offers a wonderful opportunity to share the gospel with the unbeliever who is going through tremendous stress. You can share a time in your life when you were also obsessing on a problem and thinking worst case scenarios. But now, since you have surrendered your life to Jesus Christ, you have a big-picture view of your life and realize a couple of things:

- First, someone greater and more powerful than us exists who is in control. He is an all-powerful God and Father who loves His children and will always make sure they are sufficiently taken care of.

- Second, more important than any problems we face in this lifetime is the question of eternity and where we will spend it. This life is but one short breath in time, and the problems we face are incredibly insignificant when compared to eternity.

- Third, you can give your testimony about how God helped you put your problems and worries into proper perspective. Share Romans 8:28 stories of your life and the lives of other believers, where God used something that looked tragic for the ultimate good of His children.

The ideal way to interact with people who are dealing with facts associated with strongly negative emotions is to tell them they can talk about anything and for as long as they want, especially when it comes to processing traumatic experiences. When they have a fear about the future, give them the freedom to process their fears out loud, sharing their worst case scenarios. Be praying, asking God for the right words to share with them. And as the Holy Spirit moves you, share similar experiences or fears you have encountered and how Jesus Christ has helped you gain a correct big-picture (eternal) perspective.

Key Points:

- The damage in the conscious brain is due to the strong negative emotion tied to a set of facts and can be stopped with each thought loop.

- The way to repair this damage is to lessen the strong negative emotion tied to the connecting fact, so it can be intentionally addressed.

- A way to repair damage in the conscious brain and lessen the strong negative emotion tied to it is by telling your story well to someone who is a good listener.
- Learn to be a good listener and share examples of similar situations you have faced and the new perspective you have as a disciple of Jesus Christ.

Summary

Humanist psychology teaches that man is in essence good and capable on his own of becoming even better. God's Word tells us we are sinful, evil, and corrupted before His saving grace. The only way a man can become righteous is by the saving grace of God through complete faith and trust in Jesus Christ. Psychology, the study of the human mind and its behaviors, is not in and of itself evil. However, the influence of humanist philosophy has corrupted it. By knowing how God designed our brain, heart, and conscience to work and applying the truth of God's Word, we can begin to improve our thought process and lead a life increasingly pleasing to God.

Believers have access to the Holy Spirit and can choose to use a godly thought process to repair the damage in our conscious brain. Repairing damage in our conscious brain and using a godly thought process enables us to address damage in our unconscious brain and amygdalae. We are able to slow our thought process down instead of reacting instinctively when we feel triggered by certain words or circumstances. We are no longer slaves to our fleshly thought process but are instead able to take our thoughts captive and use a godly thought process.

The new thought process the Holy Spirit develops in us by repairing our brain allows us to consistently choose righteous actions instead of sin. The new heart God has given us will confirm these choices and battle against our human conscience that has been degraded by sin and wrong teachings. As we learn to listen to our new heart and reject our corrupted conscience, our unconscious brain starts to align with our new heart. We grow in sanctification and joy, and store up eternal reward in heaven. We arrive quicker at our desired destination.

Jesus gave us a system to help us on our journey. He knew the enemy would do all he could to distract us, hoping to delay or end our journey to earthly joy and eternal reward. This enemy hopes we decide to take the journey on our own, and completely rely on ourselves. Jesus knew there was strength in numbers, so He encouraged us to travel in groups, so we could help one another stay on His path to our destination. Jesus gave us Christian fellowship, knowing we could help one another when problems arose.

Chapter Seven

STRENGTH IN NUMBERS: REAL CHRISTIAN FELLOWSHIP

Chapter objective: to learn to protect one another from deception and humanism.

As our nation grows more and more hostile toward God and His Word, churches will be faced with serious challenges and questions. Their non-profit tax status will be used as leverage to get them to conform to humanist values in place of the Bible. We need to take a step back and clearly identify what the church is and what role God has assigned to it.

As Christian thought has deteriorated in our nation, one of the words we define incorrectly is *church*. Most Christians define it as a place they go once a week to worship God and hear a sermon. But the word *church* in Greek is *ekklesia*: "assembly of Christian believers and saints."

For where two or three are gathered in my name, there am I among them. (Matthew 18:20)

Jesus placed no geographic or numeric restrictions on *church*. He said where two or more true believers are gathered, He is with them in Spirit. I am not saying we should abolish the current system we call church in America. The gathering in fellowship of tens or hundreds of Christians in fellowship on a weekly basis offers value. But church in America looks nothing like the first-century church, and in the future churches will be under pressure to conform to worldly values more and more.

> And they devoted themselves to the apostles' teaching and the fellowship, to the breaking of bread and the prayers. And awe came upon every soul, and many wonders and signs were being done through the apostles. And all who believed were together and had all things in common. And they were selling their possessions and belongings and distributing the proceeds to all, as any had need. And day by day, attending the temple together and breaking bread in their homes, they received their food with glad and generous hearts, praising God and having favor with all the people. And the Lord added to their number day by day those who were being saved. (Acts 2:42-47)

First, notice the fellowship met daily, sharing their experiences and all the possessions God had blessed them with. Second, they were devoted to learning the teaching of the apostles. They were hungry for the Word of God, wanting to grow in sanctification. Third, God added to their numbers. There was no need for mission statements or church growth plans, which are a human thought process.

Compare the early church to many churches in America today. Some modern churches are more like small businesses or corporations, where the focus is on growing the "customer base" and then making sure that customer is happy. The focus is often on the convenience and comfort of the church member, instead of focusing on growing in God. The modern church in America uses a human thought process, thinking clever marketing schemes and carefully orchestrated services will appeal to people and grow the church. The church sees itself as the cause rather than the effect of growth. Whenever God is not the cause, the growth is superficial, lacking true eternal good effects.

The system established as church in America can actually feed into hypocrisy. Professing Christians can put God in a box for an hour a week and go on living like the world the remaining 167 hours. Christianity has become something we *do* instead of who we *are*. Because we only share fellowship one hour a week, we are able to put on a mask and pretend everything is just fine in our lives. But real fellowship is intimacy between believers, as we support and challenge one another to live out our faith 24 hours a day, seven days a week, 365 days per year.

I am not anti-church. I believe the fellowship should gather for teaching, the breaking of bread, worship, and prayer as often as possible. However, many churches have unintentionally developed a system where professing Christians can put on that mask and meet for an hour or two a week but do little to ensure these people are walking in truth and victory in their lives. Accountability of professing Christians is lacking in our church system with no method to help believers live out their faith every day. As long as people show up to church once a week and financially support the church, all is well.

I am blessed to have a full-time career in Christian ministry, where I manage a staff of nine at our Christian Radio Station. Most of us spend up to forty hours a week interacting with one another. We pray together and discuss the challenges of life – encouraging, and when necessary, rebuking one another in love and truth. We hold one another accountable for our behaviors and work ethic. We realize we are only as strong as our weakest member and are committed to helping one another grow as Christians. By the biblical definition of church and fellowship, we are a more influential "church" than a group that only gathers once a week for an hour or two. We see each other living life. We experience each other at our best and worst. No employee here can bluff their way through fellowship. We are committed to helping each member become no less than what God wants him to become.

Our ministry leadership insists that each employee belongs to a Bible-believing church and insists that each employee leads a life that glorifies God in behaviors consistent with biblical teachings. But no church that gathers one to two hours a week can hold every member accountable to these standards. As a leader, I have a greater influence in the lives of my employees than a church pastor who has indirect access to them for an hour a week. They can hide at church, but not here at the ministry.

But the vast majority of Christians are not blessed to work in Christian ministry. They serve God in a secular workplace where the challenges of sharing and living their faith are more and more daunting. Therefore, we must take Christian fellowship more seriously than just an hour or two every Sunday morning. Christians in the world are under increasing pressure to conform to the ways of this world, and without a strong support network of Christians with a good thought process, growing numbers will be influenced by humanist thought and fall away from the true faith.

Many churches try to expand fellowship through Bible studies. But many professing Christians do not know how to interpret the Bible correctly, so many of these Bible studies tend to be shallow and unproductive. We gather and read the Word but do not seek to truly understand or live out the Word. Our pride prevents us from admitting there are teachings in the Bible we either do not understand or do not know how to apply in our lives. Sadly, many of these Bible studies become little more than opportunities for prideful people to impress one another with their knowledge of Scripture.

I am blessed to belong to a church fellowship that is serious about knowing, understanding, and applying the Bible to our lives. We study the what, why, and how of the Scriptures. My typical week within the fellowship includes two hours early Sunday morning where a group of men study the Word related to a particular topic such as grace, sin, humility, and prayer. These intense studies each last three or four months. Right after our Sunday morning study, we attend group fellowship, where the service usually lasts at least two hours. Our time includes a sermon, corporate worship and prayer, communion, and more study of the Scriptures, led by one of our elders. We then conclude with a time of food and fellowship where we build a culture of family with one another.

Every Tuesday and every other Saturday, we have more Bible study and discussion where we systematically learn the Bible and discuss ways we can become serious and committed disciples. We also host three to four conferences a year that address biblical prophecy, current events, and discipleship growth.

Contrast this with how many define *church*: a building we go to one hour a week. But even with the level of involvement I have within our church fellowship, it is not enough. I have a group of fellow believers I meet with regularly during the week. We share what is going on in our lives and are willing to be vulnerable with one another, sharing our temptations and challenges to use and maintain a godly thought process. We have permission to speak into each other's lives. This allows me to see myself as others see me with a fresh, objective set of eyes looking for ways we can each grow in holiness.

If we are serious about our journey as Christians, we must understand that church and fellowship are not something we do an hour a week. Expecting local church leadership to carry this burden for us is impractical and unfair. Our journey to earthly joy and eternal life with God is not a journey we can take on our own. It will require the support of a group of committed believers joining us. If you are not in a meaningful fellowship where every member is encouraged to be honest and open about our struggles, you are easy pickings for the world and the enemy of our souls to sidetrack your journey.

Be sober-minded; be watchful. Your adversary the devil prowls around like a roaring lion, seeking someone to devour. (1 Peter 5:8)

Satan loves it when Christians believe we are fine outside of fellowship and think our Christian faith is just between God and us. But the Bible repeatedly speaks to the need of regular Christian fellowship.

*Take care, brothers, lest there be in any of you an evil, unbelieving heart, leading you to fall away from the living God. But exhort one another **every day**, as long as it is called "today," that none of you may be hardened by the deceitfulness of sin. For we have come to share in Christ, if indeed we hold our original confidence firm to the end.* (Hebrews 3:12-14, emphasis added)

And let us consider how to stir up one another to love and good works, not neglecting to meet together, as is the habit of some, but encouraging one another, and all the more as you see the Day drawing near. (Hebrews 10:24-25)

The Bible encourages us to meet as believers in fellowship as often as possible. One might argue that the busyness of life with all its distractions makes this unrealistic. But this is exactly why regular fellowship is necessary, because Satan uses things of this world to take us away from the path to joy and eternal reward. If we cannot find a few hours a week for meaningful fellowship, when you consider all the other things we entertain in our lives, what does it say about our real love and commitment to God?

We were not made to travel this journey alone. Meaningful Christian fellowship allows us to see our lives from a different perspective. We all still have blind spots: a heart that is open to deception and a conscience that is not wired properly. And left to our own, these can cause serious delays and problems on our journey. Traveling in a caravan of committed believers who are looking out for each other, is crucial to our not straying from the path God has given us. But what does meaningful fellowship look like?

What is True Fellowship?

In Greek, the word *fellowship* is *koinonia*: "participation as partners; social intercourse, mutual benefit." Fellowship is openly sharing with each other for the benefit of each other. Fellowship goes far beyond talking about football or superficially discussing our lives. It is the willingness to be open, honest, and vulnerable with one another, even at the risk of appearing to be weak.

> *Obey your leaders and submit to them, for they are keeping watch over your souls, as those who will have to give an account. Let them do this with joy and not with groaning, for that would be of no advantage to you.* (Hebrews 13:17)

Who do you consider your leaders? A person in a human thought process might answer, "My pastor and church elders." A person in a godly thought process would add to that list. He would also include other believers who exemplify the true Christian life and seek to grow in holiness. Even though I spend up to ten hours a week in fellowship with my church elders, I can still fool them. I could put on a façade of holy living, convincing them I am being sanctified.

Who are my leaders? In addition to my church elders, they include my board of directors, the Christian men I meet with regularly, my employees who observe me forty hours or more every week, and my wife who sees me at my best and worst. All of these are leaders to some extent in my life, if they are serious about growing in sanctification.

Before we expand on fellowship, we must remember that each of us is ultimately responsible for our own thought process that leads to our beliefs and actions. We will not be able to blame others when we stand before God and give an account of ourselves:

> *The good person out of his good treasure brings forth good, and the evil person out of his evil treasure brings forth evil. I tell you, on the day of judgment people will give account for every careless word they speak, for by your words you will be justified, and by your words you will be condemned.* (Matthew 12:35-37)

Our own words will be used to justify or condemn us. This includes every word I speak to or about another. So I will be held accountable by God for the words I share with every other person with whom I interact.

> *Whoever causes one of these little ones who believe in me to sin, it would be better for him if a great millstone were hung around his neck and he were thrown into the sea.* (Mark 9:42)

> *Thus, sinning against your brothers and wounding their conscience when it is weak, you sin against Christ. Therefore, if food makes my brother stumble, I will never eat meat, lest I make my brother stumble.* (1 Corinthians 8:12-13)

Disciples understand that while each person will be judged by their words and actions, we have a responsibility to one another as believers, and if we cause others to sin, we will be held accountable. Fellowship is a very serious commitment to God and one another. It deserves far more attention and diligence than we give it. What are some of the necessary components of true fellowship?

Spiritual Transparency and Safety

Have you ever been victimized by prayer? Have you ever shared a confidential problem with another Christian, asking for prayer, only to find out later it became part of a circle of gossip? You open up your heart and share a problem with a fellow believer, and the next thing you know everyone and their brother is lecturing you and telling you what you need to do about your problem.

You share with Linda that you and your husband are struggling and need prayer. She asks for details, and you confidentially share that your husband is deep into pornography. The next thing you know, everyone knows of the pornography problem because Linda just had to drop a juicy piece of gossip into the prayer circle, instead of just asking her friends to pray for your marriage generally. How apt are you to ever open up to another Christian?

In order for other believers to help us on our journey, we need to be spiritually transparent about our fears, temptations, and sins. But this requires an atmosphere of confidentiality and safety. People, particularly men, fear taking emotional risks. While women are more apt to share, men have been raised to believe they are weak if they share their fears or show excessive emotion. We have allowed ourselves to be imprisoned and isolated from true fellowship, becoming easy pickings for Satan.

Unity in the Body of Believers

Some doctrines are important enough to break fellowship over, and some are not. What are the non-negotiable doctrines of our Christian faith and which should we allow discussion and disagreement over? This question has been debated for two thousand years and requires thoughtful consideration. While not a complete list, I believe the following could certainly qualify:

- The gospel: man's sinful nature and inability to save himself; confession and repentance before God; acknowledging who Jesus is and what He accomplished through His death and resurrection; salvation by the grace of God alone through faith; and a life of growing holiness by the grace of God.

- Salvation through faith and trust in Jesus Christ *alone*.

- The inerrancy and sufficiency of the Word of God.
- The truth about eternal life with God for born-again believers and the reality of hell for those who reject salvation through faith in Jesus Christ alone.
- Believing and accepting that what God identifies as sin in the Bible *is* sin and that we must not attempt to justify our sins as acceptable to God.
- Marriage exclusively as a covenantal relationship between a man and a woman.

I am not stating that these are the only non-negotiable doctrines, but we must resist the temptation to expand this list carelessly to the point we become unbiblical legalists.

But woe to you, scribes and Pharisees, hypocrites! For you shut the kingdom of heaven in people's faces. For you neither enter yourselves nor allow those who would enter to go in. Woe to you, scribes and Pharisees, hypocrites! For you travel across sea and land to make a single proselyte, and when he becomes a proselyte, you make him twice as much a child of hell as yourselves. (Matthew 23:13-15)

Remember, in 1 Corinthians 5, Paul ordered the church to break fellowship with the man living in unrepentant sexual sin. So the breaking of fellowship is warranted over an unrepentant sinful lifestyle. But again, we must remember that repent means to acknowledge our sinful actions as sin and desire to no longer indulge in them. Even the most committed of disciples may temporarily fall back into the grip of sin on occasion. As long as there is serious repentance and an effort to resist temptation, we should be slow to break fellowship. Issues that are often cited for breaking of fellowship include:

- Eternal security or the ability to lose one's salvation.
- Continuation or cessation of the gifts of the Holy Spirit.
- Timing of the rapture of the church.

- God predetermining who is saved and who is condemned vs. the free will of man.

We should be humble enough to realize that, while the Bible addresses these doctrines, we may lack the wisdom to understand these doctrines with 100 percent accuracy. A question we should ask ourselves is this: if I am willing to condemn someone as an unbeliever because of their belief in one of these areas, am I willing to be condemned if it turns out I was the one who was wrong?

When our nation and the world turn its might on us as believers, will these differences in non-salvation interpretations matter? Or will we find ourselves united in love and fellowship despite our differences? We should begin to discuss these issues now as a church, so we are prepared for the days ahead. The breaking of Christian fellowship is sometimes necessary, but we must be careful not to use our human pride and self-righteous attitudes to break fellowship when it is not biblically mandated. Wisdom and patience with one another should always trump quick, unbiblical judgment.

Strong Men as Leaders in the Fellowship

What is your definition for *man*? The first explanation people usually give relates to male organs that differentiate men from women. But a young boy at birth has these same organs. Is he a man? Here is a verse from the Bible that talks about real men:

> *And he said, If the Syrians be too strong for me, then thou shalt help me: but if the children of Ammon be too strong for thee, then I will come and help thee. Be of good courage, and let us play the men for our people, and for the cities of our God: and the Lord do that which seemeth him good. And Joab drew nigh, and the people that were with him, unto the battle against the Syrians: and they fled before him.* (2 Samuel 10:11-13 KJV)

The Hebrew word for *man* is *hazaq*: "strong, courageous, causatively strengthen." Notice that Joab says the Lord will take care of the effects. A man is someone who does the right thing regardless of the effects on himself. Men just do what is right according to God and His Word and leave the effects to God. We do not try to manipulate outcomes that are out of our control. Men should be humble enough to do the right thing, regardless if it benefits us or not.

Men often get into trouble when we try to fix things that are "above our pay grade," and lack the humility to admit when something is beyond our repair. In fellowship with other believers, we must remember that only God can truly fix anyone. As men, we should speak truth into a person's life, and point them to the knowledge, understanding, and wisdom of the Word: the correct what, why, and how.

Men, God has ordained us as leaders of our families and the church fellowship, and we need to start acting like leaders. What we see happening too often in church and Christian homes is men acting like bosses instead of leaders. A boss uses others for his own benefit. A leader facilitates the progress of others for their benefit. Godly men do the right thing because it is the right thing. We take seriously the spiritual growth of our wives, children, and other believers. We do what is eternally best for them without worrying about how it will affect us in the short term.

Bosses do not like to follow anyone. Leaders love to follow someone. Who was the greatest leader in the history of the world and whom did He follow?

> *Then Jesus was led up by the Spirit into the wilderness to be tempted by the devil.* (Matthew 4:1)

Jesus said:

> *For I have not spoken on my own authority, but the Father who sent me has himself given me a commandment – what to say and what to speak. And I know that his commandment is eternal life. What I say, therefore, I say as the Father has told me.* (John 12:49-50)

Is your church being led by bosses or leaders? Men, are you a boss or a leader? Are you doing the right thing regardless of its immediate effects on you? Do you have complete faith that if your cause is righteous, God will honor your faithfulness? How deeply do you trust God's promises? Is His Word sufficient?

> *When he had entered Capernaum, a centurion came forward to him, appealing to him, "Lord, my servant is lying paralyzed at home, suffering terribly." And he said to him, "I will come and heal him." But the centurion replied, "Lord, I am not worthy to have you come under my roof, but only say the word, and my servant will be healed. For I too am a man under authority, with soldiers under me. And I say to one, 'Go,' and he goes, and to another, 'Come,' and he comes, and to my servant, 'Do this,' and he does it." When Jesus heard this, he marveled and said to those who followed him, "Truly, I tell you, with no one in Israel have I found such faith." (Matthew 8:5-10)*

Are we men *of* authority or men *under* authority? If you consider yourself the former but reject the latter, you are no leader; you are a self-serving boss, unfit to lead and serve in Christian fellowship. God-fearing men who want to do the right thing, regardless of the immediate effects for them, are crucial to true biblical fellowship. A husband who understands the true biblical definition of being a man realizes his position of leadership is not a perk; it is a responsibility. He understands that his wife is a temporary gift God has entrusted to him as a steward. This leads us to another crucial component of Christian fellowship.

• Strong Biblical Marriages

I was speaking at a conference last year and proposed a mathematical problem to those in attendance: "In a group of one hundred people, how many potential unique one-on-one relationships exist within that group?" The answer: 4,950! I then challenged them with this question: "If we cannot get marriage right, how in the world will we ever get church fellowship right?"

Unhealthy marriages are a major impediment to vibrant church fellowship. But our pride would never allow us to admit publicly that our marriage is suffering. Men in particular tend to see themselves as better husbands than they are in reality. I want to share a story from my marriage that is still painful for me to discuss, but one that I am grateful God allowed as a wake-up call to me as a husband.

Ten years ago, Nancy had been working at the radio station with me for four years. A local Christian counselor met with us to discuss ideas about seminars for Christian couples that would strengthen marriages. As we finished the meeting, Nancy asked her if they could talk privately for a few minutes. So I excused myself but couldn't help wondering what they were talking about. The hour they spent privately talking seemed like days to me. When Nancy came out, I asked her what they had been discussing. She calmly asked if we could talk about it when we got home. The anticipation was killing me, but I agreed.

When we got home, Nancy asked me if I would just listen as she shared what they had discussed. Here is the summary of what she said to me: "Mike, I love you; but I am full of pain deep down in my heart. At times over the past four years, I have felt like I have lost my husband. I do my best to be a good worker for you at the ministry, but I feel like you place much higher expectations on me than you do on every other employee at the ministry. And when we are at home or away on vacation, the conversation always comes back to the ministry. I feel more like your employee than your wife at times. And the pain I am feeling over my loss of you as my husband is so great at times I want God to just take me home to Him."

I was devastated. And at first, my flesh and pride wanted to turn this into Nancy's problem instead of mine. Every time I felt the urge to counter what she said, I also felt the Holy Spirit urging me to just listen and really think about what Nancy was sharing. The wife who led me to Jesus Christ; the wife who nurtured and taught me as a young believer; the wife I grew to love and cherish had just shared with me that at times she felt no more important to me than any other employee in the ministry. In fact, she shared that she felt I was treating her worse than other employees by expecting a level of perfection from her at work I did not expect of others. She told me she was proud that God had used me in amazing ways within the ministry but was grieving for our marriage.

I made a commitment to my beloved wife that night after I asked for her forgiveness. I thanked her for opening up and sharing her heart with me and promised her I would never let ministry work get in the way of our marriage again. And I asked her to hold me accountable to that promise. I told her I would immediately resign from ministry if it ever got in the way of our marriage again. I had fallen into the trap many men fall into: I identified myself with what I *do* instead of who I *am*.

Since that painful day, I remind myself that I *am* a child of God and He has entrusted Nancy to me as His steward. I *do* ministry work. Have I been perfect in fulfilling my commitment? Not always, but when challenges start to rise up, we take a step back and remember that painful day and what I put my beloved wife through, because I did not understand nor fulfill my responsibility to God as Nancy's husband. For the past seven years, Nancy and I have shared an office within the ministry, which has been a tremendous blessing to both of us. We have learned how to keep a correct balance between marriage and ministry work.

I am still far from a perfect husband to Nancy, but I am humble enough to know I am unable to husband her correctly in my own human strength. I pray every day that I give up my will to God's will for her life.

> *Wives, submit to your own husbands, as to the Lord. For the husband is the head of the wife even as Christ is the head of the church, his body, and is himself its Savior. Now as the church submits to Christ, so also wives should submit in everything to their husbands.*
>
> *Husbands, love your wives, as Christ loved the church and gave himself up for her, that he might sanctify her, having cleansed her by the washing of water with the word, so that he might present the church to himself in splendor, without spot or wrinkle or any such thing, that she might be holy and without blemish. In the same way husbands should love their wives as their own bodies. He who loves his wife loves himself. For no one ever hated his own flesh, but nourishes and cherishes it, just as Christ does the church, because we are members of his body.* (Ephesians 5:22-30)

The church is to submit to Jesus as a wife does to her earthly husband. If wives do not willingly submit to their husbands, they undermine the church's submission to the authority of Jesus Christ. Marriage and fellowship are not separate issues, They have a causal relationship: great biblical marriage is a cause that leads to the effect of great biblical fellowship. Paul says wives submit to their husbands because the husband loves his wife as he loves himself. She knows that her husband has her interests at heart, not just his own desires. She knows that her husband is a leader, not a boss who is only out to gain for himself. She is confident that her husband wants what is best for her as she grows in Jesus Christ. She trusts him, so she is free to submit willingly to him.

Most churches model fellowship as men's and women's groups. These groups have value, but they allow couples to avoid transparency and accountability. They can also lead to unbiblical gossip and can turn into complaint sessions where the absent spouse is dragged through the mud without the ability to share his or her perspective on the issue being discussed. While there is value in men or women meeting separately, doing this solely without married couples being in fellowship together can cause much unintended damage.

I often meet with men who come in to get some advice on life and problems in marriage. When I ask the man to describe himself as a husband, he usually says he is a good husband. I then ask if he would mind if his wife joined our meeting, so I could get her perspective on him as a husband. Interestingly, his story starts to change. Suddenly he begins to share the ways that he is not being a good husband. The fear of accountability and another perspective drives him to a more accurate portrayal of his reality as a husband.

Whenever I am asked by a married man if I will help disciple him and the subject of difficulties in marriage comes up, I always insist that his wife joins us. If the man is unwilling to have his wife join us, I refuse to continue to meet with him because I know he is not being humble.

When we ignore fellowship where the husband and wife are both involved together, we can actually damage the marriage relationship by giving uneducated advice. If I was meeting with you, and you said you were an excellent husband and your wife was the problem, the advice I give you will be skewed. It would be like Solomon trying to decide the fate of the baby and only hearing the perspective of one of the women claiming to be the mother.

If a group of men gathers in fellowship to discuss how to be better husbands, and the men are using a bad thought process, one of two things will most likely happen. A man will portray himself as a wonderful husband who is frustrated by a wife who doesn't understand him, or he will put on a false front that everything in his marriage is perfect. Our best intentions to get men to discuss how to become good husbands actually backfires because these men either do not have an accurate perception of themselves as husbands, or they are too prideful to admit they are a big part of the marriage problem.

I would be remiss if I did not point out that the same problems plague women's fellowships that talk about marriage without husbands being there. When we operate out of a fleshly/animal or human thought process, we will always point out the specks in the eye of others without removing the planks in our own eye first. So, while separate men's and women's fellowship meetings can be valuable, they should never replace meeting as married couples in an atmosphere of honesty, safety, and accountability. Biblical marriages are a foundation for biblical fellowship.

> *Therefore, since we are surrounded by so great a cloud of witnesses, let us also lay aside every weight, and sin which clings so closely, and let us run with endurance the race that is set before us, looking to Jesus, the founder and perfecter of our faith, who for the joy that was set before him endured the cross, despising the shame, and is seated at the right hand of the throne of God. (Hebrews 12:1-2)*

> *Let us rejoice and exult and give him the glory, for the marriage of the Lamb has come, and his Bride has made herself ready; it was granted her to clothe herself with fine linen, bright and pure – for the fine linen is the righteous deeds of the saints. (Revelation 19:7-8)*

> *And they came to John and said to him, "Rabbi, he who was with you across the Jordan, to whom you bore witness – look, he is baptizing, and all are going to him." John answered, "A*

person cannot receive even one thing unless it is given him from heaven. You yourselves bear me witness, that I said, 'I am not the Christ, but I have been sent before him.' The one who has the bride is the bridegroom. The friend of the bridegroom, who stands and hears him, rejoices greatly at the bridegroom's voice. Therefore this joy of mine is now complete. He must increase, but I must decrease." (John 3:26-30)

In marriage and Christian fellowship, we must be like John the Baptist; we must decrease so He can increase. We must let the Holy Spirit speak eternal truth through us to one another: a godly thought process. Our human thought process must decrease so God can increase in our marriages and fellowship.

Just as men are to love and help their wives to bear much fruit for Jesus, we need to serve one another because every one of us is a part of the eternal Bride of Christ. We are to speak the truth in love to one another, as this helps righteous deeds of God flow through us. And if we are in a fellowship with a hundred believers with potentially 4,950 unique one-on-one relationships, how can we possibly get it right when we don't get marriage right? Strong Christian fellowship is anchored in strong Christian marriages! Men, as leaders of our wives and the church, we are the ones responsible for making this happen. We must humble ourselves as leaders, putting aside our desires and focusing on whatever God wants us to do to help others bear abundant fruit in Jesus Christ. We must decrease in our human understanding, so God can increase by His Holy Spirit and Word speaking through us.

The godly man understands delayed gratification. If we do what God tells us to do, regardless of the short-term effects in our lives, God will honor our faithfulness with eternal reward in heaven. We realize we are but stewards of our wives and the eternal Bride of Christ. We are dedicated to taking what God has given us and making it fruitful for Him.

Husbands, are we bosses or leaders at home and in fellowship? A boss uses others to facilitate his own progress. A leader invests in others to facilitate their progress. Jesus was the greatest leader who ever lived. He facilitated the progress of others (salvation), knowing the immediate effects on Him would be bad: suffering and death on a cross. But He understood that God controls all eternal effects and by following the Father's will, He would be rewarded with an eternal bride.

<u>Are our churches being led by leaders or bosses?</u> Some local churches still have dedicated men who are true leaders, but they are fewer and fewer in number these final days, as humanism has infected many churches. The only way we can return to the biblical model of church is through strong marriages led by humble husbands, leading to strong Christian fellowships, led by humble leaders.

Men, this responsibility has been given to us by God. Will we be proven to be godly men, doing the right thing regardless of the immediate effects on us? Or will we prove to be little children who boss others around for our benefit?

> *But woe to you, scribes and Pharisees, hypocrites! For you shut the kingdom of heaven in people's faces. For you neither enter yourselves nor allow those who would enter to go in. Woe to you, scribes and Pharisees, hypocrites! For you travel across sea and land to make a single proselyte, and when he becomes a proselyte, you make him twice as much a child of hell as yourselves.* (Matthew 23:13-15)

People who boss others around for their own benefit prevent others from eternal life and thus do not enter it themselves.

> *And Jesus said to them, "Follow me, and I will make you become fishers of men."* (Mark 1:17)

Are we willing to give up our plan for life and follow Jesus to benefit others?

> *And whoever does not take his cross and follow me is not worthy of me. Whoever finds his life will lose it, and whoever loses his life for my sake will find it.* (Matthew 10:38-39)

Leaders follow Jesus. We realize we must deny self and follow Him if we are to have eternal life.

Biblical Love and Submission in Marriage

> *Wives, submit to your own husbands, as to the Lord. For the husband is the head of the wife even as Christ is the head of*

the church, his body, and is himself its Savior. Now as the church submits to Christ, so also wives should submit in everything to their husbands.

Husbands, love your wives, as Christ loved the church and gave himself up for her, that he might sanctify her, having cleansed her by the washing of water with the word, so that he might present the church to himself in splendor, without spot or wrinkle or any such thing, that she might be holy and without blemish. In the same way husbands should love their wives as their own bodies. He who loves his wife loves himself. For no one ever hated his own flesh, but nourishes and cherishes it, just as Christ does the church, because we are members of his body. "Therefore a man shall leave his father and mother and hold fast to his wife, and the two shall become one flesh." This mystery is profound, and I am saying that it refers to Christ and the church. However, let each one of you love his wife as himself, and let the wife see that she respects her husband. (Ephesians 5:22-33)

Earlier we discussed understanding causality when we read the Scriptures. With that in mind, which of these is the cause and which is the effect?

- A wife submitting to her husband in everything?
- A husband loving his wife as Christ loves His church?

In other words, which comes first leading to the other? Should a husband love his wife when she submits to him in all things? Or should a wife only submit to her husband when he loves her perfectly? Both are causes and both are effects. They are spiritually intertwined, one leading to the other. We husbands need to love our wives even when they are not submissive to us as leaders. Wives need to submit to their husbands, even though they love imperfectly and make bad decisions.

It is a human thought process to make love or submission conditional. It is *agape* love and a godly thought process to love and submit without preconditions. If we claim to believe the Word of God is eternal, inerrant, and sufficient truth in all matters, we must conclude that both of these commands are unconditional causes, and one is not dependent on the other. Again, it is rooted in what I believe is the foundational characteristic of a true follower of Jesus Christ: humility.

Marriages are difficult relationships, which are nearly impossible when pride trumps humility in either party. And all of us, even as born-again believers, have remnants of pride remaining in our sinful nature. If a husband unconditionally loves his wife but she consistently does not submit, she undermines his God-given authority and problems will arise. Likewise, if a wife submits to her husband in all matters, but he abuses that authority by putting his interests above hers, the marriage will suffer.

Paul's commands are not conditional. There is no *quid pro quo* – no tradeoff – relationship in what he writes. Husbands, we must love our wives the same way Christ loves His church, overlooking her blemishes and making decisions that benefit her growth in Jesus Christ, even if it means sacrificing what we want. And wives need to submit to and trust their husbands, even though he will make bad decisions at times. Trust that God will reveal his errors to him, so he can grow as a Christian and as a husband.

I am not saying this will be easy, but then Jesus never told us life as His disciple would be easy. We must avoid the temptation to look at our marriages and the unique roles of husband and wife as conditional. If men love their wives unconditionally and unselfishly as Christ loves us (His church) and wives unconditionally submit to their husbands in all matters (unless they are being forced to do something unbiblical), our covenant of marriage will grow to be a strong, unbreakable bond in Jesus Christ.

Agape love and submission run counter to the desires of our flesh. But if we fail to do both as we are taught in the Bible, our marriages will struggle and may one day be in jeopardy. Take the initiative, whether husband or wife, to hold up your part of the covenantal relationship. We can only control our thoughts and behaviors, not those of another. But when we are faithful to God in our marriages, and husbands unconditionally love and wives biblically submit, God will bless our marriages in amazing ways. Step out in faith, do the right thing, and leave the effects to God! Christian marriages and fellowship are about helping one another through love, truth, sharing, teaching, and mutual accountability to the Word of God. Fellowship is a caravan of committed believers dedicated to helping each other reach our destination. Are you in true fellowship? If not, you are on the road all by yourself, and your journey toward joy and eternal reward will suffer.

Next, we look at how to protect our thought process and help others improve their thought process. The world wants to damage your thought process, so you can be more easily manipulated, deceived, and controlled. God wants you to be in control of your thought process, so His Spirit can guide and lead you.

Chapter Eight

GUARDING OUR THOUGHT PROCESS

Chapter objective: to protect our thought process and help others with their thought process.

Every week we hear stories of criminals who hack into government and banking databases and gather information that puts millions of people at risk. In the same way, your thought process is at risk every time you interact with any other person. If you are not using a godly thought process, you are vulnerable to being influenced by people who will damage your thought process, which delays or ends your journey to earthly joy and eternal reward. Before we discuss how to protect your thought process against others, we need to make sure we are not vulnerable to an enemy from within that will weaken our resistance when others try to infect our thought process.

Stress and Worry: An Internal Virus

Once we become born-again believers, we realize what a mess we were before we received the grace of God. While we are now free from the punishment of sin, we are still susceptible to the presence of sin in our lives. Much residual damage remains within our brain and conscience as a result of the sinful nature having its way with us for decades.

Computers can be infected by downloaded files that have a dormant virus attached, which can suddenly activate a damaging program and cause major problems. When a dormant file is activated in a computer, it usually leads to one of two effects: either the computer freezes and is incapable of doing its work, or the computer is overloaded as it tries to process its normal work while dealing with the virus. The result is the computer is stressed and incapable of performing its regular duties efficiently.

Our sinful nature is a virus waiting to damage our thought process. We covered this earlier, but it bears repeating: when we are saved, God removes our old heart and gives us a new heart that desires to love and obey Him, but He does not remove our human spirit that has rebelled against Him in the past. Our human spirit hosts the sinful nature virus that continually attacks our brain, heart, and conscience. The Holy Spirit gives us the ability to use a godly thought process to eradicate this virus, but this is a lifelong process. Circumstances and challenges of life can activate this dormant virus, which leads to contradictory thoughts. Our human spirit and sinful nature contradict the new heart and Spirit God has given us, which leads to stress and worry as we seek to be conformed into the image of Jesus Christ. We have many "viruses" we downloaded through years of feeding our flesh and sinful nature. From time to time, they will be activated and threaten to damage our thought process and delay our journey.

The godly thought process focuses us on eternity. We realize everything in this world is a temporary effect that will not carry over into eternity, but we find ourselves stressed and worried about our temporal circumstances. The virus has been activated!

Stress and worry are effects of a bad cause: a lack of complete faith in God and His promises. Before I describe biblical principles that will help us maintain a godly thought process, we need to know how we can allow the Holy Spirit to identify and eradicate these viruses that attack our thought process, causing stress and worry.

Stress and worry are always future orientated: we experience bad circumstances, and our imagination runs wild. We think of worst case scenarios, take our eyes off God, focus on circumstances, and convince ourselves that the eventual outcome will be catastrophic. Remember our lesson on thought loops? Our squirrel jumps from one tree to the next, and to the next, and on and on, until a molehill becomes a mountain. We are stuck in a destructive thought loop and damage our thought process and rob ourselves of peace and joy. We use a fleshly/animal thought process, refusing to consider a perspective different from "this is going to end in disaster." The solution is to take our thoughts captive by preventing the squirrel (our mind) from reaching conclusions that may never happen.

My experience in helping Christians has identified two major viruses we have downloaded that are activated in our brains that lead to stress and worry:

- Believing human doctrine instead of biblical doctrine.
- Accepting destructive "life commandments" from people we respected in our past.

Both of these viruses have been established as fitting in our unconscious brain and have damaged our conscience. Before we were born again, nothing within us could effectively challenge these patterns established in our unconscious brain. Unsaved people can use understanding through a human thought process to consider a different perspective, but if these destructive beliefs and patterns are deeply rooted from years of wrong teachings and experiences, the human thought process alone is usually overmatched when trying to defeat these viruses.

But believers have the indwelling of the Holy Spirit to give us a godly perspective that can counter the facts engrained in our unconscious brain. This is the internal battle for our thought process: will we allow the Holy Spirit to override and replace the damage in our unconscious brain and conscience? If we do not, we will be susceptible to others who can damage our thought process and disrupt our journey.

Chapter 4 described tools to interpret the Bible correctly, replacing any human doctrines you have embraced: causality, non-contradiction, understanding lies, deception, opinions, facts, eternal truth, and logical biblical conjunctives. The correctly interpreted Word of God is the only source for eternal truth, since God alone possesses infinite understanding.

Since the unconscious brain only responds to the five external stimuli (sight, touch, taste, smell, and hearing), when God's Word teaches you correct doctrine that contradicts the beliefs established in your unconscious brain, you must state these correct beliefs out loud repeatedly, until a new pattern is established in your unconscious brain. Consequently, this also helps to repair the faulty wiring in your conscience. Remember, the unconscious brain does not know what the conscious brain is thinking until it sees an action or hears a belief stated out loud. Reading the Word of God out loud and verbally stating correct beliefs that refute the wrong beliefs established over years in the unconscious brain is critical to eradicate the damaging virus embedded within us. We are not talking about some mystic New Age thing here. This is understanding how God designed our brain to work and allowing the Word and Spirit of God to change our beliefs and behaviors. Only God's Word and Spirit can permanently change anyone.

> *This Book of the Law shall not depart from your mouth, but you shall meditate on it day and night, so that you may be careful to do according to all that is written in it. For then you will make your way prosperous, and then you will have good success. Have I not commanded you? Be strong and courageous. Do not be frightened, and do not be dismayed, for the Lord your God is with you wherever you go.* (Joshua 1:8-9)

The word *meditate* means "to ponder, study, and speak." Speaking the Word out loud allows the unconscious brain to come into alignment with our conscious brain, so we are not double-minded. This reduces internal stress as we now consciously and unconsciously understand the truth of the Word.

Life commandments we received from others who influenced us are another dormant virus waiting to wreak havoc in our thought process when circumstances challenge us. A life commandment is something we were taught that we have erroneously accepted as truth, which has affected our outlook and decisions. Earlier I shared the example of how my father defined the perfect woman: "a lady in public and a whore in the bedroom." This life command was placed in my unconscious brain even though I did not consciously consider what my father said at that time. I looked up to my father instead of consciously questioning his life command, and I believed if he said it, then it must be truth.

People who are verbally, physically, or sexually abused by their fathers often develop a wrong definition of father in their unconscious brain. This can severely impede their ability to trust God when He is called our heavenly Father. They aren't even aware of this because this wrong definition is in the unconscious brain. The virus affects them without consciously realizing it.

> *Therefore, if anyone is in Christ, he is a new creation. The old has passed away; behold, the new has come. All this is from God, who through Christ reconciled us to himself and gave us the ministry of reconciliation; that is, in Christ God was reconciling the world to himself, not counting their trespasses against them, and entrusting to us the message of reconciliation.* (2 Corinthians 5:17-19)

*The old has passed away…*This must be our perspective as new believers; we must be willing to die to our preconceived beliefs and facts. *New creation* means we should start from square one and not be bound to former damaged beliefs and thought processes. Our inability or unwillingness to put the past behind us damages our thought process and delays our sanctification. Satan wants nothing more than for Christians to stay in bondage to our former life commandments that are viruses that attack our thought process.

> *Jesus answered him, "Truly, truly, I say to you, unless one is born again he cannot see the kingdom of God." Nicodemus said to him, "How can a man be born when he is old? Can he enter a second time into his mother's womb and be born?" Jesus answered, "Truly, truly, I say to you, unless one is born of water and the Spirit, he cannot enter the kingdom of God. That which is born of the flesh is flesh, and that which is born of the Spirit is spirit."* (John 3:3-7)

> *Do you not know that all of us who have been baptized into Christ Jesus were baptized into his death? We were buried therefore with him by baptism into death, in order that, just as Christ was raised from the dead by the glory of the Father, we too might walk in newness of life.* (Romans 6:3-4)

- Do you consider yourself truly dead to your old life? Or do you see yourself as a better version of the same old person? Let's use our analogy of a computer: when a computer is infected with a virus, there are two options to combat it. You can use a patchwork mentality, or you can wipe the computer clean by deleting all of the programs that could hold a hidden virus waiting to be activated. The first solution does not assure you that every virus has been eradicated, but by wiping the computer clean of all programs, you can start over with a clean computer.

When we allow wrong teachings and life commandments to influence our thought process, we are subject to the activation of these hidden viruses at some future time. Harmful life commandments instilled in our unconscious brain must be taken captive and wiped out. You must know who you now are because of salvation and the grace of God. You are not some improved version of an old self; you are a new creation, a new "computer" now able to receive clean information. The old you is dead, and you must eliminate all the life commandments the old you received and believed. As born-again Christians, we start from scratch, forgetting all we have learned and accepted from people who influenced us in an ungodly manner.

> *Now this I say and testify in the Lord, that you must no longer walk as the Gentiles do, in the **futility of their minds**. They are **darkened in their understanding**, alienated from the life of God because of the **ignorance that is in them**, due to their hardness of heart. They have become callous and have given themselves up to sensuality, greedy to practice every kind of impurity. But that is not the way you learned Christ! – assuming that you have heard about him and were taught in him, as the truth is in Jesus, to **put off your old self**, which belongs to your **former manner of life** and is corrupt through deceitful desires, and to be **renewed in the**

***spirit of your minds**, and **to put on the new self**, created after the likeness of God in true righteousness and holiness. Therefore, **having put away falsehood**, let each one of you speak the truth with his neighbor, for we are members one of another.* (Ephesians 4:17-25, emphasis added)

Paul speaks powerfully to the need to die to your old self and forget all the wrong things you were taught before you were born again as a new creation. Unless we take our thoughts captive and rebuke all the wrong teachings and destructive life commandments from our previous life, we will be subject to having these dormant viruses attack us and distract us from our journey. Like hidden viruses, we are not aware of them until a problem arises and one causes a malfunction in our computer (our unconscious brain). And once they are activated, we find our thought process being instantly and negatively affected, which prevents us from addressing the virus in a rational way.

Computer specialists offer virus detection software to expose hidden viruses in computers and eliminate them before they can be activated and do damage. How can we use a similar method? First, by accepting what the Word of God says about being a new creation and the passing away of the old you. And second, by discussing tension and worry we feel with someone who understands non-contradiction and identifying truth from deception and opinions – someone using a godly thought process. This is why true Christian fellowship is so important. We can still be blinded and deceived when we look at ourselves, but fellow Christians can see our thoughts, beliefs, and actions with a set of objective eyes. They can help us remove the speck in our eye if they understand and use a godly thought process themselves. They can often detect a virus that we are not even aware exists.

Worry and stress are often the effect of our conscious brain and unconscious brain trying to work through contradictory beliefs. Consciously, we recognize we are a new creation in Christ, and the old me is dead. But my unconscious brain with an established pattern of damaging life commandments still thinks I am the same old me. Unless we resolve this contradiction, we will feel continuing stress and worry every time the virus is activated. These damaging beliefs must be wiped out and replaced with a new set of beliefs based on God's truth and promises that tell us who we now are: people who are no longer in bondage but free from our sinful past and chains.

Stress and worry are signs that we are focusing on our old self instead of the new creation. Instead of focusing on the promises of God, we are stuck in a thought loop triggered by believing a destructive life commandment established in our unconscious brain. By talking through our feelings and fears with someone who understands thought processes, we can identify the damaging life commandment and start to replace it with truth from God. As we discussed, meditating (thinking and speaking) on the Word of God also helps reduce stress and worry, as we accept God's Word and promises as eternal truth.

In my case, two life commandments that I accepted as truth hindered me for years. The first, which I shared already was a destructive definition of *woman* planted in my unconscious brain by my father. The second was, "You'll never really be successful without a college degree." For years I secretly saw myself as inferior to friends and co-workers who had a college degree. I felt I was always at a disadvantage and would ultimately fail in my career because I lacked a degree. This fear was tied to a wrong definition I believed for *success*. For years I defined success as financial stability and being highly respected by my peers.

> *No one can serve two masters, for either he will hate the one and love the other, or he will be devoted to the one and despise the other. You cannot serve God and money.* (Matthew 6:24)

> *But Peter and the apostles answered, "We must obey God rather than men."* (Acts 5:29)

> *You adulterous people! Do you not know that friendship with the world is enmity with God? Therefore whoever wishes to be a friend of the world makes himself an enemy of God.* (James 4:4)

For far too long I allowed destructive life commandments to determine who I was. Now, when I start to worry about my finances or other temporal problems, I remind myself that God has an eternally true definition of success:

> *Only be strong and very courageous, being careful to do according to all the law that Moses my servant commanded you. Do not turn from it to the right hand or to the left, that you may have good success wherever you go. This Book of the Law shall not depart from your mouth, but you shall meditate on it day and night, so that you may be careful to do according to all that is written in it. For then you will make your way prosperous, and then you will have good success. Have I not commanded you? Be strong and courageous. Do not be frightened, and do not be dismayed, for the Lord your God is with you wherever you go.* (Joshua 1:7-9)

By meditating on God's Word to understand it and obey Him, I no longer turn to the distractions of this world that define success in a seductive and dangerous way. I do not allow the world to define success for me. God has given us the definition of success and told us how to achieve it.

Two-Spirited

As we discussed earlier, when James warns us against being double-minded, the Greek word actually means *two-spirited*. Before we were born again, our spirit was infiltrated and dominated by our sinful nature. But now as a new creation, the Holy Spirit wants our spirit and conscience to be aligned with God's Spirit. If we do not allow the Holy Spirit and eternal truth of God's Word to replace the destructive life commandments we have believed and have been imprisoned by, our thought process will never be able to defend itself against this world that wants us to react according to the flesh and blindly follow lies and deception. Here are some things we say or think that indicate we have a virus in our unconscious brain:

"I can never do anything right!"

"I'm so stupid!"

"I just know something bad will happen now!"

When we hear statements like this, we must look for the cause: the harmful life commandment that triggered the statement. Being in fellowship with Christians who understand thought processes will help us identify the life commandment and help us replace the deception with the truth of what God's Word says about us as a new creation. An excellent statement I have heard will help us with this: "When Satan reminds you of your past, remind him of his future." He is a defeated enemy, and the only power he has over us is the power we give him from a faulty thought process and wrong beliefs.

We are responsible for our thought process and the decisions our thoughts lead to. If we are enslaved to destructive life commandments, we will be easily deceived by people who want to treat us like an animal and train us to blindly follow them. When we allow the Holy Spirit to refute our old destructive life commandments that have enslaved us for years, we are able to use a godly thought process and be on guard against those who will try to damage our thought process.

Guarding Your Thought Process from External Viruses

Christian fellowship should be among believers who seek to use a godly thought process to help one another grow spiritually. But when interacting with unbelievers or nominal Christians, every interaction can be a threat to your thought process. Entire industries are dedicated to teaching salespeople how to manipulate the thought process of others to sell their products. False prophets and teachers are masters of getting people to forego rational thought to be manipulated and controlled.

I enjoy watching college basketball, particularly when contrasting team styles clash and one team is up-tempo while the other tries to slow things down. When this type of game is played, usually the team that can get the other to play at a tempo they are uncomfortable with wins the game. Believers using a godly thought process should slow down our thoughts to make sure our words and decisions are consistent with the teachings of the Bible. But others will try to speed us up by appealing to our flesh and emotions, hoping they can control the conversation and get us to "play" at their pace. Not allowing people in a fleshly/animal thought process to control the pace is crucial.

When I meet someone the first time, I ask questions to determine their thought process. When they state facts (whats), I ask them why questions. If they cannot give a good reason (why) for their fact (what), I know I am dealing with someone in a fleshly/animal thought process who will try to speed me up. I make sure the conversation stays at a pace conducive to my maintaining a godly thought process.

Some salesmen will state many facts (whats) and then suggest reasons (whys) they want us to accept as our own. Engagement rings are a classic example. Marketing firms have successfully equated a man's level of love for his fiancée with how expensive the ring he purchases for her is. "I can tell you love your fiancée very much and want to give her a ring that shows how much you love her…take a look at this ring…" The implication is, "If you really love her, you will buy her this expensive ring!" People can be manipulated to buy things they had no intention of buying when someone knows how to influence their thought process.

But it is not just sales situations where we must guard our thought process. Have you noticed how your mood, tone, and words are affected by the positive or negative attitudes of those you spend time with? I do not spend significant time with people with negative attitudes, because they can drag me right down with them. Peer pressure within groups is also a powerful tool for manipulating thought processes. Over the years, I have taught seminars on team building and group dynamics. I am fascinated as I watch people in a group modify their beliefs and behaviors, aligning with the strongest personality in the room. Unless a person has a strong set of values and principles and a sound thought process, he can easily be seduced by a person who sounds as if he knows what he is talking about. Religious cults begin in this way and Americans are easily swayed by politicians and people who look and sound authoritative. People want and need to be led, which is probably why Jesus referred to us as sheep.

When he saw the crowds, he had compassion for them, because they were harassed and helpless, like sheep without a shepherd. (Matthew 9:36)

And Jesus said to them, "You will all fall away, for it is

> *written, 'I will strike the shepherd, and the sheep will be scattered.'"* (Mark 14:27)

God's plan was for His people to follow Him, but as the Israelites interacted with nations of unbelievers, they developed a "better" plan:

> *Then all the elders of Israel gathered together and came to Samuel at Ramah and said to him, "Behold, you are old and your sons do not walk in your ways. Now appoint for us a king to judge us like all the nations." But the thing displeased Samuel when they said, "Give us a king to judge us." And Samuel prayed to the Lord. And the Lord said to Samuel, "Obey the voice of the people in all that they say to you, for they have not rejected you, but they have rejected me from being king over them."* (1 Samuel 8:4-7)

Jesus established the church to provide leaders who would shepherd us and point us to God and His ways. But how can we know if the leaders we follow are pointing us to God or seeking their own power? Unless we know how to protect our thought process, we will be vulnerable to self-appointed leaders who will lead us away from God for their benefit.

> *Beware of false prophets, who come to you in sheep's clothing but inwardly are ravenous wolves. You will recognize them by their fruits. Are grapes gathered from thornbushes, or figs from thistles?* (Matthew 7:15-16)

Hopefully this book helps you realize one of the greatest testimonies to a person's "fruit" is their thought process. False teachers appeal to us through deception: knowledge (what) lacking understanding/application (why/how). And if our thought process is wired only toward facts and knowledge (whats), we are vulnerable to their deception. One major characteristic of people exists with people who use a godly thought process, which makes them qualified to be true godly leaders.

Humility

No attribute is more important in the life of a Christian, particularly a leader, than genuine humility.

> *Do nothing from selfish ambition or conceit, but in humility*

*count others more significant than yourselves. Let each of
you look not only to his own interests, but also to the interests of others.* (Philippians 2:3-4)

Jesus was the most humble man who ever lived. He left heaven and took human form to live as one of us and die on the cross for our benefit. In fact, if Jesus was not humble, sinful man could not have been reconciled to God.

We are called to be conformed to the image of the One who saved us (Romans 8:29). The only way this is possible is for us to be humble like Jesus. Humility is necessary for salvation; we must acknowledge who God is (righteous, just, and holy) and who we are (hopelessly lost, sinful, and rebellious). But humbling oneself when our eternity is at stake is much easier than remaining humble after we have been forgiven and justified by God. We are then adopted sons of God, but the moment we take pride in that position and consider ourselves better than others, our mind and heart can become corrupted. We can easily become like the Pharisee who prayed:

*The Pharisee, standing by himself, prayed thus: "God, I
thank you that I am not like other men, extortioners, unjust,
adulterers, or even like this tax collector. I fast twice a week;
I give tithes of all that I get."* (Luke 18:11-12)

The first way to determine if someone is a leader that will point us to God is to see how they view themselves compared to others. I want to share an experience where God showed me I had no right to consider myself better than another. We were sharing the gospel at a county fair, and a man came up to our booth looking for an argument. He stuck his finger in my face and yelled, "Do you know what ticks me off about you Christians? You think you're better than everyone else!"

I felt the Holy Spirit give me peace and the words to speak: "Actually Sir I think I am probably worse than you. See, God has not revealed Himself to you yet – His holy, righteous, and just nature and how he despises the sin and disobedience of His creation. So you sin against God out of ignorance. But God has revealed who He is to me; I am conscious of His righteousness and disdain for disobedience. Yet I continue to sin against Him on occasion, so I am sinning consciously, while you are sinning unconsciously. That actually makes me worse than you! But here is the truth I hope God reveals to you one day: people who think they are good do not make it to heaven; people who realize how bad they are and sincerely confess and repent are forgiven and go to heaven even when we still occasionally sin."

He looked at me and said, "Thank you for your honesty. You've given me something to think about." Will this man eventually come to saving faith in Jesus? I don't know. But at least he has something to think about. God revealed to me that day that I have no right to consider myself better than anyone. Only by His grace am I spared eternal damnation.

The truly humble believer realizes he is probably the weakest of the saints he will encounter every day. He sees the continuing sin in his heart and mind and realizes the damaging things he is still capable of doing without God's Spirit and grace. When he sees others lie, cheat, steal, or hurt others, he realizes it is only God's grace that stops him from doing even worse. <u>A true leader understands this and leads from a position of true humility.</u>

If we ever try to justify our sins and bad decisions, we are not being humble. The proud man thinks he has arrived. The humble man realizes every day by the grace of God he has farther to go than he thought the day before. I call this the "paradox of grace": as the grace of God reveals hidden sin in my heart, I realize it is His way of drawing me nearer to Him. But the newly revealed sin also makes me realize I was farther from the holiness of God than I thought. I understand He is more holy and perfect than I realized, and I am more sinful than I ever imagined. But that serves to help me see the incredible beauty of what He accomplished for me on the cross, which makes me more humble.

A true leader understands he still has a sinful nature that can deceive him and others, so he welcomes feedback about his words and actions from those he leads. He is comfortable asking fellow believers what they honestly see in his life. The humble man cherishes loving criticism because he realizes he has a blind spot toward his actions. He realizes he thinks more highly of himself than he should, so he wants objective feedback from those he knows desire to help him grow and will be honest with him.

Humility is necessary for salvation:

You save a humble people, but your eyes are on the haughty to bring them down. (2 Samuel 22:28)

Blessed are the poor in spirit, for theirs is the kingdom of heaven. (Matthew 5:3)

True humility brings us earthly reward:

The reward for humility and fear of the Lord is riches and honor and life. (Proverbs 22:4)

True humility points us to those we should follow and learn from:

A dispute also arose among them, as to which of them was to be regarded as the greatest. And he said to them, "The kings of the Gentiles exercise lordship over them, and those in authority over them are called benefactors. But not so with you. Rather, let the greatest among you become as the youngest, and the leader as one who serves. For who is the greater, one who reclines at table or one who serves? Is it not the one who reclines at table? But I am among you as the one who serves." (Luke 22:24-28)

True humility saves us from disgrace:

When pride comes, then comes disgrace, but with the humble is wisdom. (Proverbs 11:2)

True humility stores up eternal reward in heaven:

At that time the disciples came to Jesus, saying, "Who is the greatest in the kingdom of heaven?" And calling to him a child, he put him in the midst of them and said, "Truly, I say to you, unless you turn and become like children, you will never enter the kingdom of heaven. Whoever humbles himself like this child is the greatest in the kingdom of heaven." (Matthew 18:1-4)

The growth of mega-churches in our nation has built a dangerous system where some pastors now view themselves as CEOs rather than servants and leaders. They insulate themselves against any questioning of the direction of the church or its teachings. If we are in a church where the pastor is not available to listen to our questions or concerns, we should consider it a red flag. But also, we must make sure we are not nit-picking over insignificant details or disagreements with our pastor or church leadership. Any concerns we have should be on important doctrines or direction, not on insignificant matters.

Jesus was the greatest leader in history and also a great follower, led by His Father and the Spirit. A fleshly/animal thought process refuses to be led by anyone. A human thought process believes certain people (pastors, politicians, or employers) are the only leaders. The godly thought process realizes we are all to be leaders, working for the benefit of others. Pastors and elders lead the church and teach men how to teach and lead their wives and families. Christian men lead other men, and Christian women can teach and lead women. But without true humility, we are not qualified to lead anyone. What is your definition of humility? If it is "willing to admit I am wrong," then Jesus was not humble because He was never wrong. Humility is not admitting you are wrong when you are not. Humility is not about being right or wrong. It is about how we view ourselves. As Christians, this relates directly to how we view ourselves compared to God and others.

Compared to God

God is eternally righteous, just, perfect, and holy. We are inherently sinful, selfish, and incapable of permanent change by our own human efforts. This is the first point of the gospel of salvation, and without real humility we will not be saved by God. Once we are born again, we have the imputed righteousness of Jesus Christ in us. Recognizing that anything righteous that comes out of me is by God's grace and not my own strength or ability is humility. Humility is an accurate self-awareness of who we are as born-again believers. We are only vessels for His righteousness. No one drinks a great cup of coffee and says, "Wow! What an amazing cup this coffee is in!" The drink is great, not the container. Humble Christians realize we are only the vessel that is used to contain and share the grace and love of God. When someone acknowledges good effects from us, we point them to God as the cause of those good effects.

But humility does not mean we think less of who God is creating us to be. We are a new creation by His grace and Spirit, and we should acknowledge the work He has done and continues to do in our lives. C. S. Lewis said it well: "True humility is not thinking less of ourselves; it is thinking of ourselves less."

Compared to Others

When we learn to think of ourselves less, we can focus our attention and thoughts more on others. A proud man wants to do all he can to make sure he always benefits from any situation, so his focus in any relationship is what is in it for him. Oh, he may be able to put on a temporary front of false humility to let others think it is not all about him, but in the end he makes sure he profits from every relationship. The man of true humility looks for ways others can benefit and grow.

> *Do nothing from selfish ambition or conceit, but in humility count others more significant than yourselves. Let each of you look not only to his own interests, but also to the interests of others.* (Philippians 2:3-4)

These verses speak to using a godly thought process to create a win/win situation. True humility within fellowship is where both members look to mutually help each other grow and benefit. If you and I are in relationship and one always gives while the other one is always the beneficiary, how long will it be until the giver gets tired of giving because he never benefits in any way? This discourages fellowship.

Marriages and Christian fellowships should be relationships where both parties grow and receive benefit when we interact. But if we are the ones always giving but never receiving, by using a godly thought process, we realize that whatever good deeds we allow God to do through us, without immediate earthly benefit, will be rewarded by God in eternity.

> *He said also to the man who had invited him, "When you give a dinner or a banquet, do not invite your friends or your*

> brothers or your relatives or rich neighbors, lest they also invite you in return and you be repaid. But when you give a feast, invite the poor, the crippled, the lame, the blind, and you will be blessed, because they cannot repay you. For you will be repaid at the resurrection of the just." (Luke 14:12-14)

A person in a fleshly/animal thought process looks to receive immediate benefits from others. The person in a human thought process sees relationships as a *quid pro quo*, where both parties exchange equal value. The person using a godly thought process knows we are eternally rewarded when our righteous deeds are not immediately rewarded. Understanding this is crucial to our relationships with everyone: spouses, other believers, and unbelievers. When we understand that God rewards us for our righteous behavior, we are free to love and help others because we know God is faithful to reward us.

Genuine humility is the most essential ingredient for strong Christian marriages and fellowship. Once we are truly humble, we are free to communicate openly, knowing we are in a place of safety where fellow believers want to help us instead of looking for ways to take advantage of our honesty and vulnerability. Effective communication is becoming a lost art in a world where we are inundated with noise and distractions. Wars have been started over poor communication, and a single careless word is often the trigger that can lead to broken marriages and fellowship. Every word we speak is important, so how can we guard our speech to avoid serious potential problems in marriage and fellowship?

Biblical Model for Effective Communication

Every time we engage in conversation, a potential conflict between thought processes exists. On average, an American woman speaks twenty thousand words a day. The average American male speaks about seven thousand words per day.[20] It is no wonder the Bible speaks volumes about the words we speak.

> *When words are many, transgression is not lacking, but whoever restrains his lips is prudent.* (Proverbs 10:19)

---

20 http://www.funtrivia.com/askft/Question97860.html

Whoever restrains his words has knowledge, and he who has a cool spirit is a man of understanding. Even a fool who keeps silent is considered wise; when he closes his lips, he is deemed intelligent. (Proverbs 17:27-28)

And in their greed they will exploit you with false words. Their condemnation from long ago is not idle, and their destruction is not asleep. (2 Peter 2:3)

The Bible teaches us consistent principles about the words we speak. A fool speaks many words without thinking; false teachers deceive people with false words, but the wise man chooses his words carefully.

You brood of vipers! How can you speak good, when you are evil? For out of the abundance of the heart the mouth speaks. The good person out of his good treasure brings forth good, and the evil person out of his evil treasure brings forth evil. I tell you, on the day of judgment people will give account for every careless word they speak. (Matthew 12:34-36)

Jesus warns us the words we speak will be used to judge us for eternity, because they are an accurate reflection of the condition of our heart. With so much riding on every word we speak, is it wise that we speak as often as we do? The argument can be made that the more we talk, the more trouble we can bring upon ourselves. But verbal and written communication is the primary way we communicate as people, and we are called to speak the truth in love, so perpetual silence is not the answer. Learning to use a godly thought process that guards our heart and leads to words and actions that honor God is the solution.

And we impart this in words not taught by human wisdom but taught by the Spirit, interpreting spiritual truths to those who are spiritual. The natural person does not accept the things of the Spirit of God, for they are folly to him, and he is not able to understand them because they are spiritually discerned. The spiritual person judges all things, but is himself to be judged by no one. "For who has understood the mind of the Lord so as to instruct him?" But we have the mind of Christ. (1 Corinthians 2:13-16)

Our words carry great power and influence in the lives of others. Many people today live shattered lives because of parents who spoke devastating life commandments into their lives. In fact, some research shows people can recover easier from physical or even sexual abuse than from destructive verbal abuse.

To grow in holiness and help others grow, effective communication is critical. **What** we say, **why** we say it, and **how** we say it is essential to effective communication and fellowship. In the Bible, godly people generally followed three guidelines in communication:

- Made statements about themselves (sharing).
- Asked questions of others (learning).
- Answered others' questions about themselves (sharing).

The ungodly interaction was the opposite:

- Made statements about others (accuse; possibly bearing false witness against another).
- Didn't ask questions of others (pride, assumed they knew what the others were thinking).
- Didn't answer the questions of others (isolate).

One of the greatest advantages to asking people questions instead of making statements about them is this: If I make a statement about you like, "You were wrong," your brain registers it as an opinion.

But if I ask you excellent questions about your behavior that leads you to state, "I was wrong," your brain registers it as a fact. Remember what we learned about the nucleus basalis, the doorway from the unconscious to conscious brain? Questions open the nucleus basalis because the person has to think to respond to your question. If I simply make a statement about you, it can stay in your unconscious brain; if the unconscious brain has a pattern that is contradictory to my stated belief about you, it can simply reject it without conscious thought.

A key to effective communication is to reach the conscious brain of the person you are talking to, so they can use their human understanding to consider the issue at hand. If the person is a true believer, this also allows the Holy Spirit to try to influence them about the issue being discussed. Making statements about another person will not accomplish this. Let me share a personal example:

Two years ago, a lady called up our radio show, to ask for advice about an issue she had with her husband. I gave her what I thought was the best advice I could, given how quickly things move in a live radio talk show. My wife came into the office a couple of hours later and made a statement to/about me: "The advice you gave that woman wasn't very good."

My flesh screamed internally! Here is what my flesh wanted to say to my wife: "Well, when you do a live talk show where things happen fast, and you have to think on your feet, I will consider your perspective. But since you have no idea what I face on air, you don't know what you are talking about." Just imagine how ugly that conversation could have become.

But I slowed down and took my thought process captive, not reacting out of a fleshly/animal thought process. I told myself that I knew Nancy loved me and wanted me to be the best talk show host I could be, so she was actually trying to help me. I calmly looked at her and said, "Sweetie, could you put your thoughts into the form of a question?"

She did, asking me, "I know things happen fast in live radio, but now that you have the time to think more on the lady's question, is there any advice you could have given her that would be even better?"

I focused on her question, using my conscious brain and asking the Holy Spirit to guide my thoughts. I was able to state three ways I could have given better advice to the woman who called. I went on the air the next day and shared these additional thoughts about how wives could talk with their husbands if they faced a similar situation.

When Nancy made a statement about me, my unconscious brain wanted to respond out of pride and a defensive posture (fleshly/animal thought process). By asking me a question, Nancy helped me open my nucleus basalis and use my human understanding, and the influence of the Holy Spirit, to guide my thoughts. Also, notice that Nancy's new question affirmed and valued me when she told me she understood how difficult doing a live radio show is. This allowed me to drop any defensive guard I wanted to put up in opposition to her question.

Remember, the unconscious brain can accept or reject a statement (a what) if it does not fit the patterns of belief established within it. But when we use our conscious brain, we can understand (why) and consider another perspective that might differ from the pattern established in the unconscious brain. And if we have the Holy Spirit, He can influence us with a great how – godly wisdom. By asking me a question, Nancy helped me use a godly thought process that benefited me and others. When we share our thoughts and feelings, we help one another grow. This is a great cause. We can give four types of causes to one another, and I have ordered them according to the amount of increasing control being exerted upon the other person.

Good: Open-ended questions or statement of fact.

"How are you doing?" or "That car is green."

Not Bad: Close-ended question or statement of our opinion.

"Did you like that movie?" or "I don't like the color of that wall."

Bad: Projection (telling someone what they think or feel) or judgment.

"You don't like that movie." or "You're stupid for liking the color of that car!"

Worst: Negate another.

"What is your favorite color?" They answer "red." You state, "No it's not, it's blue!"

The next time you talk with another couple, carefully observe how they communicate with each other. You might be shocked by how many times couples who live in continual conflict project or negate each other by telling the other person what they "really" believe. This type of ungodly communication is a cancer that eats away at healthy relationships. Telling someone else what they think or believe is always harmful and dangerous.

As we learn to become masters of biblical communication, we help people open up and share why they believe what they believe. When a person only states a what, they use their unconscious brain and neglect the use of human understanding. But a simple question such as "Why do you believe that?" opens their nucleus basalis to use their human thought process. This is crucial in understanding how to share the gospel effectively. Once we know what a person believes and why they believe it, we can ask good questions that will help us understand the depth, or lack thereof, of their stated beliefs.

Any person can state something they believe (what). If you ask them why they believe what they claim, and they cannot give you a good reason, they are in a fleshly/animal thought process. Asking good questions that lead people to state their beliefs and their reason for them is the beginning of effective evangelism and meaningful discipleship. All of us, because of our sinful nature, first want to respond out of pride. We all want to believe we are right and will seek to justify our beliefs and actions. But God has given each man a conscience that knows right from wrong. If someone states a belief out loud that both their conscience and unconscious brain know is not truth, they introduce a contradiction into their unconscious brain. God did not wire our unconscious brain to accept contradictions, so we have to process them, or we will become unsettled. By asking good questions that get people to state their beliefs out loud, we allow them to wrestle with a contradiction. If they are unbelievers, their unconscious brain will not let them be settled until the contradiction is resolved. If they are sincere Christians with a wrong belief, the Holy Spirit will work on their conscience to conform it to Him. Look at these examples to see the type of communication (godly or ungodly) that occurred:

> *And they heard the sound of the Lord God walking in the garden in the cool of the day, and the man and his wife hid themselves from the presence of the Lord God among the trees of the garden. But the Lord God called to the man and*

said to him, "Where are you?" And he said, "I heard the sound of you in the garden, and I was afraid, because I was naked, and I hid myself." He said, "Who told you that you were naked? Have you eaten of the tree of which I commanded you not to eat?" The man said, "The woman whom you gave to be with me, she gave me fruit of the tree, and I ate." Then the Lord God said to the woman, "What is this that you have done?" The woman said, "The serpent deceived me, and I ate." (Genesis 3:8-13)

God: Asked open and close-ended questions.

Adam: Shared (good); made statements about Eve and God; didn't answer the question.

Eve: Made statement about the serpent.

If God knows all things, why did He ask Adam questions? To get Adam to think and to give him an opportunity to confess and repent. God gave up control of the conversation to let Adam try to explain his actions. How can people think God is controlling? He gave Adam an opportunity to confess and repent, but Adam condemned himself and all mankind with his answer by blaming Eve and God.

Then the Lord said to Cain, "Where is Abel your brother?" He said "I do not know; am I my brother's keeper?" (Genesis 4:9)

God: Asked open-ended question. (Remember God already knew the answer.)

Cain: Deflected the question and did not really answer.

And the Lord said to Satan, "Have you considered my servant Job, that there is none like him on the earth, a blameless and upright man, who fears God and turns away from

evil?" Then Satan answered the Lord and said, "Does Job fear God for no reason? Have you not put a hedge around him and his house and all that he has on every side? You have blessed the work of his hands, and his possessions have increased in the land. But stretch out your hand and touch all that he has, and he will curse you to your face."
(Job 1:8-11)

God: Asked closed-ended question.

Satan: Two insincere questions that project; two statements about God.

We covered this earlier, but the above verse also spoke to causality.

God's causality statement:

Cause: Job is righteous.

Effect: I have blessed him.

Satan's model/point of view:

Cause: God blessed and protected Job.

Effect: Job is righteous because God blessed and protected him.

We can never be accused of judging or condemning someone when we ask sincere questions to learn something about them. Insincere questions are nothing more than disguised projections or judgments like Satan used toward God in Job chapter 1. We seek to understand others so we can help them. When we make statements about others, we can be seen as judging or condemning. When we ask the right questions, we help people think and process why they believe what they believe. This is fellowship, where we help one another grow in the knowledge and grace of Jesus Christ (2 Peter 3:18). We ought to be learning about others by giving up control of the conversation, instead of dominating it with statements.

Unbelievers think what they believe is truth. To come out with "guns blazing" and attack their beliefs without empathy for their current condition (unsaved and without the Holy Spirit) does no good. When we can understand what they believe and why they believe it, we can have fruitful dialogue and discussion without being seen as condemning. We help them use a better thought process.

I am blessed to have met with hundreds of professing Christians who, because of our radio show, seek my advice on issues they face in living the Christian life. But because of the watering down of the true gospel and the growth of Emergent theology in many churches, I never assume the person I meet with is actually a born-again believer. So I always start our conversations with the same questions I asked the young people at the Christian youth event we discussed earlier:

"Why do you believe you are a Christian?"

"Why did Jesus have to die a brutal death on the cross?"

Their answers usually tell me if they understand the gospel and who they were before salvation. If their answers indicate they have been taught a false gospel, I start from square one. We go through the gospel: God's nature and character, sinful man's condition, heartfelt confession and repentance, and what our lives as true believers should look like. If they claim to know and accept the complete gospel as truth, I ask one more question before I agree to help them: "Do you believe the Bible is the inspired, inerrant and sufficient Word of God, eternally true in all matters?"

You would be surprised how many professing Christians say no. I then ask them what their objective definition of truth is. If they state that it comes from within, I know I am dealing with a humanist, even though he may not realize it.

I have found it is often easier to help an unbeliever than it is to help a person who professes to be a Christian but has serious doubts about the truth of the Bible. The unbeliever is at least being transparent. The "façade Christian" is not humble, and he wants God's blessings but does not want to obey God's Word. He is double-minded and usually picks and chooses which Scriptures he wants to believe and which he can ignore. The Emergent Church movement has mastered this hypocrisy.

Every Christian church that is serious about its calling in Christ should go right back to square one and not assume every member is a true born-again believer. This is crucial for two reasons. First, Bible teachers will be held accountable for the growth of those they teach.

Not many of you should become teachers, my brothers, for you know that we who teach will be judged with greater strictness. (James 3:1)

Obey your leaders and submit to them, for they are keeping watch over your souls, as those who will have to give an account. Let them do this with joy and not with groaning, for that would be of no advantage to you. (Hebrews 13:17)

Second, if our churches are heavily populated by professing Christians who are not truly born again, the church is wide open for deception as times get more difficult. The sad reality is that many pastors have bought into the deception that church numbers are more important than the spiritual growth of members. And the foxes are already in the chicken coop, leading people astray with false doctrines.

Pastors and church elders should become masters of biblical communication. Many are under pressure for church growth and are taught to avoid controversy, so most decide the less communication with their members, the better. But the exact opposite is true: when we learn to communicate biblically, we are able to help people grow and handle conflict in a way that honors God, strengthens marriages, and grows the church with committed disciples.

Biblical Communication in Marriage

The busyness and pressures of life damage the spiritual intimacy God wants us to experience in our marriages. I meet with several couples who truly love God and each other but struggle in their marriages. Most come with preconceived notions about the issues they face, but almost without fail, the real problem is a lack of biblical communication in their interactions. We've already seen how Satan uses secular media and social media to distract and overwhelm us. Many people are so preoccupied with these mediums that little time is left for meaningful face-to-face conversations. When I meet with couples for the first time, I give them a series of questions to answer individually:

- On a scale of 1 to 10, with 10 being excellent, how would you rate your marriage?
- List five things that delight you about your spouse and five things he/she does or says that bother you.
- List five things you say or do that you think bothers your spouse.
- Complete this sentence: "Our marriage would be great if …"
- When you are faced with a problem, are you more successful when you think it through or verbalize it out loud with others for feedback?

I remind them that honest communication is imperative to improving marriages. Each must assure the other they are free to share everything they feel without fear of negative consequences. Wives are usually much more forthcoming in their responses than husbands are. Women tend to be proactive in communication, whereas men tend to be reactive, not wanting to take risks in communication or relationships. This information gives me a starting point for discussion in an open, honest format. I now know how each spouse sees the reality of their marriage relationship. Regardless of their answers to the first four questions, I begin by addressing question number five: how they process information to reach decisions.

Internal and External Processors

A great way to foster excellent communication is by recognizing if you and your spouse are internal or external processors. Internal processors are more comfortable with not speaking until they have completely thought through a problem. External processors need to verbalize a problem to help them understand it and reach a decision. Neither one is necessarily better than the other, but each has their unique characteristics.

If internal processors get stuck in their thought process and are unable to reach a decision, they can freeze up and obsess on the situation. The problem feels like it is more and more serious with worse and worse potential consequences. They feel anxiety or self-condemnation because they are unable to reach a decision on an important matter. They withdraw and seem distant. Left unresolved, this can lead to increasing isolation.

The external processor, needing to verbalize a problem, says what he is thinking without giving a great deal of deep internal thought to the issue. He speaks of possibilities, looking for something that feels right. Talking about the problem is his way of thinking, but internal processors around him might see his thinking out loud as communicating actual decisions.

External processors can see internal processors as cold, calculating, and unemotional. Internal processors can see external processors as emotional, impetuous, and scattered in thought. Remember, we shared data earlier that stated women speak on average twenty thousand words each day, while men speak only about seven thousand words per day. This data seems to indicate that wives are more likely to be external processors, while husbands tend to be internal processors. My experience shows me that generally this is factual. Wives want to talk things out, while husbands want to think things through before they speak. This is not saying men are smarter or superior to women but just the result of how we were raised. Often men are less forthcoming with their emotions because they've been trained that showing emotion is a sign of weakness. This lie they have accepted damages the intimacy in our marriages.

In addition to believing that sharing emotions is a sign of weakness, men also believe being wrong is a sign of weakness, making us less of a man. Think about how most sit-coms are designed for television these days: Which spouse is usually portrayed as the smarter? Women are portrayed as the smarter person while the man is often presented as the stupid one who never gets anything right until the wife or children set him straight. Is it any wonder most men clam up and internally process when the world tells us we have no right to be emotional and everything we decide is stupid?

Most men do not like to take emotional risks, so they learn to become internal processors. Wives, if you are in a marriage where you feel you have to pry words or emotions out of your husbands, a simple remedy is available: Continually assure your husband he can share everything he is thinking or feeling without worrying that you will think he is stupid. Tell him you value his thoughts and emotions. But a word of caution: you must be sincere about this. If you get him to share and you quickly discount his feelings, he will feel betrayed and will clam up all the more in the future. Marriage is about safe, honest sharing leading to mutual growth. Assure your husband he can share everything with you without fear of condemnation. Do not react with excess emotion or hurt, no matter what he says. Continue to ask great questions, seeking why he feels what he does. Help him to process his thoughts and find out the cause of the issues he struggles with.

When couples process thoughts in differing ways (external vs. internal), barriers to effective communication can emerge. Unless internal and external processors understand how to safely communicate, couples can drift apart, and our imaginations cause us to see or read into things that can damage the marriage relationship.

Nancy is an internal processor and I am an external processor. At times when I process, I think things out loud that Nancy takes as facts, because she rarely speaks until she has internally processed her thoughts and reached a conclusion. So at times she understands something I am verbalizing as a potential conclusion as something I have reached a conclusion about. On the few times we have argued about our relationship, I would think something out loud, trying to better understand things, and she would think what I stated was a fact, when in reality I was processing it as a possible fact or conclusion. In this way I would sometimes unintentionally say things that were hurtful to her.

As we learned to understand the two ways people process thoughts, we developed a communication system. If I am stuck in a thought loop, I tell her I need to process my thoughts externally and nothing I state should be taken as conclusions, only as me processing my thoughts. This has allowed her to help me think and reach correct conclusions.

When Nancy is thinking through an important issue, I used to think she was upset with me because she seemed to withdraw. So I would press the issue, insisting she open up and share with me before she was ready. This would frustrate her because she did not feel ready to talk about the issue, because internally she had not completed thinking it through. So I have learned to be patient and trust her, knowing if she needs to talk, she will when she is ready.

Marriages must be intimate relationships where we help one another process our thoughts and emotions, rather than impede one another from openly sharing. Understanding and accepting that we might process our thoughts differently and then helping each other to reach right conclusions honors God and one another.

One other truth is crucial to understand and live out: No one can make you feel anything. You alone are responsible for how you feel and react. A huge difference exists between saying, "You made me feel bad," and "When you said that, I felt bad." The first one is projecting; the latter is sharing. A key to resolving conflict in marriage and fellowship is to take responsibility for your own feelings and actions and not to project fault on the other. When both parties share what they are feeling and thinking, instead of projecting responsibility or blame on the other, their humility provides an atmosphere for mutual growth.

Finding Fault

A fleshly/animal thought process only considers one perspective: "I am right so you must be wrong." A human thought process is willing to consider that I could be partially wrong about the conflict. A godly thought process looks for ways I was wrong, so I can grow into a better spouse. This requires the ability to see my actions through my wife's perspective.

People in a fleshly/animal thought process focus on effects (whats). People using a human thought process look for the reasons (whys) of the disagreement and seek to understand why the other said or did what they did. People with a godly thought process understand that a person could have wanted to do what was right with a correct intention (why) but did not use wisdom in doing what they did (wrong how). We must get beyond effects (words, actions) and seek to find the cause/motivation for those effects. If we only treat effects, we will never understand the real issue and we will be unable to fix the root of the problem. When people argue, the issue stated is rarely the real issue at the heart of the problem. A person who uses a godly thought process looks for causes in himself and others that led to the negative effects. When we understand and address the cause, the effects will take care of themselves.

Humility is always the key attribute necessary in a Christian's life. Without humility, we will always revert to the desires of our flesh and seek to gain at the expense of others. In fact, every step I share in how to improve communication between spouses and other Christians is predicated on both parties being humble. I have developed a four-step system to help resolve conflict:

- First, give each other permission to share everything you think and feel about the situation. Commit to focusing on the problem, not on each other. Share as much information as you can, as if you are two scientists trying to seek a solution to a problem. Understand you are not adversaries; you are two people brought together by God as one in marriage. Understand the enemies are Satan and your residual sinful nature. All of this helps depersonalize the issue.

- Second, ask questions to learn why you feel what you feel and try to identify the cause of the negative effects. Once you identify the cause, spend some time together in prayer; ask God to give each a pure heart to seek His wisdom for the problem.

- Third, separate for a short time for individual prayer. Ask God to show where you are wrong, instead of asking Him to convict the other. Ask God to search your heart and fix you.

- Finally, come back together and share what God revealed where each was wrong or could have used wisdom (a better how). Focus on what you could have done better, not your spouse. When we approach God with a humble heart, wanting to know our faults, He honors our request. When we come back together, we come

> with contrite hearts, recognizing our own failures in the situation. Have you ever been in a heated argument with your spouse where accusations led to hurt feelings? Perhaps you spit verbal venom all over each other, but after tears were shed, you both asked for forgiveness. You came back together, tripping all over each other with apologies and admissions of guilt. And then you felt a tremendous emotional release and embraced each other, thankful for your marriage, which led to a wonderful night of emotional and physical bonding as you appreciated getting through the tension.

Being humble and using a godly thought process leads to a great ending – emotional, spiritual, and sometimes physical bonding without the residual hurtful words that may never be forgotten, and which lie dormant until the next heated argument.

Humility is always the crucial ingredient. Willingness to remove the plank in our own eye before we point out the speck in another's eye leads to constructive conflict resolution and a growth of mutual love and respect.

When we understand and apply biblical principles of conflict resolution to our marriage, the intimate bond between spouses is strengthened. Once we have excellent marriages, we can help develop excellent churches. The principles we shared for communication in marriage equally apply to Christian fellowship within the church, the eternal Bride of Christ.

Fellowship and marriage should be relationships where both parties benefit. If someone constantly gives yet never feels they receive a benefit in return, they are headed down the path to bitterness. The time will come when they shut down emotionally, feeling their kindness has been abused. But fellowship and marriage must never be seen as an arrangement where equal value is achieved through every transaction.

> *Give, and it will be given to you. Good measure, pressed down, shaken together, running over, will be put into your lap. For with the measure you use it will be measured back to you.* (Luke 6:38)

> *He said also to the man who had invited him, "When you give a dinner or a banquet, do not invite your friends or your brothers or your relatives or rich neighbors, lest they also invite you in return and you be repaid. But when you give a feast, invite the poor, the crippled, the lame, the blind, and you will be blessed, because they cannot repay you. For you will be repaid at the resurrection of the just."* (Luke 14:12-14)

God will see to it that every good gift we give to others will come back to us as eternal reward. In fact, in the verses in Luke, Jesus tells us it is better to give to those who can never repay your kindness. What can any man give us in this life that compares to what God will give us for eternity? This is a crucial point to remember: When both parties give without expecting anything in return, God rewards both parties. And just how is Satan able to disrupt marriages and fellowship when all parties give without expecting anything in return from the other?

When we give to others using a human thought process, we naturally expect they will one day repay us for our kindness. But as time passes, there is the possibility of bitterness taking root in our lives as our act of kindness goes unrewarded. A godly thought process actually hopes we will never be repaid while on earth. A godly thought process embraces a principle we will discuss later: delayed gratification.

Anxiety that leads to depression can occur when future expectations go unmet for a long time. One of the best ways to avoid depression is to expect nothing from anyone. Give and love freely, not expecting anything in return but knowing God is faithful to reward us far greater than any human ever can.

People in a fleshly/animal thought process are takers. People in a human thought process give, hoping they will get something in return. People in a godly thought process give and expect nothing in return from the other. They realize God will reward them in eternity in a far greater way than any human reward ever could. Are we takers, lenders, or givers in marriage and fellowship?

> *And if you lend to those from whom you expect to receive, what credit is that to you? Even sinners lend to sinners, to get back the same amount. But love your enemies, and do good,*

and lend, expecting nothing in return, and your reward will be great, and you will be sons of the Most High, for he is kind to the ungrateful and the evil. (Luke 6:34-35)

Playing "LeMay Ball"

My brother and I are baseball fans who share a common affliction: our teams have a long history of losing games. He follows the Chicago Cubs while I am a fan of the hapless Milwaukee Brewers. But nonetheless, we find some time to drive to Milwaukee and take in a couple of games surrounding a night in a hotel where we reminisce about our childhood and the close friendship we have forged.

We both grew up loving sports and would always turn any sort of ball into a friendly athletic competition. A few years ago, he brought a small beach ball on our annual trip, and we invented a new game we played in the hotel pool that he called "LeMay Ball." We stand in the pool about eight feet apart and bat the ball back and forth to see how many times we can do so without it hitting the water. Our record is 234 times, and usually as we approach the point of breaking our record, one of us will crack a stupid joke or line from a television show we watched when we were young, which causes us to laugh and lose focus.

This game taught me a lesson we can use in Christian fellowship and marriage when we try to resolve disputes. Both participants succeed when you hit the ball to the other where they are in excellent position to send it back as gently as they received it. Both parties win as we cooperate with each other toward the common goal of keeping the ball in the air. If you send the ball to the other in a way that causes them stress, the chances are they will be out of position even if they can return it. The volley back will cause the other to be out of position to return it in a way profitable to both parties to continue making progress toward the mutual goal. Neither person wins unless we both win by setting each other up to make progress.

Our conversations with spouses and Christians should embrace this win-win strategy, but often we are convinced that the only way we can win a discussion is when the other person loses. This is a prideful attitude that should have no part in Christian marriage or fellowship.

Even if I win the argument, we both really lose because our relationship could be damaged in the future.

This should also be our plan when we share the gospel with friends, family, and coworkers. But too often we really want to prove ourselves better than the other person and press issues to prove our righteousness, which damages the relationship and discourages ongoing conversations. We go for the "close" to prove we are superior, instead of sharing information and giving the other party time to think through the discussion and arrive at a logical conclusion to the matter being discussed. We are so busy trying to convince the other person we are right that we miss an opportunity to get them to open up, share, and give the Holy Spirit the chance to convict them of anything they might be in error about. We just can't resist doing the Holy Spirit's work to show how holy we are.

> *I therefore, a prisoner for the Lord, urge you to walk in a manner worthy of the calling to which you have been called, with all humility and gentleness, with patience, bearing with one another in love, eager to maintain the unity of the Spirit in the bond of peace.* (Ephesians 4:1-3)

> *Put on then, as God's chosen ones, holy and beloved, compassionate hearts, kindness, humility, meekness, and patience, bearing with one another and, if one has a complaint against another, forgiving each other; as the Lord has forgiven you, so you also must forgive. And above all these put on love, which binds everything together in perfect harmony. And let the peace of Christ rule in your hearts, to which indeed you were called in one body. And be thankful. Let the word of Christ dwell in you richly, teaching and admonishing one another in all wisdom, singing psalms and hymns and spiritual songs, with thankfulness in your hearts to God. And whatever you do, in word or deed, do everything in the name of the Lord Jesus, giving thanks to God the Father through him.* (Colossians 3:12-17)

These teachings speak to the gentle and patient way we should teach and, when necessary, rebuke other believers and even unbelievers. There is no agenda of pride or self-righteousness in the methods Paul teaches: only one person sincerely trying to help another person grow in Jesus Christ. There is no win/lose agenda, but rather a patient course of action where both people grow in love and mutual respect.

As we discussed earlier, true humility is the defining characteristic of a disciple of Jesus Christ. He does not seek to make himself look superior to another. He looks for ways to edify and encourage others to grow. He has no need to say things that will testify to his intelligence or wisdom because he realizes anything good that comes out of him is only by the power of the Holy Spirit anyway.

He never forgets that he has grown only by the grace of God. He remembers how it made him feel when other Christians chastised him so they could feel better about themselves. He is self-aware and realizes the human need to show superiority over another speaks to his lack of maturity as a believer. He plays "LeMay Ball" instead of intentionally trying to throw the other person off balance and then watching him fail to uphold his end of the discussion. He gently hits the ball back to the other and puts him in position to move forward instead of putting him in a position to fail.

He is also humble enough to realize he is not always the smartest Christian in every conversation; he actually hopes the other person will raise an excellent point he had never considered to prove he was wrong about an issue. He will discover truth and grow in wisdom and holiness. Is this what our fellowships look like? Or do they look more like prideful people trying to impress one another with our knowledge and spiritual maturity?

> *If anyone imagines that he knows something, he does not yet know as he ought to know. But if anyone loves God, he is known by God. (1 Corinthians 8:2-3)*

> *So that Christ may dwell in your hearts through faith – that you, being rooted and grounded in love, may have strength to comprehend with all the saints what is the breadth and length and height and depth, and to know the love of Christ*

> *that surpasses knowledge, that you may be filled with all the fullness of God.* (Ephesians 3:17-19)
>
> *Love never ends. As for prophecies, they will pass away; as for tongues, they will cease; as for knowledge, it will pass away.* (1 Corinthians 13:8)

We treat knowledge as king, yet the Bible tells us knowledge is not eternal. But love endures forever. In the verses before this last passage, Paul tells us we can have great knowledge, but without love it is meaningless.

> *Preach the word; be ready in season and out of season; reprove, rebuke, and exhort, with complete patience and teaching.* (2 Timothy 4:2)

Too many Christians act with a self-righteous attitude toward less mature believers, expecting them to acquire instantly the wisdom and discernment it took us years to grasp. This often happens when certain teachers and preachers are discussed. When I was a new Christian, after forty-five years of disobedience to God, I was hungry to learn all I could about Him. I attended every Christian conference I could to hear from whoever was willing to share the Word of God. I wanted to trust everything they taught, figuring they knew what they were talking about, because thousands of Christians attended their conferences.

Now, after seventeen years of seasoning, I realize some of these teachers were either wrong or flat out deceivers, but I lacked the wisdom and discernment to understand at that time. But I was blessed to be in fellowships with solid, seasoned believers who were smarter and wiser than I was. They helped me to discern truth from deception by studying and understanding the Word of God. When I talk with young believers now who are caught up following a teacher who preaches incorrect doctrine, I am patient with them. I do not come out and blast them for following deceived teachers, because I once did the same thing. Instead, I listen and ask questions and use their answers to point us to the Word of God for wisdom and clarity.

One of the questions I ask professing Christians is this: "If you believe something is truth, but the Bible contradicts your view, which would you believe?"

Most answer, "The Bible."

I then ask another question: "Do you believe any current Bible teacher is perfect in everything they teach?"

If they answer no, we are able to move forward in productive fellowship. I confirm they are correct in their answers and ask if we can study the teachings of every teacher we follow, comparing them to the Bible to see if the teachers are correct or incorrect. Notice, I did not blast the teacher they currently follow. I simply asked questions to obtain permission to study everything in light of the eternal truth of the Bible.

I share with them that there were some teachers I followed in the past but later discovered were wrong in their understanding of doctrine. I tell them I want to help them grow faster in holiness and correct doctrine than I have. I have still not criticized their favorite teacher. In fact, I encourage them to spend the next week reading the writings of that teacher, writing down any questions they have or specific points the teacher made that impressed something upon them. I encourage them to get beyond what the teacher says and look for the why/how they do or do not use. We meet and discuss the points of interest to them, and I pray and ask the Holy Spirit to give me the right questions to ask that will point them to truth.

This is important when younger believers are caught up in messages such as the false prosperity gospel or teachers who talk about all the benefits of Christianity without talking about the responsibilities. Every person's journey toward sanctification is unique. No simple, one-step formula gets us to complete sanctification. We all come to saving faith, scarred by our past experiences and destructive teachings we've learned. We need to be patient with one another as God has been patient with us.

Christians argue about many issues that lead to division where none should exist. Some break fellowship with any person who does not believe the rapture of the church happens before the tribulation. I know believers who will break fellowship with others over issues like pre-destination, the ability to lose one's salvation, or the cessation or continuation of the spiritual gifts. These attitudes can be rooted in human pride, and it often shows a heart of self-righteousness and a lack of love for other believers.

Christian fellowship should not be predicated by some arbitrary level of sanctification where everyone above the line is part of fellowship, while everyone below the line is excluded. Christian fellowship should be established with people who are saved and willing to be continually sanctified and who come together in humility with hearts to help each other grow in the knowledge and grace of Jesus Christ. We recognize we are all works in progress, at varying levels of sanctification as the Holy Spirit continues His work in our lives.

Judging One Another

No doctrine of the Bible has been more mangled than the teachings on judging one another. The unbiblical legalist judges everyone and everything. The emergent judges no one or anything. The disciple of Jesus Christ knows what to judge, why to judge, and how to judge with a godly thought process.

If we are going to help unbelievers come to saving faith in Jesus Christ and help young believers mature in holiness, we must have a biblical understanding of our responsibility and limitations in judging others. Our nation and a growing number of Christian churches are moving toward political correctness on steroids, where even the thought of judging others to any degree is considered a crime against humanity. Morality has become an individual choice, rather than based on the objective truths of the Bible. And consequently, our nation and the church have shied away from confronting people who live contradictory to God's Word, even though they are harming themselves for eternity.

> *In those days there was no king in Israel. Everyone did what was right in his own eyes.* (Judges 21:25)

America, and the professing Christian church that is supposed to keep it under God's guidance and protection, has abandoned Christian thought based on the Bible and embraced individual morality just like the Israelites did at the end of the book of Judges. A pattern repeats throughout the book of Judges:

- The people abandoned the Lord.

- God punished them by raising up a foreign power to oppress them.
- The people cried out to God for deliverance.
- God raised up a deliverer, or judge, for them.

We see America and the Christian church in this second phase patterned in Judges. We have abandoned God, and we are now being oppressed by two religious powers, which are diametrically opposed to the Word of God:

- Islam, touted as a religion of peace yet violent and oppressive in its core doctrines, is being promoted as a religion compatible with biblical Christianity, in spite of it being defined as a spirit of antichrist in John's epistles. Reports suggest that hundreds, if not thousands, of terror cells are ready to be activated when the Muslim call for jihad is given.

- Secular humanism, where individual morality replaces the standard in the Bible, has become the religion of choice in America. Christian thought is being eliminated in favor of humanist thought.

The latter is the greatest threat to America in the big picture. Islam can be refuted once its core doctrines are understood by Christians who understand the Bible. But humanism appeals to our flesh – an enemy we do not even want to acknowledge, much less wage war against. There is no greater evidence of the infestation of humanism than how we have come to misunderstand judgment in the Bible.

The Two Types of Judgment in the Bible

Jesus spoke of judging:

> *Yet I do not seek my own glory; there is One who seeks it, and he is the judge.* (John 8:50)

> *If anyone hears my words and does not keep them, I do not judge him; for I did not come to judge the world but to save the world. The one who rejects me and does not receive my*

words has a judge; the word that I have spoken will judge him on the last day. (John 12:47-48)

The Greek word Jesus uses for judge is *krino*: "to try, convict and punish." Paul uses a different word for judgment:

But with me it is a very small thing that I should be judged by you or by any human court. In fact, I do not even judge myself. For I am not aware of anything against myself, but I am not thereby acquitted. It is the Lord who judges me. Therefore do not pronounce judgment before the time, before the Lord comes, who will bring to light the things now hidden in darkness and will disclose the purposes of the heart. Then each one will receive his commendation from God.
(1 Corinthians 4:3-5)

The Greek word for judge in this verse is *anakrino*: "to scrutinize, investigate and determine." *Anakrino* is used fourteen times and translated in the following way in the ESV New Testament:

Examine: Luke 23:14; Acts 4:9; Acts 12:19; Acts 17:11; Acts 24:8; Acts 28:18; 1 Corinthians 9:3.

Question: 1 Corinthians 10:25, 27.

Discern: 1 Corinthians 2:14.

Judge: 1 Corinthians 2:15; 1 Corinthians 4:3, 4.

Account: 1 Corinthians 14:24.

So *krino* judgment is to "try, convict, and punish"; *Anakrino* is to "scrutinize, investigate, and determine." Let's use a modern day example from the American justice system to explain the difference. A trial jury is a group of people who hear evidence and determine the guilt or innocence of an accused criminal. They can also impose a sentence if they determine the person is guilty. But a grand jury has less authority and power. They gather to look at evidence to see if there is sufficient reason for a person to be charged with a crime. If their verdict is that evidence warrants a formal charge, they make their recommendation to the court, and their work is finished. They have no further legal jurisdiction over the case. It is then presented to the judge and jury for consideration of guilt or innocence.

We can compare this example to when and how we as Christians should judge others. But in both instances, God is the only One qualified to judge the eternal guilt or innocence of any person. He alone is righteous and just to proclaim a final verdict, and when necessary, sentence a guilty party to eternal damnation.

Judging Other Believers

Believers can be considered members of a "grand jury" for one another. We look at evidence in the life of each other as believers and make recommendations on how we can bring our beliefs and actions in alignment with God's Word. When necessary, and always in an appropriate way, we judge the visible fruits of one another to help each other grow in holiness. This benefits the individual and the church as a whole.

No issue causes more destruction within the church than members who either believe judgment has no place in the church or believers who judge others with a wrong motive (why) or method (how). Judging other believers is a serious matter that must be conducted using biblical principles.

- First, our motive must be to help one another, not to make ourselves look more righteous than the other person. We make judgments about the behaviors of another to help him grow in sanctification, along with helping him avoid worsening consequences because of his choices. Pride doesn't enter into the equation.

- Second, judging others must always come from a position of true humility. We must be aware of and willing to admit our own shortcomings as believers. Jesus warned us of the consequences if we judge others for the same sins we commit without confession and repentance:

Judge not, that you be not judged. For with the judgment you pronounce you will be judged, and with the measure you use it will be measured to you. (Matthew 7:1-2)

Let's not diminish what Jesus is saying here. If we condemn someone struggling with a particular sin, while we carry a similar unrepentant sin in our own lives, the judgment we pronounce on the other person will be used to determine our guilt when we stand before God. In fact, this form of unrighteous judgment is a major reason so many younger people have left the Christian faith; they see it as legalistic and hateful.

No sin has caused more problems and divisions within the church than sexual sin. Every week we read the next sad story of a pastor or well-known Christian falling into the grip of sexual sin. And one of the reasons youth cite for their disillusionment with Christianity is the hypocrisy in judging sexual sin.

For years the church singled out the sin of homosexuality as an abomination, while excusing extra-marital affairs and addictions to pornography by members and leaders. All sexual sin is an affront to God. And if we continue to condemn people over one sexual sin, while continuing to live as unrepentant sexual sinners ourselves, God will judge us with the same measure we used on others.

A young man who listens to our radio show called me one day to tell me that he was a practicing homosexual, and when he heard us refer to homosexuality as sin, he got very angry. But one day God showed him that he was sinning as a homosexual, and he confessed and repented to God. He realized it was a sin and was committed to walking away from the lifestyle.

About six months later, he called me, clearly upset. He had been out at a bar, had too much to drink, and succumbed to sexual temptation, having a one-night affair with a young man. He wondered if God could ever forgive him for this relapse in judgment. I asked him, "How do you feel about what you did?"

"Horrible! I've betrayed God and myself. I feel [terrible]! I know what I did was wrong."

He had confessed and repented (admitted guilt and turned from it) about his sexual sin six months earlier. He had avoided the temptation for six months and then, in a moment of weakness, sinned. He again sincerely confessed and repented to God with all his mind and heart. Would you consider him a true believer? If your answer is no, then you must understand that when you sin after you have confessed and repented, God can hold you to the same standard when you stand before Him.

The difference between a born-again believer and an unbeliever is not that one doesn't sin and the other does. The difference is that the born-again believer acknowledges his sin is wrong, confesses, repents, and by the power of the Holy Spirit seeks to stop sinning. The unbeliever justifies his ongoing sin, while the believer acknowledges his sin (confession), grows to hate it (repentance), and desires deliverance from it.

Judaizer/legalists exceed the restrictions the Bible puts on judging others. They also judge others with a higher standard than they allow themselves to be judged. Gnostic/emergents reject the Bible's commands to judge the behaviors of others. They hide behind a flawed definition of love to excuse their sins and the sins of others. Believers who use a godly thought process know what to judge, why to judge, and how to judge. And our *how* always tries to help others, not condemn them.

Another important reason to use biblical wisdom in judging others is the damage it can do to our unconscious brain and conscience when we judge another for something of which we are also guilty. Our unconscious brain sees this as a contradiction, and we will feel unsettled when we are hypocritical. Our unconscious brain knows we are not being just, and we open a potential stronghold for the enemy to use to lead us to feel condemned when we give in to similar sin. We damage our thought process when we judge others in a hypocritical way.

> *It is actually reported that there is sexual immorality among you, and of a kind that is not tolerated even among pagans, for a man has his father's wife. And you are arrogant! Ought you not rather to mourn? Let him who has done this be removed from among you. For though absent in body, I am present in spirit; and as if present, I have already pronounced judgment on the one who did such a thing. When you are assembled in the name of the Lord Jesus and my spirit is present, with the power of our Lord Jesus, you are to deliver this man to Satan for the destruction of the*

flesh, so that his spirit may be saved in the day of the Lord. (1 Corinthians 5:1-5)

When professing Christians say, "The Bible says we should never judge," they choose a human thought process over a godly thought process. They are guilty of preaching human doctrine over biblical doctrine, just like the Pharisees. They are so adamant about not judging others because they realize they themselves would be found guilty if others judged them. But Paul is telling the church at Corinth to pronounce this man guilty and expel him from the church for two reasons:

- First, for the benefit of the church. The Corinthian church struggled mightily with issues of sexuality, as evidenced by Paul's letters to them. Paul was concerned that this man, a blatant, unrepentant sinner whose behavior was worse than that of pagans, would infect the body of believers.

- Second, Paul tells them to publicly admonish him and throw him out of the church *to deliver this man to Satan for the destruction of the flesh, so that his spirit may be saved in the day of the Lord.* Paul tells them to do this for his benefit. If this unrepentant man had been allowed to stay in the church, many others would have become infected and would be judged and convicted by God on judgment day.

The most unloving thing a church can do is to allow unrepentant sinners to remain in the church. The sinner is given a false sense of eternal security, and the people in that church open themselves up to temptation and sin. Did Jesus teach the same thing?

If your brother sins against you, go and tell him his fault, between you and him alone. If he listens to you, you have gained your brother. But if he does not listen, take one or two others along with you, that every charge may be established by the evidence of two or three witnesses. If he refuses to listen to them, tell it to the church. And if he refuses to listen even to the church, let him be to you as a Gentile and a tax collector. (Matthew 18:15-17)

The unrepentant sinner should be admonished by the church for his failure to confess and repent. Only after he has seen the error of his ways, confesses, and repents, should he be allowed back into the fellowship. Again, this is for his benefit. When we learn how to live out what the Bible teaches us about how to judge, we can start to rebuild and grow the church.

Judging Unbelievers

I wrote to you in my letter not to associate with sexually immoral people – not at all meaning the sexually immoral of this world, or the greedy and swindlers, or idolaters, since then you would need to go out of the world. But now I am writing to you not to associate with anyone who bears the name of brother if he is guilty of sexual immorality or greed, or is an idolater, reviler, drunkard, or swindler – not even to eat with such a one. For what have I to do with judging outsiders? Is it not those inside the church whom you are to judge? God judges those outside. "Purge the evil person from among you." (1 Corinthians 5:9-13)

Notice that Paul wrote these verses following his command to throw the unrepentant sexual sinner out of the church. Paul is saying to judge the fruit of a man who claims to be a Christian through his participation in the church, and if his fruit is bad and he does not repent, throw him out. Then, you should no longer judge him because he is not a true believer. You have done the job of the grand jury, leaving him to the responsibility of God to judge his eternal soul.

It is futile for Christians to focus our efforts on judging and condemning unbelievers. Rather than focus our anger and judgment on government, media, public education, or Hollywood, we should focus our attention on professing believers in the church. If their values and lifestyle consistently line up with the world, then we confront them in their errors. If they act out of pride and refuse to confess and repent, we treat them as unbelievers and remove them from the church for the benefit of the church and the individual.

Not judging unbelievers does not mean we do not share the gospel with them. We can see the unique relationship between believers and unbelievers in some interesting verses where Jesus said:

> *"If anyone hears my words and does not keep them, I do not judge him; for I did not come to judge the world but to save the world. The one who rejects me and does not receive my words has a judge; the word that I have spoken will judge him on the last day. For I have not spoken on my own authority, but the Father who sent me has himself given me a commandment – what to say and what to speak."*
> (John 12:47-49)

We must approach these verses in the same way we approach John 3:16-19. Remember, the emergents claim the first two verses of that passage as proof of universal salvation. But when we understand verses 18 and 19, we understand the truth that many will be condemned. In the same manner, progressive Christians claim John 12:47 is proof that "since Jesus did not come to judge the world, neither should we." But when we read and understand the Bible in a non-contradictory manner, we understand Jesus will one day judge all men. Consistent with His life, Jesus is saying that the first time He came as God in human form and offered salvation to all men. But the second time He comes, the Word (Jesus) will be the instrument of judgment for all men.

> *For the word of God is living and active, sharper than any two-edged sword, piercing to the division of soul and of spirit, of joints and of marrow, and discerning the thoughts and intentions of the heart. And no creature is hidden from his sight, but all are naked and exposed to the eyes of him to whom we must give account.* (Hebrews 4:12-13)

> *From his mouth comes a sharp sword with which to strike down the nations, and he will rule them with a rod of iron. He will tread the winepress of the fury of the wrath of God the Almighty.* (Revelation 19:15)

> *And the rest were slain by the sword that came from the mouth of him who was sitting on the horse, and all the birds were gorged with their flesh.* (Revelation 19:21)

Jesus' first coming was to offer salvation to men, not to condemn them. His second coming will see Him judge every man and nation, swiftly and justly.

> *Or do you not know that the saints will judge the world? And if the world is to be judged by you, are you incompetent to try trivial cases? Do you not know that we are to judge angels? How much more, then, matters pertaining to this life!* (1 Corinthians 6:2-3)

Paul was teaching the need for Christians to make correct judgments with one another when they have disagreements; this is church discipline. Again, unless we learn to understand the Bible in a non-contradictory manner, we can develop bad theology. After all, this same Paul in the verses of 1 Corinthians 5:12 asked, "*What do I have with judging outsiders?*" The key is we will judge the world and even angels after Jesus returns to establish His everlasting kingdom. Just like Jesus, in this lifetime we are not to judge unbelievers, but rather point them to Jesus as the only means of salvation. We should show them how they can be saved, just as Jesus did when He came. Those who reject our plea on behalf of Jesus will be judged and condemned when He returns.

The gospel is good news, not a message condemning fallen man for that which his conscience already knows: that he is sinful and lost. The good news is Jesus has come to rescue them.

> *For everyone who calls on the name of the Lord will be saved. How then will they call on him in whom they have not believed? And how are they to believe in him of whom they have never heard? And how are they to hear without someone preaching? And how are they to preach unless they are sent? As it is written, "How beautiful are the feet of those who preach the good news!"* (Romans 10:13-15)

In Romans 1, Paul says every man's conscience knows he is a sinner and he deserves the eternal death penalty. If you were meeting with a man in prison who had been sentenced to death, which message would he be interested in hearing: "You know you are going to die," or "There is a way out if this death sentence; confess, repent, and call on the name of your judge, Jesus Christ, for mercy and forgiveness."? If you were that man, which message would pique your interest?

Unrepentant sinners will be eternally judged one day. Little can be gained by us reaffirming that reality. Jesus came the first time to save, not condemn, people. As ambassadors of the good news, we must use the same method as Jesus. We correctly judge others for their benefit, leaving the final, eternal judgment to Jesus when He returns.

Christians who use a godly thought process know what to judge, why to judge and how to judge. Judging others is always done for their benefit, not to exalt ourselves.

Key Points:

- Sharing about yourself and learning about others through questions fosters growth in the relationship.

- Making statements about others and refusing to share (not answering their questions) leads to isolation and conflict. When we project, negate, or judge another, we act out of pride, thinking we know them better than they know themselves. This is abuse.

- Expecting unsaved individuals who do not have the Holy Spirit to know what we know is prideful and unproductive. If we can learn what they believe and why they believe it, we can establish a productive framework for discussion about God and the Bible.

- Participating in a fellowship should be a win/win scenario, where both parties share and grow.

- Looking for faults in others is a human thought process. A person in a godly thought process looks for his own faults.

- Understanding the role of judging one another is

characteristic of a mature Christian. He knows who to judge, what to judge, why to judge, and how to judge.

Summary

Our thought process is under constant attack by the world, which looks to deceive, manipulate, and control us. If we cannot guard our thought process, we are vulnerable to deception that can lead us away from God's truth in His Word. By using a godly thought process, we can protect ourselves and help others understand the eternal truth of God's Word.

Effective communication has become a lost art in a world where we are busy chasing the latest fads and things we think will bring us happiness. Do not allow people in a fleshly/animal thought process to rush you. Learn to control the conversation in a constructive way by asking great questions to help others improve their thought process while protecting yours.

Next, we look at principles that will help us maintain a godly thought process when life brings its inevitable challenges.

Chapter Nine

FOCUSING ON ETERNITY

Chapter objective: to apply biblical principles to keep us focused on eternity.

Guarding your thought process and helping others improve their thought process are what marriage, fellowship, and sanctification are all about. Principles in God's Word remind us how to take our thoughts captive and trust in God no matter what circumstances we are facing.

Principle #1: Knowing the difference between who you are and what you do.

Try an experiment the next time you meet someone: after you have been introduced, say, "Tell me about yourself." With near certainty they will tell you where they work, that they are married, or what they like to do in their free time. Listen and then politely say, "No, not what you do, but who you are." Most likely you will receive a blank stare that says something like, "I just did!"

This malady doesn't only affect unbelievers, because most Christians will tell you what they do instead of who they are when you first meet. This may not seem like an important distinction, but not understanding the difference between who we are and what we do as Christians leads to serious problems in the church, including the exodus of millions of young Christians as they become adults.

Earlier we discovered the difference between who God is and what He does: He is always righteous, holy, and just. His "do" is loving, merciful, judging, forgiving, patient, and always consistent with His nature. When we confuse who God is (His nature) and the effects of His nature (His actions and behaviors), we are perplexed when deceivers or unbelievers challenge our beliefs.

For example, if we say God's nature is love, how do we respond when an unbeliever says, "Then your God is a liar because He ordered the deaths of tens of thousands in the Bible and wiped out most of humanity in a flood. Your 'god' is not love. He is a petty, spoiled little child who destroys others when he does not get his way!" I witnessed this, and the evangelizing Christian was dumbfounded, not knowing how to respond. He was a laughing stock to everyone who witnessed his attempt at evangelizing.

But when we know who God is, we can respond with truth; whether the person accepts or rejects that truth is up to him. But at least we did not allow an unbeliever to make us look foolish and dishonor God by misrepresenting him with our witness.

The world is watching us. Not only is God on trial in their eyes, but so are we. The world loves nothing more than to call us hypocrites who judge others by standards to which we are unwilling to be held ourselves. And if we cannot understand and accept what the Bible teaches about the difference in who we are and what we do as Christians, we set ourselves up for a life of discouragement, worry, failure, and the self-condemnation Satan wants us to believe to render us ineffective as ambassadors of Jesus Christ. Paul reminded us in Romans chapter 7 of the difference between who we are and what we do.

Romans is an amazing treatise of biblical doctrine, and it gives us tremendous insight on how the mind and heart of the believer wrestle with temptation and sin. It presents a perfect picture differentiating who we are in Christ and what we do as believers; we are people who are not above temptation, sin, and moral failure. Many Christians, including people we see in church every Sunday, cannot distinguish between how God judges who we are versus what we do. This dilemma robs us of our joy and hinders the fruit God wants to bring forth in us. It probably causes more people to leave their Christian faith than anything else. An enemy out there, Satan, wants nothing more than to condemn us and render us ineffective in our testimony for the gospel. And if we cannot distinguish between who we are and what we do as Christians, we will fall for his clever deception and lies.

The two great lies Satan will use against us when we sin as believers are these:

> "How can you claim to be a real Christian when you have confessed and repented but still go on sinning?"

> "Don't worry about your sin; you're saved so it doesn't matter anymore."

Unless we combat these lies with the truth of the Bible, we will either give up and go back to our sinful lifestyle or believe the lie that our sins no longer matter and go back to our sinful lifestyle! We need to understand that while all sin is reprehensible to God, He responds differently to the person who has humbled himself before Him in comparison with how he responds to the person who remains prideful and arrogant about their sins. The first person avoids eternal punishment in hell; the second will spend eternity in hell.

Second, we need to understand that even as born-again believers, we will have to pay a price for any sins we commit if we do not continue to confess, repent, and humble ourselves before God. But unlike the unbeliever, who will pay the price for his sins with eternal damnation, the true believer will pay the price with a loss of eternal reward in heaven.

There are two separate judgments at the end of the Bible:

> *Then I saw a great white throne and him who was seated on it. From his presence earth and sky fled away, and no place was found for them. And I saw the dead, great and small, standing before the throne, and books were opened. Then another book was opened, which is the book of life. And the dead were judged by what was written in the books, according to what they had done. And the sea gave up the dead*

> *who were in it, Death and Hades gave up the dead who were in them, and they were judged, each one of them, according to what they had done. Then Death and Hades were thrown into the lake of fire. This is the second death, the lake of fire. And if anyone's name was not found written in the book of life, he was thrown into the lake of fire.* (Revelation 20:11-15)

We will be judged by a righteous and just God in two different ways: by what we do and for who we are. Who we are will determine our eternal destination. For the true believer, "do" represents eternal reward.

In Romans 7, Paul distinguishes between who we are and what we do as believers. Paul points out who he is: a man who loves God and wants to obey Him. He points out that his actions (sins of commission and omission) contradict who he truly is (a new creation in Christ). His *do* does not consistently match up with his *are*, and he laments his ongoing sinful actions that contradict his love of God. He is desperate for ultimate deliverance from the sins he cannot stop committing, to the point he cries out, *"Wretched man that I am! Who will deliver me from this body of death?"* (Romans 7:24). And at this height of hopelessness, the Spirit of God gives Paul the answer: *Thanks be to God through Jesus Christ our Lord!* (Romans 7:25). Jesus knew no sin but became sin for our sake, taking the wrath of God upon Himself for our benefit. Paul then states a crucial truth we must understand and live out:

> *There is therefore now no condemnation for those who are in Christ Jesus. For the law of the Spirit of life has set you free in Christ Jesus from the law of sin and death. For God has done what the law, weakened by the flesh, could not do. By sending his own Son in the likeness of sinful flesh and for sin, he condemned sin in the flesh, in order that the righteous requirement of the law might be fulfilled in us, who walk not according to the flesh but according to the Spirit.* (Romans 8:1-4)

But how can we know that we are walking in the Spirit and not the flesh? After all, don't we all return to our flesh when we choose to sin?

How can we know for sure we have not been deceived by our wicked human heart and have a false sense of security?

> *The heart is deceitful above all things, and desperately sick; who can understand it? I the Lord search the heart and test the mind, to give every man according to his ways, according to the fruit of his deeds.* (Jeremiah 17:9-10)

Notice in these verses God stated a question and gave us a way to answer the question. If we try to provide our own answer to His question, we use a sick and deceitful tool (our human heart) to judge if that same heart is good or wicked. That would be like a judge pronouncing a verdict at his own trial. Of course, our deceitful heart is going to deceive us once again and tell us it is good.

So the Lord searches the heart and tests the mind to show us truth. A God who is always righteous and just is the only one qualified to render a correct verdict of guilt or innocence. So how does God search the heart and test the mind? What does He provide to prove our hearts are no longer wicked? How can we know for sure we have received a new heart and spirit from God and are walking in the Spirit and not the flesh?

> *This God – his way is perfect; the word of the Lord proves true; he is a shield for all those who take refuge in him.* (2 Samuel 22:31)

> *I bow down toward your holy temple and give thanks to your name for your steadfast love and your faithfulness, for you have exalted above all things your name and your word.* (Psalm 138:2)

> *But he answered, "It is written, Man shall not live by bread alone, but by every word that comes from the mouth of God."* (Matthew 4:4)

> *The one who rejects me and does not receive my words has a judge; the word that I have spoken will judge him on the last day.* (John 12:48)

> *All Scripture is breathed out by God and profitable for*

teaching, for reproof, for correction, and for training in righteousness. (2 Timothy 3:16)

So the Word of God is true; it is a shield; it is exalted above all things; it is the bread of eternal life; it will judge us on the last day; it is profitable for teaching, reproof, correction, and training in righteousness. But is hearing it alone enough for salvation?

When anyone hears the word of the kingdom and does not understand it, the evil one comes and snatches away what has been sown in his heart. This is what was sown along the path. (Matthew 13:19)

<u>We must hear it, believe it, understand it, and completely trust in it.</u> It is not enough to recite or memorize it. We must understand it, trust in it, and live it.

Who you are determines whether you inherit eternal life with God or are cast into darkness for eternity. But isn't what you do a testimony to who you really are? Absolutely! This presents quite the conundrum for those who do not understand what the Word teaches about sin, confession, repentance, salvation, and sanctification. If what we do is a testimony to who we are, does that mean our ongoing sin proves we were never really saved to begin with? We know that is not true because Paul and Peter would not be saved, since both confessed to still sinning. So how do we discover the truth of the Word in what appears to be a sea of confusion? How can I know who I am, either a sinner saved by grace who walks in the Spirit or a false convert who applies cheap grace to justify my ongoing walk in the flesh?

If we say we have no sin, we deceive ourselves, and the truth is not in us. If we confess our sins, he is faithful and just to forgive us our sins and to cleanse us from all unrighteousness. If we say we have not sinned, we make him a liar, and his word is not in us. (1 John 1:8-10)

Remember, this letter is written to and for believers. John says anyone who claims that he no longer sins is deceiving himself and the truth is not in him. The pride of the individual who claims he is now sinless immediately proves he has not humbled himself before God and has not received God's grace or Spirit.

> *Everyone who makes a practice of sinning also practices lawlessness; sin is lawlessness. You know that he appeared in order to take away sins, and in him there is no sin. No one who abides in him keeps on sinning; no one who keeps on sinning has either seen him or known him. Little children, let no one deceive you. Whoever practices righteousness is righteous, as he is righteous. Whoever makes a practice of sinning is of the devil, for the devil has been sinning from the beginning. The reason the Son of God appeared was to destroy the works of the devil. No one born of God makes a practice of sinning, for God's seed abides in him, and he cannot keep on sinning because he has been born of God. By this it is evident who are the children of God, and who are the children of the devil: whoever does not practice righteousness is not of God, nor is the one who does not love his brother.*
> (1 John 3:4-10)

But then John says that anyone who goes on *practicing* sin is of the devil. Is John contradicting himself? The Word of God, like God Himself, is never contradictory. We may be conflicted about Scriptures that seem to give differing messages, but this is simply the result of our own human failings in understanding the complete context of the Word, something these principles will help you overcome.

The key is making sure we apply God's definitions for words He uses instead of supplying our flawed human definitions. The key word in this verse is *practice*. The Greek word used is *poieo*: "to agree with; to abide in; bind together with; to perform willingly without delay." This is what Paul meant when he talked about walking in the flesh. We plan to sin, agree with sin, and rush head on and enjoy our sin. Anyone who habitually does this is walking in the flesh and does not have the Holy Spirit in them. Understand, we may sin suddenly without giving it a second thought on occasion, but that is not who we are. As true believers, like Paul, we love God and want to honor and obey Him. Walking in the Spirit, we want to love Him with our entire heart, mind, soul, and strength, but we will occasionally fail to do that.

But look again at our first quote from this epistle, as John gives us the remedy: *If we confess our sins, he is faithful and just to forgive our sins and to cleanse us from all unrighteousness* (1 John 1:9). This is who we are as born-again believers; we love God more than anything, and in our spirit we want to honor and obey Him, but we still fail at times. When we fail, we confess our sins again. He continues to sanctify us through our ongoing confession and repentance.

The true believer who grows in holiness is the one who is more aware of his sins each day, which leads to a godly sorrow of confession and repentance. One more word we must revisit and make sure we accurately define by what God says instead of applying a wrong human definition is *repentance*.

> *From that time Jesus began to preach, saying, "Repent, for the kingdom of heaven is at hand."* (Matthew 4:17)

Christians who condemn others ultimately damage or condemn themselves by changing the definition of *repentance* to "stop sinning." The word *repent* in Greek is *metanoeo*: "to think differently afterwards." When we apply the harmful human definition, we damage others and ourselves; we feel hopeless because we claim to repent but still keep sinning. When we truly repent, we think differently of the sins we used to justify. We now realize we were wrong and see those sins as offensive to God; we ask Him for more grace to help us resist future temptation and sin. We may commit those same sins on occasion, but each time we do, we should feel worse and worse. And if we continue in the same sin we have repented of, God will discipline us, and we will welcome His discipline because we will know He disciplines us for our benefit.

> *For the grace of God has appeared, bringing salvation for all people, training us to renounce ungodliness and worldly passions, and to live self-controlled, upright, and godly lives in the present age, waiting for our blessed hope, the appearing of the glory of our great God and Savior Jesus Christ, who gave himself for us to redeem us from all lawlessness*

> *and to purify for himself a people for his own possession*
> *who are zealous for good works. Declare these things; exhort*
> *and rebuke with all authority. Let no one disregard you.*
> (Titus 2:11-15)

Who are we as born-again believers? Sinners who are humble enough to acknowledge our hopelessly lost sinful state, who throw ourselves on the mercy of God and have complete faith and trust in who Jesus is and what He accomplished on the cross. We are people who realize more each day how sinful we are as the grace of God that saves us also reveals hidden sin, which leads us to continuing confession and repentance and further sanctification by the Holy Spirit.

Knowing this, we move forward, saved by God's grace and sanctified through continuing confession and repentance, no longer under the false accusations of Satan that say we are either not really saved or our sin no longer matters because we are saved. We grow in the knowledge and grace of Jesus Christ, and become more sanctified for the glory of God and the benefit of others. We enter through the narrow gate of eternal life.

This first principle: knowing the difference between who we are and what we do is essential to applying the Word of God in our lives. When we know who we are through God's grace and forgiveness, we can begin to apply other principles from His Word that will lead us to lives of joy, peace, and fruit.

Principle #2: God cannot lie and He knows the future.

The perfect accuracy of God's prophecies in the Bible proves He knows the future. He has spoken through prophets such as Moses, Isaiah, Ezekiel, Daniel, and Jeremiah with 100 percent accuracy on future events. Isaiah goes into incredible detail about the birth, life, and death of Jesus Christ that only a fool would deny that God is who He says He is. No prophecy of God that has reached its time of fulfillment has gone unmet. So we can be 100 percent confident that God is faithful and what He tells us is going to happen will happen in His perfect timing.

Jesus Christ has laid out specific promises of what we can expect in this life and for eternity. Nothing man or demon can do will foil

God's plans for us and His creation. God is also true to His nature and is incapable of lying:

> *God is not man, that he should lie, or a son of man, that he should change his mind. Has he said, and will he not do it? Or has he spoken, and will he not fulfill it?* (Numbers 23:19)
>
> *So when God desired to show more convincingly to the heirs of the promise the unchangeable character of his purpose, he guaranteed it with an oath, so that by two unchangeable things, in which it is impossible for God to lie, we who have fled for refuge might have strong encouragement to hold fast to the hope set before us. We have this as a sure and steadfast anchor of the soul, a hope that enters into the inner place behind the curtain, where Jesus has gone as a forerunner on our behalf, having become a high priest forever after the order of Melchizedek.* (Hebrews 6:17-20)

Accepting that God knows the eventual outcome of everything and is incapable of lying should bring us great peace and joy. Remember our example of reading a murder novel? When you know the outcome, you are able to relax, read the story and appreciate the beauty of the author's work. This is exactly what we must do with the Word of God: a God who cannot lie and has already told us how the story ends.

When I meet a professing Christian, I often ask, "What does the world look like just before Jesus returns and what does He do when He returns?" The Bible tells us the world will be full of evil and under control of Antichrist, one who proclaims himself as god. Jesus returns when all looks lost, destroying evil with a word from His mouth and establishing His everlasting kingdom. If someone gives me an answer that contradicts the Bible, I know they are either deceived, not knowing or trusting God, or they are a deceiver, misrepresenting Him for their own purposes. If we do not know how the story ends, we will be like a person who reads a murder mystery looking for clues but discovers there is no end to the novel. We go on and on reading, but we never discover the conclusion.

The Bible is not that complex when you understand the big-picture story. God created man in His image to live forever in fellowship with Him. Man chose sin and disobedience and lost his spiritual covering. God desires to redeem and restore man to his original standing – what he had when he was created (salvation/eternal life under God's covering). He does this through Jesus Christ, who returns one day to destroy evil and restore those who have put their complete faith and trust in Him. It is that simple, so let's stop making it more complex than it should be. The writings between Genesis and Revelation are the continuing story of that reconciliation. The ending has already been written by a God who cannot lie and who transcends time.

Worry and stress are always the effect of a lack of complete trust in God and His promises. When we grow in faith and trust God, confident of His eternal promises, we are able to reduce stress over our earthly circumstances. One day we will be in heaven with God, and the troubles of this life will be a distant memory, if we remember them at all. When we allow stress and worry to rob us of our joy, Satan gets a foothold in our lives to distract and overwhelm us. Knowing how the story ends leads us to peace and joy, and we are confident in the eternal outcomes.

Principle #3: God loves you as an adopted son through Jesus Christ and He cares about your happiness and future.

We damage people when we falsely state, "God doesn't care about your happiness!" Nothing could be further than the truth. The problem is we use contradicting definitions for the word *happy*.

The Beatitudes we covered earlier summarize the life Christians should lead. They first speak to the need for humility (poor in spirit) and conclude with the best evidence of happiness a person can attain – being persecuted for the sake of Jesus Christ. It goes against our flesh to look at persecution as leading to happiness. The word *blessed* begins every Beatitude – the Greek word *makarios*: "fortunate, happy."

> *Seeing the crowds, he went up on the mountain, and when he sat down, his disciples came to him. And he opened his mouth and taught them, saying:*

> "Blessed are the poor in spirit, for theirs is the kingdom of heaven.
>
> "Blessed are those who mourn, for they shall be comforted.
>
> "Blessed are the meek, for they shall inherit the earth.
>
> "Blessed are those who hunger and thirst for righteousness, for they shall be satisfied.
>
> "Blessed are the merciful, for they shall receive mercy.
>
> "Blessed are the pure in heart, for they shall see God.
>
> "Blessed are the peacemakers, for they shall be called sons of God.
>
> "Blessed are those who are persecuted for righteousness' sake, for theirs is the kingdom of heaven.
>
> "Blessed are you when others revile you and persecute you and utter all kinds of evil against you falsely on my account." (Matthew 5:1-11)

We miss something critically important when we don't understand the progression of these teachings. They begin with teaching humility, which leads to confession, repentance, and salvation. They transition into how we should live as true believers (sanctification) with growing humility as vessels of God's righteousness, grace, and mercy toward others. And they warn us that as we grow in Christ, we will be hated and persecuted for our beliefs and lifestyles as believers. But you may have noticed there is one verse remaining in the Beatitudes that gives us the *why* of what Jesus just said:

> *Rejoice and be glad, for your reward is great in heaven, for so they persecuted the prophets who were before you.* (Matthew 5:12)

Rejoice in Greek is *chairo*, meaning "cheerful; calmly happy." *Glad* is *agalliao*, meaning "to jump for joy; exceedingly happy." When we are hated and persecuted by the world for our faith in Jesus, we are to be calm and exceedingly happy. How can we be happy when all these things happen? Jesus gave us the answer in verse 12: by maintaining an eternal big-picture view of our lives.

Principle #4: Learn to walk into the future backwards.

The wisdom is simple in this old Jewish saying: "None of us knows what tomorrow will bring, but when we walk into it backwards, we look back and see all the times God was faithful during past trials." The other thing about walking backwards is this: it forces you to slow down and walk more carefully. We live life at a hectic pace beyond anything our ancestors could have imagined. A simple trip down a freeway will drive this point home. Everyone is in a rush and only focused on getting where they are going as quickly as possible. We talk on our phones, text, eat, and perform other duties while we drive – just to save a few minutes but putting ourselves and others at risk. We cut one another off in traffic as if our life depended on arriving at our destination one minute earlier.

In addition to our actions being done at breakneck speed, our minds also race a million miles an hour, and we literally wear ourselves out and age prematurely. Studies show teenagers today have "old brains" because of video games, texting, and a constant barrage of social media. We are burning ourselves out, raising our level of stress, and living at such high speeds that we have forgotten how to relax. Little time is given to deep thought or engaging conversation, as we sacrifice our physical, emotional, and spiritual health all for the "American Dream" of wealth and fame.

When was the last time you shut off all the noise and slowly read your Bible, asking God to reveal the magnificent truth and beauty of His Word? When was the last time you took a few hours to turn off the television or computer and have an engrossing conversation with your spouse or children about God?

Walking backwards into the future forces us to slow down and walk carefully and deliberately. We can look backwards, see God's faithfulness, and thank Him that while we are not yet the Christians we should be, we are grateful for the work He has done in us. This is particularly important in helping us put our latest crisis into proper perspective. We worry ourselves to death while we try to stay ahead in this rat race we call life; we put out fire after fire and treat every challenge we face as a crisis. But when we look back and see that in the past, we were always protected by God and our worst fears never materialized, we gain perspective and wisdom. We realize a couple of important life changing truths:

- First, we grow when we handle challenges the right way. We are wiser for the difficulties that have come our way when we handle them consistent with God's Word.
- Second, the world is watching us, and when we handle difficult situations by trusting God, they notice.

The year 2015 probably held more ministry challenges for me as a leader than the previous ten years combined, but I learned to trust God through the trials. He wanted me to realize no problem was insurmountable for Him when I give up control to Him. He wanted my faith to grow. By His grace I now look back and am actually glad I faced the challenges I did because my trust and faith in God has grown. By learning to walk into the future backwards, you are forced to slow down, relax, and learn to trust God more and more. We always say, "God is faithful." Let's practice what we preach to others.

Principle #5: Learn to engage your brain before using your tongue.

> *If anyone thinks he is religious and does not bridle his tongue but deceives his heart, this person's religion is worthless.* (James 1:26)

> *So also the tongue is a small member, yet it boasts of great things. How great a forest is set ablaze by such a small fire! And the tongue is a fire, a world of unrighteousness. The tongue is set among our members, staining the whole body, setting on fire the entire course of life, and set on fire by hell. For every kind of beast and bird, of reptile and sea creature, can be tamed and has been tamed by mankind, but no human being can tame the tongue. It is a restless evil, full of deadly poison. With it we bless our Lord and Father, and*

> *with it we curse people who are made in the likeness of God. From the same mouth come blessing and cursing. My brothers, these things ought not to be so. Does a spring pour forth from the same opening both fresh and salt water? Can a fig tree, my brothers, bear olives, or a grapevine produce figs? Neither can a salt pond yield fresh water.* (James 3:5-12)

How many times do we speak a careless word that does irreparable damage to others, our Christian testimony, and ourselves? James was not exaggerating when he said the uncontrolled tongue is a world of unrighteousness. One word spoken in haste can damage people and relationships for life. We are quick to speak and slow to listen and think. In this fast-paced world we are all walking time bombs when we don't slow down and consider the powerful consequences of the words we speak.

> *A fool takes no pleasure in understanding, but only in expressing his opinion.* (Proverbs 18:2)

> *A fool gives full vent to his spirit, but a wise man quietly holds it back.* (Proverbs 29:11)

> *The words of a wise man's mouth win him favor, but the lips of a fool consume him.*

> *The beginning of the words of his mouth is foolishness, and the end of his talk is evil madness.* (Ecclesiastes 10:12-13)

> *But I say to you that everyone who is angry with his brother will be liable to judgment; whoever insults his brother will be liable to the council; and whoever says, 'You fool!' will be liable to the hell of fire.* (Matthew 5:22)

The key to controlling our tongues before we become fools is humility. We must realize we are just not that important, and in spite of what our flesh tells us, we are not God's gift to humanity or the answer to everyone's questions or problems. A good rule of thumb to remember is that God gave us two ears but only one mouth; so let's learn to listen twice as much as we speak. Few, if any, people ever got in trouble for not speaking, but every time we open our mouths, we risk getting ourselves into hot water. We must learn the discipline of thinking before we speak and save ourselves a lot of trouble.

Principle #6: Learn to think more highly of others and more accurately of yourself.

The most important characteristic a man must have to be saved and sanctified by God is one principle that is taught throughout the Bible. Adam and Eve violated this principle, and every problem we see, along with the growing evil in this world, is a result of this violation. Also, our lack of growth and sanctification as Christians is because we continue to violate this most important godly principle: humility.

Who was the most humble man who ever lived? Of course, the answer is Jesus. He sets the standard for the humility toward which we should aspire.

> *Say to the daughter of Zion, "Behold, your king is coming to you, humble, and mounted on a donkey, on a colt, the foal of a beast of burden."* (Matthew 21:5)

In this verse *humble* is the Greek word *praus*: "*mildness of disposition, gentleness of spirit, meekness.*"

> *Or do you suppose it is to no purpose that the Scripture says, "He yearns jealously over the spirit that he has made to dwell in us"? But he gives more grace. Therefore it says, "God opposes the proud, but gives grace to the humble." Submit yourselves therefore to God. Resist the devil, and he will flee from you. Draw near to God, and he will draw near to you. Cleanse your hands, you sinners, and purify your hearts, you double-minded.* (James 4:5-8)

In Greek, the word *proud* is *hyperephanos*: "appearing above others; haughty." *Humble* is *tapeinos*: "humiliated in circumstances or disposition." So pride is considering yourself greater than you actually are, and humility can be seen as realizing who you are but actually presenting yourself as less than that for the benefit of others. True humility is that willingness of a man, who is secure in his position with Christ, to set aside his status and reputation for another's benefit.

Because we have the Holy Spirit, we are capable of great love, compassion, and righteousness. The proud man slips back into his flesh and loves the accolades of others who praise his good deeds. As others praise him and tell him how wonderful he is, he begins to believe he is the source of strength within himself that allows these righteous acts. And once pride gets a foothold in our hearts, it spreads like cancer through the body, eventually consuming us and hardening our hearts toward God and others. We become like the Pharisees, portraying ourselves as righteous and just – the very nature of God Himself. When we act out of pride, we commit idolatry and worship ourselves for our good deeds and knowledge instead of acknowledging that God alone is the source of everything good. We elevate ourselves as the standard for righteousness instead of realizing that without the Holy Spirit working in us, we are the worst of sinners.

The humble man realizes that every act of love, compassion, and righteousness is by the grace and Spirit of God alone. He realizes he is fully dependent on God for his next breath, but he also does not portray a false humility that says, "I'm wicked and depraved. I can do nothing good." Rather, he realizes that by the grace and Spirit of God alone, he is able to bear the fruit of the Holy Spirit. When I hear Christians make statements like, "We're all haters of God" or "We're all wicked and depraved," it breaks my heart. Denying the power and promises of God through the sacrifice of Jesus Christ is a sad testimony to the world. Certainly we are still capable of sin and wicked behavior, and we once were haters of God in our human spirit, but that is not who we are now as adopted children of God. Instead, it is something we still do on occasion.

> *Therefore, if anyone is in Christ, he is a new creation. The old has passed away; behold, the new has come. All this is from God, who through Christ reconciled us to himself and gave us the ministry of reconciliation; that is, in Christ God was reconciling the world to himself, not counting their trespasses against them, and entrusting to us the message of reconciliation. Therefore, we are ambassadors for Christ, God making his appeal through us. We implore you on behalf*

of Christ, be reconciled to God. For our sake he made him to be sin who knew no sin, so that in him we might become the righteousness of God. Working together with him, then, we appeal to you not to receive the grace of God in vain.
(2 Corinthians 5:17-6:1)

True humility can be seen as a realistic view of who we are and who we are not. We are no longer unbelievers who hate God and love ourselves more than anything, but we also realize that without the grace and Spirit of God, we would be lost pagans. We realize we are capable of acts of love, kindness, and compassion, but only by the grace and Spirit of God working in and through us. We are a new creation, but one that is 100 percent dependent on God's grace and Spirit. When we see unbelievers living a life of debauchery, we have compassion for them, truly saying and believing, "But for the grace of God that would be me!"

Genuine humility looks like this: by God's grace alone I am a new creation, saved from hell and being sanctified by God for eternal life with Him. By grace, I am capable of acts of love and compassion, but I am still capable of thinking, saying, and doing bad and destructive things – the exact opposite of what God wants of me. The new heart and spirit God gave me loves Him and wants to obey Him. But at times I still choose to obey the residual sinful flesh within me. I am an adopted child of God, learning what it means to honor that title and privilege. I need my brothers and sisters to help me not think more highly of myself, nor think of myself as less than God has made me by His grace and Spirit. I want to live as my Savior lived when He was on earth, willing to humble myself and put the good of others ahead of my own desires. I have been given freedom by Jesus, but I am willing to set that freedom aside for the benefit of others. I am aware of who I was but also who I am now through grace, and I know how often I fail to live as God wants me to live. I give fellow Christians permission to teach, correct, and rebuke me for my benefit, the benefit of others, and the glory of God.

Pride is thinking more highly of ourselves than reality. Prideful Christians are not aware of who they are without the grace and Spirit of God. Humble Christians have a truthful self-awareness of who we are in Christ and who we would be without His forgiveness and grace. But true humility never denies who we are by the Spirit of God – a new creation by His grace. Humility recognizes we are capable of letting God bear fruit through us for the benefit of others, all to glorify God by pointing others to Him.

Principle #7: Embracing delayed gratification.

Our souls never die, and life on this earth is but one speck of sand on an endless beach. When our bodies cease to exist in their current form, we simply continue to exist for eternity in some other form and place. So whatever challenges or trials we face in this lifetime are meaningless in the light of eternity.

When I was thirteen years old I "fell in love" with a pretty girl named Carol. She was from Pennsylvania, visiting neighbors in Wisconsin, and we spent a lot of time together. She was pretty, smart, and fun. After two weeks it was time for her to go home, and I knew our relationship was over. I was heartbroken and thought I would never love anyone again.

The day after she left, I was in our basement, pouting. My father, a tough ex-Marine, saw me and asked, "What are you pouting about?"

I opened up and shared my hurt, pain, and fears. His response? "Stop acting like a stupid little child. Some other pretty face will come around and you'll forget all about Carol!"

I was so mad at my dad I wanted to hit him, but he was right. Less than two weeks later, I "fell in love" again with a different pretty face, and Carol had become a distant memory.

When we face worries in this lifetime or think we need something now, we have a heavenly Father who:

- Is older, smarter, and wiser than us.
- Knows us better than we know ourselves.
- Knows the ultimate outcome of every situation we will ever face.
- Truly loves us and wants us to be joyful.

We cannot see into the future with any certainty, but God already knows the future. When we ask Him for something we think is best for us, He knows what is best for us, both now and in the future. When we embrace the principle of delayed gratification, we find peace, knowing the one with the final decision to give or withhold knows the ultimate effects, positive or negative, of receiving what we ask of Him.

I have very serious sleep apnea, and if I do not use my sleep machine, I could possibly die in my sleep. Even with it I wake up about every hour of the night. Could God heal me this minute of my sleep apnea? Unquestionably, and I have asked him to do so. He has not so far, and I am fine with it because I understand He knows me better than I know myself, and He knows the effects of anything He gives me. God will heal me one day, either on earth or in eternity. He has chosen not to do so yet, and I believe it is for my benefit. I trust Him and embrace the principle of delayed gratification, knowing He knows what is best for me, but I don't.

> *Do not lay up for yourselves treasures on earth, where moth and rust destroy and where thieves break in and steal, but lay up for yourselves treasures in heaven, where neither moth nor rust destroys and where thieves do not break in and steal. For where your treasure is, there your heart will be also. (Matthew 6:19-21)*

> *And as he was setting out on his journey, a man ran up and knelt before him and asked him, "Good Teacher, what must I do to inherit eternal life?" And Jesus said to him, "Why do you call me good? No one is good except God alone. You know the commandments: 'Do not murder, Do not commit adultery, Do not steal, Do not bear false witness, Do not defraud, Honor your father and mother.'" And he said to him, "Teacher, all these I have kept from my youth." And Jesus, looking at him, loved him, and said to him, "You lack one thing: go, sell all that you have and give to the poor, and you will have treasure in heaven; and come, follow me." Disheartened by the saying, he went away sorrowful, for he had great possessions. (Mark 10:17-22)*

Embracing delayed gratification is a sign of maturity. Little children want everything they ask for right now, and they pout or scream when they do not receive it. But what loving parent would give their child something before the child is prepared to handle correctly? What wise parent would give a sixteen-year-old a high performance sports car to drive, knowing he or she lacks the maturity and experience to handle a vehicle that could cause serious injury or death? What parent would give a five-year-old a gun for Christmas? If we as flawed human parents understand the wisdom of not giving our children things they want that could be dangerous to them and others, why would we expect God to do any less?

Recently the Power Ball Jackpot reached $1.5 billion, and people were scrambling to buy tickets in the hopes of striking it rich. I was meeting with some friends the day of the drawing, and two of them had bought tickets. When they asked if I had purchased a ticket, I said, "No, I wouldn't trust myself with that kind of money." I am concerned that if I were suddenly rich, I would retire and become lazy and ineffective for God. I accept the wisdom that the Bible teaches about lusting after money:

> *No one can serve two masters, for either he will hate the one and love the other, or he will be devoted to the one and despise the other. You cannot serve God and money.*
> (Matthew 6:24)

I would much rather God continue to provide for my basic needs on earth and store up treasure for me in heaven, regardless of what that treasure is. None of us knows exactly what those treasures in heaven will be, but because we know God's nature and His promises, we can be assured of two things:

- They're far greater than anything we can imagine in our human understanding.
- They will be with us for eternity, and no one will ever be able to take them away from us.

Embracing the principle of delayed gratification is not noble; it is smart.

It lessens your desires of the flesh and focuses you on eternal life and reward with God.

Principle #8: <u>Know what you can control and what you cannot.</u>

We get stressed and can become depressed when we try to control things we really have no control over. I worked at an insurance agency for nine years and received raises and promotions for my performance. Then one day our agency was bought by a large bank, and I lost my job due to the reorganization. Something negative happened to me beyond my control. I did all I could do as a hard-working, effective manager, but I lost my job. Looking back, I was blessed by what happened because God allowed circumstances that would lead me to saving faith in Jesus and give me the opportunity to lead a Christian Radio Station.

When we try to control effects or the behavior of others, we set ourselves up for disappointment and possible depression. Sometimes we can do the right action (cause), but the short-term effects are negative. But when we trust God, the one who controls eternal effects, we find peace in the midst of life's storms. Remember, Jesus said good causes lead to good eternal effects: reward in heaven. When we give up trying to control the effects and focus on doing the right cause, God rewards us in His perfect timing.

We can really only control what we believe, think, say, and do. These are effects of the cause we live for, which is to know, love, and obey God. When our cause is just, the eventual effects will bless us. One of the ways marriages and relationships are strained is when we try to control what others believe, think, say, or do. This only leads to frustration and bitterness and leaves us rooted in pride and trying to control others.

I refereed football, baseball, and basketball for years. Good referees focus on what they can control – knowing the rules and enforcing them equally. People would ask me how I could referee and not be affected by upset fans who screamed at officials when they made correct but unpopular calls. I would tell them, "Look, all I can do is know the rules and try to enforce them consistently for both teams. I realize that when I make a difficult call, half the people will think I am a genius, and half will think I'm an idiot. All I can control is what I do and call the game professionally and fairly as I see it."

Hosting a Christian Radio Show for nearly six years has helped me realize that if you are swayed by every person who disagrees with you, you will not last long. When we try to control what others believe, say, or do, we become disappointed, frustrated, and angry. Focus on what you can control, your beliefs and behaviors, and let God deal with the effects. You will have a better marriage and peaceful relationships with others. When you try to control the behaviors of others, you will only become frustrated, judgmental, and bitter. Become *cause* driven, not *effects* driven. Strive to love God with all your strength and love others, not trying to control effects which are out of your control. When you expect others to do what you think they should do, you will find yourself growing in anger and frustration. Control what you can control – your thoughts, words and action – and trust God.

Summary

Understand, memorize, and apply these important principles so you can take your thoughts captive when facing times of trouble. These are applications (hows) that will help you embrace godly wisdom on your journey to happiness and eternal reward.

- Know the difference between who you are and what you do.
- God cannot lie and He knows the future.
- God loves you as an adopted son through Jesus Christ and He cares about your happiness and future.
- Learn to walk into the future backwards.
- Learn to engage your brain before using your tongue.
- Learn to think more highly of others and more accurately of yourself.
- Embrace delayed gratification.
- Know what you can control and what you cannot.

These principles are essential to correctly interpret the Word of God and learn how to take your thoughts captive in obedience to Christ. They will help you find joy and allow you to help others to find it in Jesus Christ. They will also help you to spot dangerous false teachings that will mislead you.

Final Chapter

LIVING AS CHRISTIANS IN A DYING WORLD

The world around us is spinning into chaos and evil. Islamic terrorism is on the rise; war is expanding in the Middle East; man is growing more callous and evil and the governments of the world are lining up, ready to follow Antichrist to their ultimate, eternal destruction. It is easy to get caught up in the fear and uncertainty of the times in which we live. We can take our eyes off eternal issues and obsess on the here and now, which is exactly what Satan wants us to do, so we must resist the urge to live in fear and uncertainty. We know how the story ends!

Humanism, the belief that man is essentially good and capable of improving himself and the world, is the greatest threat we face as professing believers. It appeals to our flesh and desire to worship self instead of submitting to God and His Word. The world, and many in the church itself embrace humanism, glorifying the wisdom of man that God calls foolish. If we cannot distinguish between godly and human wisdom, we are susceptible to the great deception and to the falling away spoken of in the Word of God. The thought process you use continually testifies to the wisdom you embrace – either the flawed wisdom of man or the eternal wisdom of God.

The Bible is clear that one day every nation will unite against God.

Evil will continue to grow and mankind will increasingly ignore God and seek its own solutions to the problems we face, contrary to the teachings of the Bible. We are aliens living in a world increasingly strange to us, and that world will do all it can to conform us to its values and thought process. It will seek to control our minds and hearts by training us to react according to the flesh instead of thinking like rational human beings. One look at the world around us gives testimony to how they are succeeding. The world, and the nation we love, is rapidly headed toward a moral, social, and economic cliff, and as much as we would like to be the agents of change who reverse this slide, the Bible tells us that the world will bring itself to the very edge of destruction just before the return of our Lord.

The sad reality is that as Christian thought has been attacked, many churches and professing Christians have fallen for the subtle lies of humanism. The word *Christian* has collectively lost any real identity. It has become a word identified by a hodgepodge of diverse and contradictory beliefs with little resemblance to true biblical Christianity. And if you fall for the subtle lies and deceptions growing in these times, you may be one of those Jesus rejects when He returns in glory. So where do we go from here?

It would be wonderful if God just decided to zap everyone with a godly thought process, and we would see the church and our nation restored to greatness, but that is not how He works. He has given every individual man a free will to think and act, and each man will face the appropriate consequences based on their choices. We face difficult challenges as true Christians living in a fallen world. We must accept the reality of our situation: our nation and the professing church may have gone too far down the road of humanism to come back under submission to God. This is where you must develop and use a godly thought process, looking at the big-picture perspective.

We use the *mind of Christ* we were given to influence one person at a time and leave the effects to God. If He is willing to exhibit patience toward our nation, giving us time to participate in a spiritual revival, we praise and thank Him. One day, every nation on earth will be destroyed and replaced with the everlasting kingdom of God. Our eternal calling is not to save a nation or restore a church that is such in name only. We fight for the eternal souls of men. This battle will be won by using a godly thought process to help others come out from the bondage of fleshly/animal thought that has enslaved them. By understanding important principles in the Bible, you can think with a godly thought process and find the peace that surpasses human understanding. If we can use a godly thought process to help others improve their thought process, we can share the gospel effectively and help believers become disciples, which fulfills the Great Commission.

Helping Others with Their Thought Process

What I share here is in abbreviated form, because complete detail would require another entire book. If you are serious about teaching others about thought process, more information is available at www.michaeldlemay.com. Here is a very brief synopsis:

Helping someone who truly wants to improve their thought process is not difficult, once you understand thought processes. People using a fleshly/animal thought process deal in effects (whats). People have been trained to speak in *effects* instead of sharing the *cause* behind their beliefs (why/how). When they state an effect (belief), ask them why they believe what they claim. If they can give you a reason (why) that is truth, you have already helped them use a human thought process. Help them by challenging their reasons (whys) if they are not truth, in a non-threatening way. Help them see new and deeper perspectives on how they perceive truth. Look at every conversation you have as an opportunity to help other people think rationally; encourage them to engage their conscious brain rather than remaining slaves to their unconscious brain with all its wrong life commands and bad teachings.

When you continue to talk with people, help them move from the *what* to the *why*. Once they begin to think with a human thought process, they have the ability for rational thought and can consider another perspective about any issue. This helps unbelievers consider the perspective of the gospel of salvation. We must understand that choosing to be humble and confessing to God is a human thought process, as you use human understanding to choose an option that will benefit you. Then, before you say, "Well, that's not enough! How can we be sure they are sincere?" remember you probably confessed to God for the very same reason of saving your eternal soul! Most of us humble ourselves and confess to God for our benefit, and there is nothing wrong with that. If a person confesses and repents with a sincere heart, they receive the Holy Spirit and are now able to utilize a godly thought process as you teach them about thought processes.

Learn to slow down your conversations with others and ask many good questions to learn more about them and their beliefs. Ask questions that will help you determine if they are prideful and self-righteous or humble and willing to learn. One great question to ask to that end is, "If you found out you were wrong about your belief, how would it make you feel?" If they say they would be mad, they are in pride. If they say they would be glad, they are humble.

Open-ended questions are always best when trying to learn about someone and what they believe. And one subject everyone has questions about is what happens to us when we die. When you ask someone this question and follow up with, "Why do you believe that?" it will give you a great deal of insight into them as a person and their belief system. If they claim to be a Christian, and their belief about eternal life is incorrect according to the Bible, a great follow-up question is, "If the Bible gave a different answer than your belief, which would you believe is truth?"

One very important thing when trying to help others is not to pressure them too hard. Our job is not to convict anyone of anything. Only God can truly convict the hearts of men. Our job is to give them something to think about. Remember, God gave every person a conscience that has a basic knowledge of right and wrong. When a person states a belief out loud that their conscience knows is wrong, they will feel unsettled about their statement, unless their conscience is completely seared. If it is seared and they are unwilling to even entertain the possibility they could be wrong, they may be eternally lost and beyond anything you can do for them. Walk away and "knock the sand off your sandals." If you try to persist once their conscience is seared, it will only serve to frustrate you and negatively affect your thought process.

Do not let people in a fleshly/animal thought process rush you. Do not get sucked into emotional and irrational arguments. Think before you speak and carefully consider the impact of your words. Do not let disagreements over spiritual issues and doctrines become their opinion versus yours. What we think is not eternally important, but what God says is. If they espouse clearly unbiblical doctrines, use the correctly interpreted Word of God to counter their arguments gently but effectively. If they persist on arguing, let their argument be against God, not you.

Start to slow down when you read the Bible. Learn to understand it, not just able to recite a couple of verses. Look for the understanding (why) and application (how) of the Scriptures. Start looking for ways you could be wrong about your preconceived notions and beliefs. Read the Bible in correct context, applying the principles we shared earlier to see where you may have strayed into human doctrine instead of biblical doctrine. None of us will ever have perfect understanding of every doctrine, but by reading the Bible with the principles we shared your understanding of scripture will grow. Look for opportunities to grow by allowing the Word of God to prove your preconceived notions were wrong. God will honor your humility and reveal more truth in His Word to you. It is perfectly fine to admit you do not have all the answers. In fact, you should run away from any teacher of the Word who claims to have God all figured out as fast as you can.

Learn to challenge the thought processes and beliefs of everyone with respect, starting with yourself. Here is an example that might help you:

> *Because, if you confess with your mouth that Jesus is Lord and believe in your heart that God raised him from the dead, you will be saved.* (Romans 10:9)

We know this verse is truth, and if a person does this, they will be saved. But does this verse also mean that someone who does not do this is automatically going to hell? If you believe that, then don't you also believe that every aborted baby will go to hell? Do you know beyond any uncertainty how God deals with the eternal souls of aborted babies or children who die tragically at a very young age? And if you believe that their inherited sinful nature automatically condemns them without an opportunity to confess and repent, what would you say to parents who tragically lost their baby to a birth defect or illness? How would you feel if you were a parent of a child who died at a young age and someone told you they knew for sure your baby was going to hell? Humility, and a willingness to acknowledge we do not always have all the answers, is always our best path.

What I know for sure is this: God is always righteous, perfect, holy, and just, and every soul will end up where God determines it belongs. When we try to answer questions that only God can answer, we may be guilty of trying to elevate ourselves to the level of God.

> Now concerning food offered to idols: we know that "all of us possess knowledge." This "knowledge" puffs up, but love builds up. If anyone imagines that he knows something, he does not yet know as he ought to know. But if anyone loves God, he is known by God. (1 Corinthians 8:1-3)

Always be humble enough to admit what you don't know. If you pursue knowledge over understanding, wisdom, and love, you are on a treadmill, going nowhere fast.

When you disagree with another person on an important issue, try to understand their perspective and why they believe what they believe. This does not mean you have to agree with their perspective, just that you can understand why they believe it. This will help you in leading them to truth. The Bible teaches us that Jesus was tempted in every way. By seeing things from their perspective, Jesus understood why people could be tempted and sin. Strive to do this with unbelievers and fellow Christians.

When you share a belief with someone or ask someone to do something, always try to give them a very good reason (why) so they can understand your intent. People in a fleshly/animal thought process will often supply their own wrong reason (why) because they will assume you are like them, trying to manipulate others for your benefit. I have found this very helpful with my employees when I have to ask them to perform a duty in the ministry they might be uncomfortable with. When I can share the motive and how the duty will benefit them and the ministry, they see the value in my request.

Husbands, your *why* as leader of your homes should always be to glorify God and benefit your wife and children, and to help them grow in Christ. Wives, as hard as submission is at times, your *why* should be to glorify God by lovingly and patiently submitting to your husband as the Bible commands. Nancy always tells wives she meets with that "even if I cannot always trust that Mike will make the right decision, I trust that God will work through him to convict him and grow him as a leader." Wives, be patient with your husbands, giving God time to work in and through him.

If your marriage is in need of help, begin by humbling yourself before God and asking Him to search your heart to reveal anything you are doing in your marriage that is not honoring God or your spouse. Husbands, if you claim God reveals nothing to you then you are prideful, claiming to be the perfect husband. Once God reveals areas you need to confess and change, go to your wife at a time when you can be alone together for a lengthy conversation without interruption. Tell her you want to be a better husband and you are grateful for the gift she is from God. Then ask her a great open-ended question: "Honey, what can I do to be the best husband possible for you?" Use the biblical communication model we shared in this book and do not act defensively about anything your wife shares with you. The goal is not who is right or wrong; the goal is to improve communication and better understand one another. Make regular, meaningful communication a part of every day, even if it is only for twenty minutes.

Of course, wives should do the same thing with husbands. But men, you are the spiritual leader of your family, so I urge you to start acting like a leader, taking the initiative to improve your marriage. Rebuke the lies of this world, open up, and take an emotional risk with your wife, sharing your thoughts and fears. Tell her you need her support, understanding, and wisdom as the wife God has chosen for you. Learn what is important to her and what you can do to show her how much you value and appreciate her.

Even if you believe the problem in your marriage lies primarily with your wife, do not underestimate the power of what God can do when you have a humble heart. God honors humility, and He will work in your wife to humble her about where she is wrong. But men, we carry the ultimate responsibility in improving our marriages, and we must take the initiative to improve them.

As we open up honestly to one another, we take the risk that information will be shared that surprises or even hurts us or our spouse at first. Use a godly thought process and humility to get over pride, understanding that effective communication can be painful at first, but that it will lead to great effects if both parties are humble and focus on the issue of improving the marriage.

A great place to start a meaningful conversation is by having your spouse read this book, which opens up the opportunity for discussion on the things we covered. Talk about the principles and teachings of this book and share your thoughts. Look for practical examples in your life where this book can help you with communication and understanding the Word of God.

I have been blessed by God to share what the Bible teaches about thought processes. It has been amazing to see how the Holy Spirit works in people once they truly confess and repent to God. I currently meet with twenty people on a regular basis to teach them how to use a godly thought process. I have seen God restore marriages, help people off alcohol and drugs, and learn to trust God with their finances and life by sharing the principles of the Bible we shared in this book.

Final Thoughts

I do not know if our nation has one more great spiritual revival in it before the Lord calls His church home to Him. He could call us home any day, or it might be decades before we are caught up to Him. We should approach our lives with the latter perspective – with the hope that we have time for another meaningful spiritual revival that can lead many more people to salvation and discipleship. As true believers, we must be committed to setting aside the noise and busyness of this world and focus our attention on the things of God, because every eternal soul is precious to God. We are talking about the eternal destiny of human beings who will either end up in heaven or hell. Nothing should be more important to us than the battle for the eternal souls of men.

This battle will be fought one person and one church at a time. The thought processes of many people have become so damaged by decades of secular humanist indoctrination that the hope of seeing our church and nation turn around quickly may not be practical. But with God, all things are possible. So we do all we can to build one strong marriage, then one strong fellowship, then one strong church at a time, and leave the effects to God.

Living in this world is not easy, but always remember that this life is but a grain of sand on an eternal beach. We will each spend eternity in the presence of God or in separation from Him in eternal hell. So will your family, neighbors, and friends. In the end, eternity is all that really matters. So keep a big-picture perspective in your life. Do not let temporary circumstances or suffering distract you from keeping your eyes focused on Jesus. Learn to use a godly thought process to protect your heart and mind, and help others to do the same. The eternal benefits will be amazing.

We must always remember that the god of this world, Satan, will seek to destroy us, stopping at nothing to separate us from God for eternity. The thought process we choose to use will either draw us nearer to God's truth or lead us away from it. When you fall for clever deception and start to think like the world thinks, you place yourself in extreme danger and separate yourself from the blessings and protection of God.

Remember to glorify God in all circumstances, even the difficult ones. Jesus never promised us life would be easy. But he promised He would never forsake us. Always remember, no matter how bad things get in this world, God wins. Jesus Christ is returning soon. To Him be all glory, honor, and praise!

Visit Michael online at:

www.michaeldlemay.com

MEET THE AUTHOR

Mike LeMay is an author, radio talk show host and General Manager of Q90 FM Christian Radio Station in Green Bay, WI. He has extensively covered and studied news, trends and issues pertaining to the Christian life, pointing people to the truth of God's Word.

His latest book *The Death of Christian Thought: The Deception of Humanism and How to Protect Yourself* has received critical acclaim for its insight into how Humanism damages the thought process of many people and leads to a life of anxiety and worry instead of peace and joy.

Mike is also owner of Christian Thought Consulting, LLC, and meets with families and business professionals to help them find joy, peace and purpose in a world that tries to overwhelm and distract us. He can be reached at 920-676-7083 or www.michaeldlemay.com.

ALSO BY MICHAEL D. LEMAY

"Are You Really Saved?" is a book that will challenge everything you think you know about God, eternal life and hell. Far too many professing Christians cannot explain why they believe what they claim to believe, relying on others to explain the teachings of God. Jesus Christ is very clear that the path to eternal life with God is very narrow, and few people find it. Yet most professing Christians do not think twice about these words of Jesus. They think because they were baptized as a baby, or attend a certain church, that they are destined for eternal life in heaven. But the Bible tells a much different story. Jesus said unless we love Him with all our heart, mind and strength, we will not enter eternall life with Him. Yet most professing Christians know more about their favorite sport team or television show than they do the teachings of the One who came to save us. This book will challenge you to the very essence of your soul.

Available where books are sold

American Christianity is dying a slow death at its own hands. Instead of positively affecting the secular culture, we are being infected by it under the guise of being "seeker-friendly" and "loving." Soon, the church may be an exact mirror of the culture that seeks to destroy us.

With a lack of strong, principled leaders, and with followers who want their ears tickled instead of being challenged to pursue righteousness, American Christianity is writing its own epitaph as it slowly dies. Unless we reverse course by embracing the complete, absolute truth of God's Word and stop trying to redefine God in our selfish human image, only a remnant will remain from a once-powerful church.

Do we have the courage to challenge our leaders and ourselves to reject secular culture and its influences? Or will we continue to die a slow death at our own hands as we continue to inhale the cancer of secular humanism? Time is running out.

Available where books are sold

ALSO BY THE PUBLISHER

ANEKO
PRESS

There are consequences when God's people take the path of least resistance and back out of culture. One only needs to look at our society to see we are living with those consequences today.

- Why do you think so many Christians pursue comfort over commitment to Christ?
- Do you sometimes feel overwhelmed by the darkness and moral decline in society today and wonder what happened to the salt and light?
- How have we reached a point where Christians who do preach the gospel and speak up about sin are called hateful, intolerant, or judgmental?

Christian in name only, America has become an epicenter for the culture war as too many of us keep ducking the issue of sin. Due to decades of Christians being silent, failing to preach the gospel and speak the truth in love, we've reached a tipping point in which political correctness refuses to coexist with religious freedom. Why do you think Christians who defend God's Word are often called hateful, intolerant, or judgmental? There are consequences in this life and for eternity, when Christians take the path of least resistance. We cannot reverse the moral decline, but we can choose to stand for righteousness as we pray for revival and be the salt and light Jesus called us to be while we're still here.

Available where books are sold

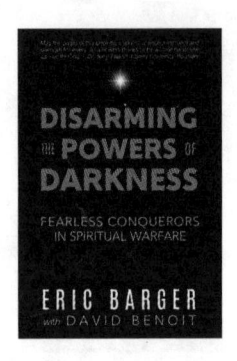

Scripture is clear: the spiritual battlefield is real and the Enemy is determined.

But most Christians are ill-equipped and unprepared when attacked, and even fewer are on the offensive. Still others write off spiritual warfare as irrelevant today, while on the other extreme some credit Satan for every imaginable problem in life. The purpose of this book is to provide biblical balance and clarity in order to establish a proper battle plan – exposing the Enemy for who he really is and showing Christians how to win this war with the spiritual weapons already at their disposal.

Disarming the Powers of Darkness **answers critical battleground questions:**

- Does Satan know my thoughts and hear my prayers?
- Where exactly does spiritual warfare take place?
- How do we deal with spirits of fear and uncertainty?
- How can we be victorious in a culture that is increasingly dark?

Available where books are sold

To have found God and still to pursue Him is a paradox of love, scorned indeed by the too-easily-satisfied religious person, but justified in happy experience by the children of the burning heart. Saint Bernard of Clairvaux stated this holy paradox in a musical four-line poem that will be instantly understood by every worshipping soul:

We taste Thee, O Thou Living Bread,
And long to feast upon Thee still:
We drink of Thee, the Fountainhead
And thirst our souls from Thee to fill.

Come near to the holy men and women of the past and you will soon feel the heat of their desire after God. Let A. W. Tozer's pursuit of God spur you also into a genuine hunger and thirst to truly know God.

Available where books are sold